Praise for *The Art of Doing Business Across* cult...

"There has never been a time in world history when communicating across cultures has been more important. Technology now allows us to contact each other but fails to support the type of communication needed for real global conversations. Craig Sorti's new book, *The Art of Doing Business Across Cultures*, creatively guides each of us in effectively communicating across the many cultures that form our global community."

> —Nancy J. Adler, S. Bronfman Chair in Management, McGill University, Canada
> Author, *International Dimensions of Organizational Behavior and Leadership Insight*

"Craig Storti has once again created a resource that bridges the complexity of cultural differences in a way accessible to individuals new to cultural exploration yet also of use to intercultural experts. Each dialogue alone is of value yet the inclusion of the culture-specific context and situation-specific explanations to each scenario provide a holistic quality of great benefit to the reader. His book is useful for myriad purposes, including as a standalone resource for individuals to gain understanding about cultural interaction in working life as well as embedded as part of a facilitated training program. It is a worthwhile addition to anyone's reading list."

> —Holly Emert, Ph.D., President, Society for Intercultural Education, Training, and Research (SIETAR USA), 2017-2018

"*The Art of Doing Business Across Cultures* is a tremendous resource. Craig Storti not only describes cultural differences in fascinating and enlightening ways, he also provides straightforward tactical advice on how to navigate them. In doing so, *The Art of Doing Business Across Cultures* not only gives its readers fish, it teaches them how to fish in today's multi-cultural business world. It is a great read for business leaders and students alike!"

> —Sarah Miller, Assistant Dean & Director of Graduate Business Student Affairs at Washington University in St. Louis.

"A wonderful guide about how to conduct business with representatives of various countries and cultures!"

"Craig Storti gives us insights, simple to read yet complex in thought, about cross-cultural challenges which arise in our everyday lives. Whether you work domestically or internationally, whether you wish to better understand a particular culture or to gain a broader understanding of our global world, you will surely benefit from this fascinating, enjoyable and enlightening book."

"Using his powerful dialogue technique, Craig Storti brilliantly illuminates common cultural missteps that occur between Americans and those from 10 other cultural backgrounds. The strength of this book is in its clarity of writing and in highlighting "a fix" for moving forward in working through cultural difference. Indispensable for Americans working across the 10 featured cultures, this book can also be used by anyone who works with people from different cultural backgrounds. Storti demonstrates throughout what it means to interact successfully across cultures and build one's cultural competence."

THE ART OF
DOING
BUSINESS
ACROSS
CULTURES

THE ART OF
DOING BUSINESS ACROSS CULTURES

10 Countries, 50 Mistakes, and 5 Steps to Cultural Competence

CRAIG STORTI

INTERCULTURAL PRESS
an imprint of Nicholas Brealey Publishing

BOSTON • LONDON

First published in the USA in 2017 by Intercultural Press
an imprint of Nicholas Brealey Publishing

21   20   19   18   17   1   2   3   4   5   6   7   8   9   10

Library of Congress Cataloging-in-Publication Data

Names: Storti, Craig, author.
Title: The art of doing business across cultures : 10 countries, 50 mistakes, and
     5 steps to cultural competence / by Craig Storti.
Description: Boston, MA : Intercultural Press, [2017] | Includes bibliographical
     references.
Identifiers: LCCN 2016034441 (print) | LCCN 2016042989 (ebook) | ISBN
     9781941176146 (pbk.) | ISBN 9781941176160 (ebook)
Subjects: LCSH: Management—Cross-cultural studies. | Corporate culture—
     Cross-cultural studies. | Business etiquette. | Intercultural communication. |
     Cultural competence. | International business enterprises.
Classification: LCC HD62.4 .S766 2017 (print) | LCC HD62.4 (ebook) | DDC
     338.8/8—dc23
LC record available at https://lccn.loc.gov/2016034441

ISBN 978-1-94117-614-6
U.S. eBook ISBN 978-1-94117-616-0
U.K. eBook ISBN 978-1-47364-532-5

Printed and bound in the United States of America

Nicholas Brealey Publishing policy is to use papers that are natural, renewable and recyclable products and made from wood grown in sustainable forests. The logging and manufacturing processes are expected to conform to the environmental regulations of the country of origin.

Nicholas Brealey Publishing
Carmelite House
50 Victoria Embankment
London EC4Y 0DZ
Tel: 020 7122 6000

Nicholas Brealey Publishing
Hachette Book Group
Exchange Place, 53 State Street
Boston, MA 02109, USA
Tel: (617) 523 3801

www.nicholasbrealey.com

Dedication

To Fanchon Silberstein,
mentor, dear friend, soul mate

Contents

"It is a luxury to be understood."

—Ralph Waldo Emerson

Acknowledgments

I am grateful to several people who read individual chapters to critique my cultural observations: Xia Zhi, Peter Franklin, and Helena Obendiek on China; Peter Franklin on England and Germany; Tomoko Sano on Japan; and Aksana Kravtsova on Russia and Brazil. All five of my readers not only corrected mistakes but also made excellent suggestions for points I could add and subtle changes that would enhance some of my explanations. The book has been much improved by their efforts.

Foreword

by Peter Franklin

Checking rather jet-lagged into the hotel on the first evening of my first ever trip to the US, the smiling, friendly receptionist said to me, "Your room is on the first floor, Mr. Franklin." I thanked her and inquired where I could find the lift. At least slightly better acquainted with British English than I was with American English, she replied, "You won't be needing the elevator, Mr. Franklin. Your room is on the first floor." Musing whether this odd reply was an acknowledgment of my apparently good physical condition and my ability to take the stairs, or an indirect piece of advice not to use some regrettably unreliable equipment, I soon found the lift, which was in perfectly good order, but not my room, which—it finally dawned on me—had to be on the ground floor, as we Brits would say.

Not only language differences, as in the exchange above, but also cultural differences are tucked away in every cross-cultural conversation. They are a hidden hindrance to mutual understanding and are thus not obviously a potential problem which might need to be tackled in advance. Cultural differences may become obvious retrospectively when they have already led to unsuccessful communication, when the goal of the exchange has not been achieved or achieved only with difficulty. Equally undesirable, cultural differences can cause collateral damage. They can lead to negative feelings—such as irritation, disappointment, and frustration—and to disharmony in the relationship between the parties to the conversation.

This insight, which is the driving force behind this new book by Craig Storti (and many of his others), is invaluable in helping people to communicate and behave effectively and appropriately when they are working, managing, and leading across cultures at home and abroad, but also when they encounter foreigners in their neighbourhood or on holiday (or on vacation, as Americans would say and as we Brits probably wouldn't).

Normally culture—what we share in the way of values, attitudes, norms, behaviors, and practices with other members of our cultural group—is a hidden helper in constructing the meaning of what others in our group say and do. Our cultural guide switches itself on automatically and without our noticing supports us in interpreting, understanding, and assessing other people, their words and actions.

The British know that when a fellow Brit says, "It is cold in here," the utterance can be interpreted in at least two ways. The speaker could perhaps be referring to the climatic condition of the room, or he may well be inquiring whether it is okay with the other person if he turns up the heating.

The help offered by culture works fairly effortlessly as long as we share more or less the same national culture. Another culture we have in common—an organizational or professional culture, for example—may help us as well. We are generally able to work out what other people mean when they say or do something because literally and metaphorically speaking we know where they come from.

But our cultural compass may let us down, and regularly does so, when we are dealing with people from other cultural settings. A comment made by a member of the German culture, for example, about the coldness of a room may well initiate an interesting conversation about the subjective experience of cold and heat in that particular case and in general but will not necessarily result in the person addressed understanding that getting the room warmer is the intention of the person making the comment. Some accompanying nonverbal signals or a more direct, explicit inquiry may be necessary to make that certain to happen.

Examples of what is at first sight not obviously dysfunctional cross-cultural communication and the keys to understanding what is really meant are at the heart of this book. In fifty "brief encounters with cultural difference," as the subtitle of one of his earlier books nicely puts it, the reader witnesses U.S. Americans interacting in dialogues with non-Americans from ten countries or areas of the world and failing to construct the right meaning of what the foreigners say. Business and management are the broad contexts of the cross-cultural dialogues, which center on topics common to all work settings.

In detailed and insightful explanatory notes written with charm and humour, Craig Storti elaborates on the regularities of various national cultures—their values, attitudes, norms and behaviours—which lead to the dysfunctionality lurking between the lines of the dialogues. The reader learns not only about what makes other cultures tick but also a lot about what drives U.S. American culture as well—the things that remain hidden helpers in monocultural, U.S. encounters. And in chapter's "The Fix" section, the reader also finds out how the two sides to the dialogue can best avoid the mistake that the cultural difference provokes.

Certainly the most generally applicable insights in the book are Craig's essential "Five Steps to Cultural Competence," in which the knowledge and wisdom derived from his many years as an internationally renowned intercultural consultant and writer shine through. In this chapter, he elaborates on a five-step, self-help methodology readers can apply to identify cultural differences and thus to communicate and act across cultures more effectively and more appropriately. The crucial second step— "Identify the key assumptions and values of your own culture"— is described in detail and helps readers to understand the hidden hindrances of their own cultural group. This step is the crucial one because it makes clear to readers that it is not just the others who are "different"; they themselves are "different" as well.

Craig wears his wisdom lightly: his prose flows smoothly and easily, using the jargon of the expert only to enlighten and not to obfuscate. You don't have the feeling that Craig is lecturing to you about foreigners and their peculiarities but rather that he is talking to you kindly and with empathy about people who are a bit different from you. And that is the delight of this book: the recognizably knowledgeable author is also obviously a very nice bloke—as the British would say and the Americans probably wouldn't.

Introduction

> I think there is nothing barbarous and savage except
> that each man calls barbarism whatever is not his own
> practice; for indeed it seems we have no other test of
> truth and reason than the . . . opinions and customs of
> the country we live in.
>
> —Montaigne

Business went global some time ago, but many businesspeople
have yet to follow. They may now work every day with people from other countries—suppliers from China, IT support in
India, virtual team members in Germany and Japan—but they're
unaware of key cultural differences between themselves and
their international colleagues. Not understanding these differences, these folks become confused and frustrated in some of
their most common everyday interactions. If you are regularly
confused and frustrated by the things people you work with
every day are doing, that's not the basis for a good business
relationship. In the end it means you succeed, when you do
manage to succeed, more by accident—and a lot of trial and

error—than by design. And when has trial and error ever been a good business strategy?

But these are smart people. If they have not "gone global" along with their companies, if they have not become "culturally competent," it is only because they have not yet read the books, consulted the websites, or attended the intercultural training that could make a difference. And even if they *have* sought out guidebooks or websites, most resources only describe the target culture but fail to contrast it with one's own culture. To become truly culturally competent, businesspeople need to know how they are different from people in other cultures. These differences, after all, are what lead to the misunderstandings—the mistakes, confusion, and frustration—that undermine good business relations.

Using a technique known as a "cultural dialogue," this book describes the most important differences between Americans and ten foreign cultures: the Arab Middle East, Brazil, China, England, France, Germany, India, Japan, Mexico, and Russia. These are ten of the largest economies and markets Americans do business with, and the issues addressed in the dialogues, five per country, are the most common cultural differences Americans will encounter.

What Is a Dialogue?

A "dialogue" is a harmless conversation that causes great harm, a conversation with a mistake. In a brief exchange of six to twelve lines, speakers from two different cultures encounter a cultural difference that causes a significant misunderstanding (the mistake). However, because the two speakers are not aware of the difference, neither are they aware of the mistake. And neither is the reader.

The cultural mistakes in these pages have various causes: an unknown value difference, a misinterpretation, an inaccurate assumption, a mistaken projection, and occasionally a genuine faux pas. But they all lead to the same unfortunate results: they undermine business relationships and disrupt productivity. Mistakes, in short, have consequences.

The mistakes embedded in the dialogues are not obvious, just as mistakes are not obvious in real life; *otherwise you wouldn't make them in the first place*. If readers fail to spot the mistake, they must accept that they could have had that same conversation and made that same error. Indeed, many people have told the author they *have* had conversations nearly identical to those in this book.

Since adults don't appreciate being made fools of, most readers are upset when they finish reading a dialogue and can't figure out what they missed. Nor do they soon forget the humbling truth that goes along with this feeling: when you work with people from different cultures, you're probably not as smart as you think you are.

This observation is in fact the central lesson of all intercultural communication: When you interact with someone from another culture, never assume you know what's going on. To be sure, there are many other things you should know about culture, but this first truth is paramount. The rest is details.

Why Dialogues?

The power of the dialogue technique lies in its immediate emotional impact, which is difficult to overstate. It's no exaggeration to say that these innocuous conversations are the closest you will come in any print-based medium to an actual cultural encounter. While there may be a puzzle or riddle at the heart of every conversation, a dialogue is not an intellectual exercise; it is an emotional incident. You don't learn anything when you read a dialogue; you experience something. Nor do dialogues clear up any confusion; *dialogues are the confusion*. And that confusion, as we'll see, is the first step to becoming culturally competent.

If we eavesdrop for a moment on Carl and Krishna, this will all become clearer.

CARL:	Hey, Krishna. I just called to see if we're still on track to fix that bug by the first of next week?
KRISHNA:	I'm glad you called. It's going quite well, but there have been one or two unexpected problems.
CARL:	Boy, I know how that is.
KRISHNA:	I'm glad we understand each other.

The first thing readers will notice is how completely natural and authentic the conversation sounds. This really is how people talk. If you haven't had this conversation yourself, you can easily imagine having it. Readers identify immediately with the dialogue.

The second thing readers notice is . . . *nothing*. They see no mistake nor any evidence of a misunderstanding. And if they can't see the mistake, then of course they could easily *make* the mistake. The hook is in. Readers quickly turn to the explanation to find out what they missed.

This conversation is explained at length in "I'm Glad You Called" (Dialogue 32), but suffice it to say here that—Krishna's last comment notwithstanding—these two men do not "understand each other." Krishna seems to think Carl understands and accepts that the deadline will be missed. However, Carl actually believes the opposite—that Krishna knows he's still expected to fix the bug and is willing to work overtime to get the job done. These two part ways with radically different interpretations of the exchange. Bottom line: It won't be pretty next week when Krishna cheerfully misses the deadline and Carl is caught completely off guard.

It's a simple, unfortunate chain reaction: cultural differences cause misunderstandings, and misunderstandings undermine smooth working relations. When the dust settles, Carl and Krishna will be quite wary of each other to say the least. And this is just one incident. What if they continue to have these conversations and misinterpret one another? It won't be long before their relationship breaks down altogether.

How Was I Supposed to Know That?

There is one other important feature in every dialogue: a clue or hint—if the reader can find it—that alerts the speaker to the mistake that's being made. After all, if readers (like the speakers in the dialogues) have to be in possession of specific cultural information in order to avoid the mistake, then the dialogue doesn't work; that is, readers would never identify with a mistake they could not possibly have avoided. But if the clue is there and readers simply miss it, then shame on them.

In the encounter above, the clue is when Krishna refers to "unexpected problems," suggesting that somehow they would be a universally acceptable excuse for missing a deadline. Carl cannot be expected to know *why* Krishna thinks this way (that will be made clear in the explanation that follows the dialogue), but if he is listening closely, he should realize Krishna is telling him something important.

How Is This Book Going to Help Me?

When all is said and done, a dialogue is primarily a pretext for discussing cultural differences—a clever and compelling pretext, perhaps, but a pretext nonetheless. The differences are what matter. Accordingly, each of the dialogues in this book is followed by the "explanation," a brief analysis that reveals where the misunderstanding occurred, the cultural differences that caused it, and the origin of those differences. In this example, the difference has to do with the extent to which Indians and Americans believe they can control external circumstances and, therefore, the degree to which it is acceptable to miss a deadline.

When people realize that misunderstandings are the result of legitimate cultural differences—of a value or belief that makes perfect sense in one culture but not the other—then they will see that no one ever *tries* to confuse or frustrate anybody else. And that in turn means that no one is "to blame" for what happened because neither party knew what was happening. Are you going to be upset with someone just because he or she comes from a culture?

This realization changes the entire dynamic of any cross-cultural interaction. When the two parties realize that no one was trying to confuse anyone else—that Carl was not trying to misread Krishna and Krishna was not trying to mislead Carl—this takes most of the emotion out of the encounter. Instead of two people who are angry with each other, we now have two people slightly embarrassed by their mistake. Angry people find it difficult to work together, but embarrassed people are willing to try again.

The Fix

If this were the end of the story, we could all go home; but it's not. Carl and Krishna may be best buddies again now that they understand what happened last week, but they still have some work to do. They still have to come up with what in this book is called "The Fix," which comprises the last few paragraphs of every dialogue explanation. Realizing that nobody was trying to frustrate anybody else certainly takes the sting out of Carl and Krishna's encounter, but that realization doesn't change the facts on the ground: namely, that these two men have very different notions of what a deadline is and what it means to miss one.

Carl and Krishna now understand what happened last week, but that understanding by itself won't keep something like this from happening again. Carl and Krishna may indeed have progressed from not realizing they think differently to realizing they do, but that's not quite the same as thinking alike. What they have learned about each other's culture has not changed what's going on between these two men; it has only changed how they feel about it. A change for the better, to be sure, but not a solution to their problem. We can all cheerfully accept that these things happen—and still wish they wouldn't happen next time.

What's needed now is for Carl and Krishna to reconcile their cultural differences and find a way to work together. It's not realistic to expect either man to adopt the worldview of the other, even if that were possible, but they do have to move toward each other, culturally speaking. The ideal fix involves finding a middle ground that does not require either party to venture much further outside his/her comfort zone than the other party, a behavioral compromise that spreads the pain around more or less equally. In the fix we have proposed for Carl and Krishna, for example, Carl adjusts the way he sets deadlines, while Krishna takes on some of Carl's urgency about meeting them.

But ideal fixes are the exception; in most cross-cultural standoffs, the burden of adapting is usually greater for one party than the other. And as for which party has to do more of the adapting, that almost always depends on circumstances. If we assume that Krishna works for a vendor with a contract with Carl's company, then it makes sense that the vendor adapts to the client, in which case Krishna is going to have to clean up his act regarding deadlines. If the tables were turned and Carl is working for Krishna, then the logical fix would be for Carl to stop obsessing about losing a day here and there.

We might add here that while circumstances are everything in a cross-cultural standoff, a typical dialogue contains almost no description. If dialogues are going to work *as conversations*, they can have very little context. Context is taken for granted when two people are talking; they're *in* the situation, so why would they have to explain it? But if we started trying to slip additional details into our dialogues (setting, work titles), they would no longer sound natural. And their *complete naturalness* is the only reason dialogues work as well as they do.

And that's how this book is going to help you: It's going to show you:

1. That there's always a reason why people do the strange things they do;
2. That the reason is hardly ever to upset you; and
3. That when everyone calms down, there's always a way forward.

What if I'm Not an American?

Readers will observe that one of the two speakers in *every* dialogue in this book comes from the United States. That would seem to suggest that this book is exclusively for an American audience, but there are several reasons why this is not the case.

Let's start with readers who do not come from the United States or any of the ten other countries featured in these pages.

It doesn't matter; so long as you do business *with* Americans, every explanation in this book contains useful tips. And then there are those ten other countries. Do you do business with any of them? If so, you will find valuable information in the relevant chapters. Finally, while your particular country might not be included, a country from your region of the world—say, Asia-Pacific or Latin America—does have a chapter here. To the extent that your culture is similar to others in your region, that chapter will have relevance to you.

Then there are readers who come from the ten featured countries. To begin with, an entire chapter is dedicated to the most common mistakes Americans make when they work with you— and vice versa. If you do business with any of the nine other countries in this book, you should probably read those chapters as well. To be sure, the chapter on U.S.-Mexican differences may not contrast *your* culture with Mexico, but you'll still learn about both Americans and Mexicans.

And now a special message for northern Europeans. Most intercultural experts agree that—at its core—America is a northern European culture. This is unsurprising given that more Americans claim ancestry from northern Europe, especially Germany and the United Kingdom, than from any other part of the world. We hasten to add that northern Europeans are not all alike; indeed, we could easily write a book of dialogues featuring Finns talking to Brits and Germans talking to the Dutch. Moreover, people from northern Europe are unlike Americans in many significant respects—significant enough that there are U.S.-England, U.S.-France, and U.S.-Germany chapters in this very volume!

So what do we mean when we say America is a northern European culture? There are many similarities between Americans and northern Europeans concerning personal identity, management style, communication style, attitudes toward rank, and the concept of universalism—all cultural topics we discuss at some length. That being the case, there are many dialogues where the American speaker could be replaced by someone from Germany or perhaps Denmark. The particular attitudes or behaviors illustrated often apply to more than one culture.

And so it is that northern European readers—and here we mean Germans, the Dutch, Scandinavians, the British, and people from the so-called Anglo cultures (Canada, New Zealand, and Australia)—might easily identify with the American in many of these dialogues. They are encouraged to read the explanations and might very well find observations that apply to them.

So I Only Get One Mistake?

Some readers may wonder if a single cultural mistake can really be *that* serious, if a single misunderstanding means we are guaranteed to lose the contract, alienate the locals, or otherwise poison the cross-cultural well. It does not. We should remember, however, that a dialogue depicts only one mistake, made in one moment in time. But if we interact with folks from another culture every day or every week, we'll have a chance to make numerous mistakes. So, no: one mistake is not a deal breaker, but before long an accumulation of misinterpretations and misunderstandings begins to have real consequences.

Can You Really Say These Things?

Many readers may wonder about the value of cultural generalizations—as well they should. Not because such generalizations are normally inaccurate but because they're generalizations. You're never going to meet a "general" person or find yourself in a "general" situation. Be that as it may, it's also true that individuals raised in the same physical, social, economic, and cultural environment will probably be more like their peers than like people raised in other environments. In short, this group of individuals is likely to have some things in common, and it's those commonalities which confer a certain legitimacy and accuracy on generalizations made about the group. But "group" is the key word here: While generalizations can and often do accurately describe a certain *type*, you're never going to meet a type, only individuals.

How Should I Read This Book?

To compile this book I selected ten of the world's largest economies/major markets, and for each country I identified five of the most significant cultural differences between that country and the United States, differences which cause the most common misunderstandings and undermine successful business relations. Next I created five scenes (the dialogues) to bring the differences to life in common business interactions. I then wrote the "explanation" for each dialogue, a short essay revealing the embedded cultural mistake and describing the cultural differences behind the misunderstanding. In effect, then, this book consists of 50 essays on various characteristics of American culture (five per chapter) as contrasted with five key cultural characteristics of the featured country for that chapter.

With that as background, I make the following suggestions:

American readers:	Read the whole book (it doesn't take that long) because every chapter contains information about your culture that you should be aware of if you do business globally. To be sure, you can focus on the countries you work with most often, but every essay in the book contains valuable information for American readers.

Readers from the ten countries:	While you will probably want to start with the chapter that compares your culture to American culture, you will find important insights into the American mindset in other chapters as well.
All other readers:	You should read the whole book (for the reasons described above). If you do business with one of the ten featured countries, read that chapter more closely. If there is a featured country in your region of the world (Latin America, for example, or the Pacific Rim), read that chapter more closely. It may actually describe cultural differences that would also apply when Americans do business in your country.

Alfred Kraemer

If I've felt free to make a number of flattering observations about dialogues in this introduction, it's because I deserve no credit for "inventing" this marvelous technique. All credit is due to the late Dr. Alfred Kraemer, a sociologist who was chief of research and development for the U.S. Army. Dr. Kraemer sought to illustrate to U.S. Army personnel how their own culture influenced their behavior in dealing with local nationals overseas. He wrote and then filmed a number of dialogues and used them to train men and women in the military. I came across the scripts for these filmed sequences many years ago, was completely captivated by the concept, and started writing my own dialogues. And I've never looked back. I am as grateful to Dr. Kraemer now as I was the first time I was exposed to his ingenious technique in the early 1980s.

• • •

But enough preliminaries. Let's meet a few foreigners, embarrass ourselves, and start down the road to cultural competence.

1

The Arab Middle East

> Arab thought tends more to move on an ideal level,
> divorced from the Procrustean bed of reality.
> —Raphael Patai

One of the greatest passages in all of travel literature comes
from one of the greatest of all travel narratives: *Eothen* by A. W.
Kinglake. ("Eothen" means "from the East.") The book is an
account of a journey the Englishman Kinglake took in the late
1820s from the Danube through Turkey and the Middle East,
as far as Egypt. The passage occurs when Kinglake crosses the
Sava River, the boundary at that time between what he calls
"wheel-going Europe" and the Ottoman Empire, or, in his words,
"the Splendour and Havoc of the East" (1). Not long after leaving Christendom behind and passing into Ottoman lands, while
approaching a Turkish fortress, Kinglake writes that

> *presently there issued from the postern [city gate] a group
> of human beings—beings with immortal souls, and possibly
> some reasoning faculties, but to me the grand point was*

this, that they had real, substantial, and incontrovertible turbans. (1982, 3)

It is that single word "incontrovertible" that secures this passage a place in the pantheon of timeless cross-cultural observations. These are human beings with immortal souls and the power of reasoning—to that extent they are like you and me—but then come those "real, substantial, and incontrovertible turbans." Until that detail, we are in the realm of the familiar, but the turbans change everything. They cannot be denied, cannot be gainsaid; that's the brilliance of "incontrovertible." You and I and no one we know on our side of the river has ever worn a turban. *These people are not like us.*

2

The people Kinglake saw were probably Turks, not Arabs*, but it is fitting this scene took place in the Middle East, for of all the peoples profiled in these pages, the Arabs of that region are the least understood by Americans. Americans cannot relate to the geography: dry, barren, and hot. They don't think much of their forms of government: monarchies, dictatorships, and military states. They don't understand their religion: Islam. And they find their societies closed and very often anti-Western. Ask Americans their opinion of Arabs, and the most likely response is that they are either cruel or dishonest. What Americans *do* know about the Middle East usually has something to do with Israel.

The gap between Americans and Arabs is incontrovertible, but it is not unbridgeable. Read on.

---

* In this chapter, "Arab" refers to citizens of Arabic-speaking countries such as Saudi Arabia, Jordan, Syria, Lebanon, Iraq, Egypt, and the other countries of the Arabian peninsula. It does not include the non-Arab people from other Muslim countries in the region such as Turkey, Iran, Pakistan, and Afghanistan. In the author's experience, most of the observations made in this chapter also apply to the Muslim countries of North Africa: Libya, Algeria, Tunisia, and Morocco.

1. A DAY IN THE DESERT

MARTHA: Kevin, you're back early. How did your visit with the Saudis go?

KEVIN: Not that well, actually.

MARTHA: What happened?

KEVIN: Well, I gave my presentation the first morning, but they stopped me after an hour and gave me a tour of their facility. I met a lot of senior people, and we had a very long lunch. But no one asked about our proposal. It's like I had never even given the presentation.

MARTHA: Really?

KEVIN: And the next day was more of the same. We went on an all-day excursion to this village out in the desert. I met the head man of the tribe, and everyone was very nice, but no one said anything about our offer.

MARTHA: No one?

KEVIN: Nobody. And after that they didn't schedule any more meetings, so I decided to come home a day early.

MARTHA: Did you hear? We got an e-mail from them this morning.

KEVIN: Really?

MARTHA: Yes, they want us to sign a contract.

In several of the countries featured here, business is personal, *very* personal, and nowhere more so than in the Arab Middle East. The terms of the deal matter, of course, but not nearly as much as the character and personality of the dealer. Kevin, who does not know he has been tested, much less that he has passed the test, is using American criteria to evaluate the success of his visit to the Saudis, and by those criteria his trip has been a failure. His pitch was cut short, no comments were made about his proposal, people went to a lot of effort not to talk about business, and a three-day series of meetings and discussions was reduced to two.

Kevin would have good reason to be discouraged if the Saudis were primarily interested in his proposal, but they're not. Having done their due diligence, the Saudis already knew that Kevin's company could execute the job even before inviting him to visit. The presentation was just a formality, and one hour was more than enough to satisfy propriety.

In short, the Saudis had already made up their mind about Kevin the business; now comes the important part, deciding about Kevin the man, which explains everything that happened next. They showed him around their facility primarily so he could meet the senior people. During their long lunch together, the key players took Kevin's measure and decided whether they can work with him. The reports must have been very favorable because the Saudis then conferred the ultimate honor on Kevin by inviting him out to the ancestral village for a meal. This was also an opportunity for the head man of the tribe to size Kevin up and have the final say. That too must have gone well, for no more meetings were needed and Kevin got to go home early.

That great Arab-watcher Raphael Patai traces much of Arab behavior back to the concept of familism, which he defines as "the centrality of the family in social organizations [and] its primacy in the loyalty scale" (282). A key goal of Kevin's visit from the Saudi perspective, then, was to introduce him to the family, including the work family (all those "senior people") and the founding family, especially the patriarch (head man). This

4

determined his suitability to join the business, which is seen as an extension of the family. Patai writes that for Arabs

> *to encounter someone not known to [them] from before is quite an unusual event; if it occurs both sides will spend considerable time discussing their ancestry and relatives in the hope of finding somewhere a connecting link; only thereafter will they approach the subject that brought the stranger in the first place to the . . . tribe. (283, 84)*

In Kevin's case, there were no common relatives, of course, and "the subject that brought him to the tribe"—business—had already been discussed. Clearly the Saudis' priority was to establish a personal connection, a link that would bind Kevin and the "family," however broadly defined.

"In business relationships," Margaret Nydell writes in *Understanding Arabs*,

> *personal contacts are much valued and quickly established. Arabs do not fit easily into impersonal roles, such as the "business colleague" (with no private socializing offered or expected) or the "supervisor/employee" roles (where there may be cordial relations during work hours but where personal concerns are not discussed). For Arabs, all acquaintances are potential friends. A good personal relationship is the most important single factor in doing business successfully with Arabs. (35)*

The difference here is one of degree, not of kind. Americans also consider the personal when making business decisions; they would not give a contract to Company A solely because their terms were more favorable than Company B. But it is certainly true that the personal factor influences the decision much less than it does in the Arab Middle East.

The Fix

When working with Arabs, Americans should be prepared to spend much more time on "pleasantries" before getting down to business. Indeed, until Arabs decide whether it will be pleasant to work with you, business may not be an option. "In strongly relationship-based societies," Erin Meyer writes, "the balance of social talk to business may tip heavily to the former" (191). You should assume that proposals have been closely studied and vetted before any face-to-face meetings are scheduled, so there is usually no need to spend very long discussing the deal. Do not interpret social invitations as time-consuming distractions; they are what matter most. Arab presentations may be quite general and even vague, so you should ask for more details if necessary.

If you are an Arab working in an American context, you should not be surprised or offended if Americans fail to extend many social invitations; that does not signal any lack of interest. Meanwhile, you should spend much more time fleshing out the details of your proposal. Because you believe the personal relationship matters so much more than the terms of the deal, your business proposals often appear quite vague to Americans. "What are details between friends?" Arabs will say. "If we're friends, there will be no problems." To which most Americans would reply, "If there are no problems, we can be friends."

2. SARAH IN CHICAGO

PETER: Before you all go, I was wondering, Ali, about that risk assessment. It's due tomorrow, I think.

ALI: Yes, sir.

PETER:	Are we on track with it?
ALI:	Yes, sir, but I am still waiting for a woman named Sarah in Chicago to answer my e-mail.
PETER:	That's right. She works in risk assessment. Did you try calling her?
ALI:	Yes, sir. But she did not return my call.
PETER:	I can help you with that, Ali. I'll give her a call. I know Sarah.
ALI:	Thank you, sir.

It all sounds very civil, doesn't it? Unless you're Ali, of course, in which case you've just been ambushed by your boss and made to look a complete fool. Arabs have an exquisite sense of personal dignity and a correspondingly acute nose for any slights to their self-esteem. Raphael Patai has written of "the single issue which seems to be the overriding moral aim of the Arab: the preservation of his self-respect" (100). Ali will have a hard time forgiving Peter for what he has done here.

Where to begin? The first mistake Peter made (but arguably not the biggest) was to bring this whole matter of the risk assessment up during a meeting. We learn that Ali may in fact miss the deadline while he waits for an answer to his e-mail. To admit this in front of everyone at the meeting is deeply humiliating for Ali. Which is bad enough, but so far as Ali can tell, Peter's behavior is completely gratuitous since he could have waited to discuss the issue after everyone else had left. If Ali is the least bit paranoid, as sensitive Arabs can be, then he probably thinks Peter brought this up on purpose to shame him.

The next slight occurs when Peter asks Ali if he tried calling Sarah. Whether Ali did or did not, this question suggests (to Ali, anyway, and to the other Arabs at the meeting) that Peter doubts Ali is actually trying to resolve the delay. Why else would he ask? And how else could this be interpreted than as a vote of no confidence in Ali? In this context, we should note that Ali does not know Sarah, referring to her as "a woman named Sarah." He would probably feel uncomfortable calling someone for help with whom he has no personal relationship or, more to the point, would not expect a stranger to offer any help even if he did ask. The fact that he actually *did* call Sarah is a mark of Ali's desperation to keep this project on schedule and please his boss. And for his efforts, he gets a public slap on the wrist.

Peter makes his worst mistake when he reveals that he actually knows Sarah. If Ali was mostly embarrassed up to this point, now he is genuinely angry. It turns out none of this was necessary: Peter knows Sarah, he knows she works in risk assessment, and he knows Ali is working on that topic. Why wouldn't he have offered to call Sarah before now, one day before the deadline? And come to think of it, if Peter has a personal connection with Sarah, why hasn't he helped from the very beginning to smooth the way for Ali? What kind of boss is so uninvolved in the work of his staff?

Some readers are probably wondering if we're not being a bit unfair to Peter. All he has done, after all, is ask one of his staff for an update and then offered to help. Isn't Ali perhaps being a tad overly sensitive? Possibly, but there are numerous accounts of Americans making what they see as the mildest possible critical observations or suggestions to their Arab colleagues that nonetheless sent the Arabs into deep depression. "Because one's self-respect is so vulnerable to treatment by others," Patai has written, "the Arab is extremely wary of being slighted and sees personal insults even in remarks or actions which carry no such intent" (100). Even if Ali is a mite overly sensitive, the lesson here is that one man's suggestion can easily become another man's slight.

"Pride is one of the main elements on which Arab individualism rests," Sania Hamady writes in *Temperament and Character of the Arabs*,

> *since it is sheer being that is primarily respected. To establish a good rapport with an Arab one must be aware of the fact that foremost in the Arab view of the self is his self-esteem. It is important to pay tribute to it and to avoid offending it. The Arab is very touchy and his self-esteem is easily bruised. It is hard for him to be objective about himself or to accept calmly someone else's criticism of him. . . . Facts should not be presented to him nakedly; they should be masked so as to avoid any molestation of his inner self, which should be protected. (Nydell, 38, 39)*

9

Americans are not immune to feeling slighted or embarrassed, but an American's self-esteem comes largely from within. It is more a function of how the individual sees herself than of how others see her, founded on personal qualities and achievements. Hence, slights and criticism—the unfavorable judgments of others—make less of an impact and cannot easily undermine an American's ego. In the Arab world, however, where self-esteem comes largely from the respect and approval of society, public criticism automatically triggers a loss of dignity and undermines personal honor.

The Fix

Criticism still must be communicated in the Arab Middle East, as it must in all cultures and business environments. But in the Arab world, anything that could even remotely be construed as criticism—and that's a very big list—must be handled with great care; in especially delicate cases, a third party is used.

If you have to criticize someone or make a suggestion face-to-face, begin with positive feedback and a healthy dose of flattery to reassure them that the coming blow is not the whole story. "The foreign supervisor is well advised to take care when giving criticism," Margaret Nydell observes. "It should be indirect and include praise of any good points first, accompanied by assurances of high regard for the individual. . . . The concept of constructive criticism truly cannot be translated into Arabic—forthright criticism is almost always taken to be personal and destructive" (37, 38). Meanwhile, if you find yourself on the receiving end of extremely mild criticism, or even just the absence of any praise, then sit up and take notice.

While it's a tall order, Arabs working with Americans should try not to take suggestions or mild criticism personally. If you can't quite manage that, at least try to understand that Americans would hardly ever knowingly insult a colleague. Realizing that slights are unintentional can sometimes mitigate hurt feelings. For your part, when you have criticism to give to Americans, you will have to be more direct.

3. THERE MUST BE MONEY

KHALIL: My dear friend Alex. Wonderful to see you.

ALEX: Hi, Khalil. How are you?

KHALIL: Excellent, thanks be to God. By the way, we had a very fine meeting about your bridge proposal yesterday.

ALEX: Great.

KHALIL: It is a beautiful proposal. Everything is very promising. And we are sure the minister will approve it.

ALEX: But I thought you said the post was vacant at the moment?

KHALIL: Yes, unfortunately there is no minister right now.

ALEX: What about the cost?

KHALIL: It's very reasonable for a design so beautiful.

ALEX: Ah, so there *is* money in the infrastructure budget, after all?

KHALIL: Actually, we don't quite have an infrastructure budget at the present time. But there *must* be money.

On the whole, the Arabs have never cared that much for reality. And who can blame them? For one thing their physical reality is stark and forbidding. In his travel classic *Eothen*, A. W. Kinglake exaggerates perhaps, but not by much, when he writes of Arabia that "the hills and the valleys are sand, sand, sand, still sand, and only sand, and sand, and sand, again." Change "sand" to "rocks" and the statement is just as accurate. Life in such an empty, bleak environment is often harsh, unsatisfying, and disappointing. To survive is hard enough; to prosper, even harder. Things frequently do not turn out as we want them to or for the better. Who would live in such a world if something else were available?

And for Arabs, luckily, something else always is: the world of the possible, of what might be—and certainly of what *should* be—instead of what is. In his book *The Empty Quarter*, St. John Philby describes an "Arab national characteristic" he calls

the constant anxiety to be the announcer of good or pleasing news. It is less objectionable, of course . . . but it has a

*tendency in Arabia to discourage the purveying of true news,
which is more important, and to encourage exaggeration or
even suppression of material facts. (Yapp, 12)*

When things are not the way Arabs would like, they have a
way of denying reality and subscribing fully to an alternative
set of facts. If these facts have the unfortunate drawback of not
being altogether true, who can say that the reality they describe
is not just around the corner? And even if it is not, then surely it
is more pleasant to ponder the ideal than to face an often disappointing reality. How nice it would be, in short, if there *were* a
minister in place and a budget for infrastructure. We could have
our beautiful bridge, and you would get your lovely contract.

Unfortunately, none of this is presently true; indeed, looked
at objectively, the current situation is anything but "very promising." There is no one in charge, and there is no money for
bridges. Nor is there any reason to think that the minister will
sign the proposal since we do not even know who the minister is
yet. Bridges may not be his priority. From an American perspective, then, Alex could be forgiven for accusing Khalil of being
misleading at best and even dishonest. To which Khalil would
reply that all he has said is quite true; the only problem is that
reality has not yet had time to catch up to the truth.

Raphael Patai has observed that Arabs tend "to express ideal
thoughts and to represent that which is desired or hoped for as
if it were an actual fact in evidence rather than cleave to the
limitations of the real. Arab thought processes are relatively
more autonomous, more independent of reality, than the thought
processes typical of Western man" (311).

Needless to say, Arabs use language very differently from
Americans, believing that words do not merely describe what

is real but that they *confer* reality. Simply saying something, in other words, makes it so. "Once the intention of doing something is verbalized," Patai continues,

> *this verbal formulation itself leaves in the mind of the speaker the impression that he has done something about the issue at hand, which in turn psychologically reduces the importance of following up by actually translating the stated intention into action. . . . The verbal statement of intention achieves such importance that the question of whether or not it is subsequently carried out becomes of minor significance. (64, 65)*

Nowhere in the dialogue is this Arab tendency—to prefer the perfect world to often tainted and imperfect reality—more apparent than in Khalil's last statement: "But there *must* be money." Whether there *is* money is irrelevant; there just *has* to be money because the alternative, the deeply painful truth that Alex's beautiful bridge may never be built, is simply unthinkable.

To be sure, Americans are an optimistic people, hoping for and even expecting the best, but this is not because they would rather not face reality; they do so because they believe they can shape reality. It is also true that Americans tend to exaggerate, minimize obstacles, maximize possibilities, and generally describe things as much more positive and hopeful than they are. But once again they behave in this manner not because they refuse to acknowledge obstacles to success, but because their national experience has taught them that there is no problem that cannot be solved and no obstacle that cannot be overcome if people want something bad enough and are willing to try hard enough.

The Fix

Americans should first listen to and then quietly subtract 50 percent of what their Arab colleagues promise. Try to understand that the motive behind their exaggeration and enthusiasm is not to deceive or mislead but to be polite—and also to not usurp Allah's prerogative to work the occasional miracle. For your part, feel free to exaggerate as much as you like and not worry that Arabs will take you literally or hold you to outlandish promises. Indeed, if you do not exaggerate, Arabs may not take you seriously or they may think you're not interested in the matter under discussion.

Arabs, meanwhile, should realize that Americans often take exaggerations much more literally than fellow Arabs ever would. Accordingly, you should be careful not to make grand promises and likewise temper some of your natural enthusiasm. Too much exaggeration and enthusiasm come across as insincere to Americans; they will think you're being dishonest or just flattering them to win their favor. If Americans do not exaggerate enough for you, do not interpret that as a lack of enthusiasm or interest; they're just trying to be honest and not mislead you.

4. JUST TRYING TO HELP

CHARLES: Hi, Khadija. How did it go with the people at DHL?

KHADIJA: Sir?

CHARLES: What did they say when you asked them about the shipments?

KHADIJA: I didn't talk to them.

CHARLES: But when we spoke, you said you could help me and would call them.

KHADIJA: Yes, sir.

CHARLES: But you didn't call them.

KHADIJA: I didn't know anyone there.

CHARLES: I don't understand.

KHADIJA: No, sir.

Arabs like to be helpful and responsive. They will agree to almost any request, quite apart from whether or not they can actually do what's being asked. Since you cannot possibly know whether you can actually do something at the moment you're being asked, the thinking goes, it would be wrong to say no, not to mention impolite. God works in mysterious ways, after all, so who are you to say that something is just not possible? Even if you know something is not possible at the present time, it may become possible later on. So how can you say no?

I encountered a version of this phenomenon on my first trip to Rabat, the capital of Morocco. (Moroccans are not Arabs, exactly, but their culture is certainly Arab influenced.) I wanted to see the king's palace, and I asked several people I met on the street for directions. After following the first set of directions for a few minutes, I sensed I might have misunderstood, and I stopped a second person. This happened two more times before I finally arrived at the palace. Later I learned that, for Moroccans, it is more polite to give wrong directions than to be rude and unhelpful and say you don't know. "After all," as one Moroccan told me, "our directions *could* be right!"

This is the sentiment Charles has run into in this dialogue. Reading between the lines, we can see that some days back Charles asked Khadija if she could help him sort out a problem he was having with the company DHL. And Khadija obviously said yes, thinking she might know somebody who works there or, if not, then somebody she knows may know someone at DHL. There are always possibilities. "When Arabs say yes to your request," Margaret Nydell writes, "they are not necessarily certain that the action will or can be carried out. Etiquette demands that your request has a positive response. The result is a separate matter" (31).

Readers might wonder that if Arabs always say yes, how do they know whether the other person really means yes or is just being polite? If you follow the Arab logic here, the answer is easy: If the person is able to follow through on their agreement, they will of course come back and let you know what happened. Similarly, if they do not check in after a reasonable period of time, that means nothing happened, the person can't help you, and neither party will refer to the matter again. This is why Khadija is quite surprised at the beginning of this dialogue (all she can manage is "Sir?") when Charles asks her how it went. If she hasn't reported back to him, then it did not go well, and he should know better than to embarrass her by asking. When Charles presses her, causing even more embarrassment, she finally tells him that she "didn't know anyone" at DHL, meaning she was not in a position to solve his problem.

As they have been miscommunicating all along, it's quite likely Charles and Khadija walk away with very different notions of how things now stand. From her perspective, Khadija assumes Charles is pleased with her willingness to help him, although it came to nothing, and accordingly, she expects to have risen somewhat in Charles' esteem. For his part, Charles is disappointed with Khadija for misleading him—and might even think she lied. He probably feels he can't altogether trust her going forward.

Margaret Nydell explains part of this cultural difference when she notes that in "Western culture actions are far more important and more valued than words. *In Arab culture an oral promise has its own value* as a response. If an action does not follow, the other person cannot be held entirely responsible for a failure . . ." (31, 32).

The "value" Nydell refers to here is that Khadija's promise clearly demonstrated her willingness to do Charles a favor, and that is significant because favors are the lifeblood of the Arab business world. Doing favors for others and then calling in those favors when needed is a standard business practice and often the only way around burdensome official regulations. And simply the promise of a favor, even if it is not executed—the mere intent to act—carries great weight in the Arab world.

Americans like to do favors too, of course, but they are not central to the conduct of business; in some cases they must even be refused for ethical reasons. Nor do Americans like to refuse requests or otherwise appear unhelpful, but they would never agree to a request if they knew they could not carry it out. Indeed, if Americans are not reasonably sure they can fulfill a request, they will typically qualify their acceptance, just in case.

The Fix

When Arabs promise to help, Americans should graciously accept the offer while not assuming anything will come of it. One way to evaluate the offer is by gauging the amount of enthusiasm that accompanies it. If your Arab colleague simply offers to "try," without specifics, that's probably pure politeness, but if she goes on at some length and provides details, then there is a good chance the offer is genuine and could produce results. If you don't hear back fairly soon, in a day or two, about how the efforts are proceeding, that is usually a sign that nothing will happen, and you should pursue other options.

Arabs should not feel obliged to promise help to an American unless you are quite sure you can deliver on it. Remember that while your Arab colleagues can distinguish a genuine offer from a merely polite one, Americans cannot. You will disappoint and probably annoy them if you make an offer that has nothing behind it. Moreover, because Americans do not routinely make promises themselves, you will not come across as uncooperative if you abstain from such promises. If Americans are not regularly offering help to you, meanwhile, do not interpret this as unwillingness or being unfriendly; it just means they are not in a position to help and don't want to give you false hope.

5. THE NAKED YES

HAMID: How did it go with Mr. Ben Aziz?

ALISON: Very well, I think. He said my presentation was excellent and that he really liked my ideas.

HAMID: He said he liked them?

ALISON: Right. He called in his deputy and told him I had made a very good proposal and he should read it and offer his opinion.

HAMID: He said the proposal was good?

ALISON: Right.

HAMID: Did you ask for another meeting?

ALISON: I did, and he said yes.

HAMID: Yes. That's it?

ALISON: No, he also said he needed to check his calendar. But he was almost sure we could meet again next week to talk further.

T. E. Lawrence wrote that "the Arabs inhabit superlatives by choice" (Yapp, 12). To be sure, Arabs are an exuberant, enthusiastic, emotional people—in their actions, of course, but even more so in their speech, which tends toward exaggeration and repetition. It's as if their physical environment offers so few avenues for indulgence that they compensate for it in their speaking style, which is much abetted, it turns out, by certain features of the Arabic language. Patai has explained that much

> *of the predilection for exaggeration and overemphasis is anchored in the Arabic language itself. It is well known that the Arabic verb has various emphatic forms (the so-called modus energeticus). . . . [Also] the third person pronoun is [frequently] inserted between subject and predicate, which lends the statement an emphatic character. . . . [And] the Arabic adjective is often used to intensify expression. (52, 53)*

This tendency to exaggerate makes it difficult for Westerners to understand how Arabs actually feel and how enthusiastic they truly are about suggestions or proposals. A quick guide to Arab reactions goes something like this: The absence of any enthusiasm or positive comments is a sure sign of a negative reaction, especially given the fact that Arabs, unfailingly polite, rarely indulge in overt criticism. Modest enthusiasm, a few pieces of mild praise, signals a neutral reaction, neither positive nor negative. Effusiveness, exaggerated enthusiasm, and hyperbolic praise all indicate a positive response. In this context, readers might notice the exaggeration in nearly every one of Khalil's comments in Dialogue 3: "my dear friend Alex," "wonderful to see you," "a very fine meeting," "a beautiful proposal," and "very promising." Khalil can't deliver on all this enthusiasm, of course, but that's not the point. "[E]xaggeration is not to be taken literally," Patai continues, "but only serves the purpose of effect" (49).

All of which explains why, if we could see Hamid's face during this dialogue, we would see signs of growing concern. Alison has in fact had a very unsuccessful meeting with Mr. Ben Aziz and almost certainly will not be called back. She missed all the clues, as she misses them in this dialogue, although by the end of the exchange, thanks to Hamid's relentless litany of doubt—"He said he liked them?" "He said the proposal was good?" "That's it?"—even Alison is probably replaying the meeting in her mind.

Alison's first comment is immediately worrying on two accounts: Mr. Ben Aziz did praise her "presentation," but this was most likely a way of avoiding the substance—and we know what not saying anything implies from our quick guide to Arab reactions above. If there were any doubt about what Mr. Ben Aziz actually thinks of the substance, that is erased by what he said next, that he "really liked" Alison's ideas. Hamid picks up immediately on the word "liked," ignoring, as well he should, the obligatory "really." Of all the words Mr. Ben Aziz could have used to express enthusiasm, "like" is among the mildest and most perfunctory. And once again we know what that means from our Arab guide.

Next Mr. Ben Aziz called in his deputy, telling him Alison had submitted a "very good" proposal and asking him to read it and offer his opinion. There's a great deal of information in this gesture. Hamid immediately zeroes in on Mr. Ben Aziz calling the proposal "very good." Once again, "good" is probably the least effusive, least enthusiastic, and least emphatic piece of vocabulary available to Mr. Ben Aziz. Moreover, the fact that Mr. Ben Aziz asked his deputy to review the proposal suggests either that Mr. Ben Aziz is unsure of the proposal and needs another opinion (not a good sign) or that the whole matter interests him so little he's dumping it on his subordinate (also not a good sign). Naturally, it could also be that Mr. Ben Aziz is so excited that he wants his deputy to start implementing the proposal right away, but there is nothing here to support that interpretation and much that contradicts it.

Hamid's concern grows when he hears that when Alison asked for another meeting, all Mr. Ben Aziz said was "yes" and nothing more. Let's let Raphael Patai explain what that means:

A simple assent from an Arab can be, for him, nothing more than a polite form of evasion, while the same word may mean for his English-[speaking] interlocutor a definite, positive commitment. A simple "yes" or "no" is for the English speaker a definitive statement. His Arabic interlocutor, however, conditioned as he is by the exaggeration and overassertion that are the rule in his own mother tongue, is simply incapable of understanding such brief and simple statements in the same sense. For him "Yes" only means "Perhaps." Only if the English speaker had said: "Yes, I am telling you definitely, yes; I assure you positively and emphatically, yes; my answer is irrevocably and permanently, yes!" would the Arab have got the point that what the English speaker really meant was "Yes" (56, 57).

Point taken.

To be fair, Mr. Ben Aziz did say one more thing after his naked "yes": that he needed to consult his calendar but was "almost sure" he could meet with Alison next week. In the days of laptops and electronic calendars, surely Mr. Ben Aziz could have checked his schedule on the spot and given her his answer. Or, if he doesn't keep his own calendar, his scheduler was standing right there and could have done the deed. And in any case, "almost sure" is certainly a troubling qualifier. If Mr. Ben Aziz has any interest in meeting again with Alison, he would be much more than "almost sure."

We have noted elsewhere that Americans are themselves prone to exaggeration and unwarranted enthusiasm. (See Dialogue 28, "A Great Pleasure.") But this does not prepare Alison to accurately read Mr. Ben Aziz's remarks; from an American perspective, modest enthusiasm is still enthusiasm, still a positive reaction, and definitely not considered neutral. And it likewise requires the presence of negative comments *and not merely the absence of positive ones* to convey an unfavorable opinion to an American. American enthusiasm, in short, is not strategic; it's the real thing.

The Fix

Americans should not apply their standards for measuring enthusiasm to the Arab playbook. You should, rather, discount obligatory enthusiasm for the mere politeness it usually is. If something better does not materialize, you should be suspicious. In addition, you should be careful not to mistake true Arab enthusiasm, that effusive praise that borders on hyperbole, for what it sounds like to most people in America: insincere flattery. It's not. When you speak to Arabs, you might want to indulge in more flattery than makes you comfortable and exaggerate just enough so they know you're serious. "Those interested in presenting the American point of view to literate Arabs," E. T. Prothro writes, "should note that a statement which seems to be a firm assertion to Americans may sound weak and even doubtful to Arabs" (Patai, 58).

For their part Arabs would do well to remember that Americans are suspicious of too much enthusiasm and exaggeration; it sounds insincere and phony, like what sycophants do. You should, accordingly, cut way back on your rhetoric, exaggerating only slightly to communicate enthusiasm. Americans will refrain from hyperbole when they are talking to you, but you should not interpret this as lack of commitment or interest. Nor will they engage in flattery, which they regard as a kind of dishonesty.

2

Brazil

Anyone who does not get along with Brazilians had
better examine himself; the fault is his.
—Jack Harding, I Like Brazil

There has always been something aspirational about Brazil, a
sense of possibilities not quite realized, of a bright future always
just out of reach. As Charles de Gaulle famously said, "Brazil is
the country of the future—and always will be."

Oddly enough, most Brazilians would agree, not because they
lack pride in their country but because they cheerfully accept
that they never quite seem to reach their considerable potential.
"There was once a sanguine vision of Brazil," Thomas Page writes,

> that held that the nation possessed sufficient human and
> natural resources to enable it to overtake the United States
> as an economic power; that while the twentieth century has
> been the "American century," the twenty-first would belong
> to Brazil. Looking with great anticipation beyond tomorrow
> has long been a shared article of faith for Brazilians who

embraced the slogan "Brazil, country of the Future." How-ever, with typical self-deprecation, many were wont to add such caveats as "but the future never comes," or "ours is a land of unlimited impossibilities." (5)

There is a common Brazilian saying that "Brazil is a large gold mine that only the Brazilians have not yet discovered."

A large part of the explanation has to be that many Brazilians live for the present moment and worry less about the future, what Phyllis Harrison has described as "a relaxed approach to the world and to problems in it and a willingness to take things as they are" (17). This carpe diem attitude probably explains another famous (possibly apocryphal) remark de Gaulle is said to have made after a visit to Brazil in the 1960s: "Brazil is not a serious country," suggesting that a serious country would not merely accept things as they are but try to make them better.

Brazil is once again experiencing a wild swing from prosperity and rapid development to economic and social disruption. For ten years or more, Brazil has proudly been one the BRIC countries (Brazil, Russia, India, and China), a quartet of high-potential emerging economies on the cusp of explosive growth. Now growth has stalled, the government is in turmoil, and public protests are daily events. Brazil may very well dig itself out of this hole, but for the moment it appears Brazilians have once again misplaced their map to the gold mine. Meanwhile, as Elizabeth Herrington reminds us, Brazilians take everything one day at a time. After all, she writes, "God is Brazilian, the country is beautiful, and the weather is nearly always amenable, so why worry?" (30)

6. VACATION

BRAD: The Ministry turned down our license
          application.

MARIA:	I know.
BRAD:	We need to find out why.
MARIA:	I know why. We didn't meet all the requirements.
BRAD:	Why didn't you say something?
MARIA:	I did. I told you we should wait a week.
BRAD:	But all you said was that you had a friend at the Ministry.
MARIA:	And I told you he was on vacation until next week.

Brazil is one of those countries that frustrates by-the-book Americans, who assume that as long as you have all the proper documents and follow all the regulations, the system works. In Brazil, if you know how to work the system, you don't need to worry about documents and regulations. "Americans tend to approach business as a system of rules and procedures," Harrison writes, "whereas Brazilians often approach business as a particular kind of social interaction" (72). Put another way: In America, the system is fair; in Brazil, it all depends.

Fairness is one of the deepest American values, which is unsurprising in a culture that is so strongly egalitarian. But what does it mean to say a system is "fair"? To an American, a fair system is a set of regulations and procedures applied uniformly across the board, regardless of circumstances, who you are, or whom you know. These regulations and procedures are expressly designed to create a "level playing field," affording the same chances for success to everyone regardless of background or connections. A fair system is transparent, accountable, and completely impersonal. There are consequences for deviations, and no one receives special treatment. Moreover, a fair system is a closed circle; there is no way to manipulate or "get around" such a system. The only way to get a different result from a fair system is to amend the system. (This concept is known as "universalism" in the intercultural field; its opposite, "particularism," is more common in Brazil, as described below.)

Is it any wonder Brad can't imagine what relevance Maria's two statements in this dialogue could possibly have: that she knows someone in the Ministry and that her acquaintance is on vacation? In what universe could these facts have anything to do with whether or not his license application was approved? As thrown as he is by these statements, Brad was already reeling from Maria's first observation: that she knew all along the license would be turned down because Brad's company "didn't meet all the requirements." Brad naturally asks why Maria didn't say anything, and when she responds ("I did. I told you we should wait a week."), Brad suddenly finds himself on the far side of the looking glass.

So how does the system work in Brazil, then? In a word: It doesn't. Things do get done in Brazil, but it's in spite of the system not because of it, the essence of what is sometimes called particularism. To be clear, there *is* a system in Brazil: countless rules and regulations, numerous policies and procedures, lots of paperwork, thousands of bureaucrats—and next to nothing to show for it. "Brazilians have been burdened with draconian laws," one observer notes, "and an inert bureaucracy. Rather than struggle against impossible odds, Brazilians find ways to cheat the system" (Morrison, 88). In the end, the real system in Brazil, the way to get things done, is to accumulate and then call in favors.

There is even a name for this alternative or shadow system: *jeito* or its diminutive, *jeitinho*. While *jeito* literally means "way," as in *jeito Brasileiro*, meaning the Brazilian way of doing things, it carries the sense of finding a way around a rule or law without actually breaking it. That way, as Jacqueline Oliveira has observed, often involves doing favors. *Jeito*, she writes, "is an intricate system of giving and receiving favors in order to accomplish a task" (64). Most Brazil-watchers consider *jeito* untranslatable, but "favors" or "little favors" (*jeitinho*) is the default translation.

"Brazilians characteristically seek subtle ways to circumvent difficult situations," Joseph Page writes.

> *Instead of resorting to confrontation, they prefer to use what they call the jeito or jeitinho, a difficult to translate term referring to what a French scholar once described as "an ingenious maneuvre that renders the impossible possible; the unjust just; and the illegal legal." It is a rapid, improvised, creative response to a law, rule, or custom that on its face prevents someone from doing something. The jeitinho personalizes something ostensibly governed by an impersonal norm. (10)*

In particularist societies everything depends on whom you know. Which is precisely where Maria's "friend at the Ministry" fits into this picture. If favors are the grease that lubricates the bureaucracy, then friends who owe favors are the linchpins of *jeito*. Needless to say, if your favor-owing friend is on vacation, now is not the time to submit your license application.

It should be noted here that Maria is well aware that her company does not meet the requirements for a license, but significantly that's *not* the reason she insists on delaying the application. Nor does she suggest they wait until the requirements are met. The point, of course, is that in the Brazilian system it's not about the requirements or, more accurately, not *only* about the requirements; it's also about the favors. Indeed, without the favors it's entirely possible Brad and Maria would still not get the license even if they did meet the requirements!

We hasten to add here that Brad doesn't need to know anything at all about *jeito* to avoid the mistakes he makes in this dialogue. He just needed to listen to Maria and figure out what she meant. Clearly, Maria was not simply babbling; when she mentioned she had a friend in the Ministry, Brad should have realized there was a reason for her to bring this up, even if he did not know what it was. When she went on to mention the friend was on vacation, Brad should again have realized that there's something important about this friend. Brad could not be expected to know *what* this was, but he should at least have realized that something else was going on.

The Fix

If business in Brazil revolves around favors, then Americans need to start doing favors so they can collect them when the time comes. Alas, this will not come easily or naturally to many of you; while the practicalities of doing favors may not be especially challenging, the ethics are. The emotional and psychological distance you will have to travel to embrace *jeito* is best illustrated by the fact that in American culture the word "favoritism" is unfailingly pejorative. There is not a single context in which it is looked upon positively. Everything favoritism stands for—preferential treatment, going around the system, influence peddling—is reprehensible to Americans. After all, it was the desire to escape the favoritism of the inherently unequal European feudal system that drove many Americans to the New World in the first place.

Be that as it may, if business in Brazil dances to the music of *jeito*, then you must come to terms with trading favors. And there is at least one sense in which that may come easily; If the official system is unfair, or, more accurately, if the rules and regulations are applied inconsistently and arbitrarily—if everyone stands a more or less equal chance of being mistreated—then indulging *jeito* may not feel so unfair. But one word of caution if you start down this road: Brazilians do not see favors quite the same way you do. To an American, doing a favor is as much a gesture of kindness as it is the incurring of a debt. While it would be nice if the other person returned the favor, it is not a moral obligation. Brazilians take favors more seriously and expect reciprocity.

For their part, Brazilians who deal in an American business context should not expect *jeito* to work or to find it necessary. Indeed, Americans are likely to be offended at the mere mention of favoritism, at least when it refers to preferential treatment or circumventing the system. In America the system works, more or less, so there's no need to go around it.

7. FIRST VISIT

RUBEM: George, I was just going to call you.

GEORGE: Hi, Rubem. I just thought I'd check with you about the pipe fittings before I go home for the weekend. They're still going to be delivered on Monday, right?

RUBEM: Ah, George, perhaps not. My wife's cousin and family came to us on Sunday.

GEORGE: Right.

RUBEM: We had no idea they were coming.

GEORGE: No, of course not.

RUBEM: It is their first time down here to São Paulo.

GEORGE: Right. How nice.

RUBEM: So we lost two days.

GEORGE: How's that?

Much has been written about the South American attitude toward time, that people south of the U.S.-Mexico border are—take your pick—relaxed, laid back, casual, erratic, or not serious about time. Of course, most of this has been written by Americans and Canadians, people north of the border, which suggests this is at best a relative judgment. But even Brazilians joke about being late. So it's not that Brazilians don't understand what it means to be on time or don't know, for example, when they are missing a deadline or showing up late for a meeting. They do know, and they will usually apologize.

So what's going on? A variety of explanations are regularly put forth to explain this phenomenon, and while they differ in specifics, they all agree on one point: Being on time is often not a high priority for Brazilians. To put it another way, Brazilians place a lower value on punctuality than virtually all of the North American and northern European cultures. Wherever it conflicts with certain other Brazilian values, punctuality does not prevail. In many cases Brazilians believe there's no sense worrying about time.

One of those cases—and one of the most important of those other Brazilian values—is on display in this dialogue. George actually receives three increasingly specific explanations for why Rubem cannot make his deadline—and why that's okay. But George, who places punctuality much higher on his list of priorities, is ill equipped to pick up on these hints. The first comes when Rubem says his wife's cousin and family have come to visit. Family takes priority over almost any other consideration in Brazilian culture, including Brazilian business culture; indeed, at their core, many businesses in Brazil are family enterprises, meaning the line separating business and family is almost nonexistent. Hence, the moment Rubem used the word "family," George should have known his delivery was in trouble and cheerfully acquiesced.

30

George's reply—the innocuous "Right"—surprises Rubem, who expected something closer to "How nice! Never mind about the fittings. Have a nice weekend and call me on Monday." George's odd response compels Rubem to offer more details to this obtuse American: "We had no idea they were coming." We were caught off guard, in other words, and did not have a plan in place to permit us to deal with this situation (such as asking other family members to look after the visitors) and stay on schedule with the pipe fittings.

When George fails to pick up on this clue, Rubem brings out his biggest gun: "It is their first time down here," meaning as they are family, and as we were not expecting them, and as they have never visited São Paulo before, what choice did we have but to take a couple days off and fulfill our family obligations? Rubem doesn't say this, but he might also have added that sooner or later looking after family is always good for business. It might mean that George has to wait for his pipe fittings in the present instance, but in the future Rubem might call on his wife's cousin to do George a big favor. Seen in this light, is it really so bad George has to wait two extra days? Moreover, is it altogether fair to say that Rubem doesn't care about deadlines?

The primacy of family and the ingroup (including close friends) in their value system explains more Brazilian behavior than any other single factor, including why punctuality cannot always take priority. The "family unit is the cornerstone of life and revered in Brazilian culture," Oliveira writes. Brazilians "may forgo a business obligation if a family matter arises. . . . For the most part Brazilian coworkers and employees understand and acknowledge the employee's decision to put family first" (21, 22).

Phyllis Harrison, another Brazil-watcher, makes the same point about close friends:

When a friend arrives a Brazilian drops whatever he is doing to visit, even if he is busy with matters a North American would consider to have precedence. A woman described a Brazilian friendship as "a constant sacrifice." One might hint about a pressing engagement . . . but one would not make any direct statement to indicate that business is more important than a visit from a friend. Brazilians are hurt and offended by the North American assumption that business comes first. . . . Likewise a visit from a friend is a legitimate excuse for lateness in Brazil. (87)

But family is not the only reason why deadlines are not taken as seriously in Brazil as in the United States. Surely another is the deep sense of fatalism that pervades Brazilian culture, the belief that many things that happen in life are outside anyone's control—except God's, of course—and simply must be accepted. Fatalism, along with its close cousin resignation, influences punctuality in two ways.

The most obvious is the fact that if people cannot always control what happens to them, then neither can they be held responsible when schedules are adjusted. This is not to suggest that fatalism causes Brazilians to be late or even that it excuses *deliberate* lateness, which it does not. But it does help explain the greater tolerance of lateness when it occurs. Brazilians, in short, appreciate it when people are on time, but there is a much broader range of acceptable justifications for being late.

Fatalism also shows up in the carpe diem syndrome almost all Brazil-watchers have described, the idea that since they cannot know or control the future, Brazilians don't worry about it and live in the present moment. Herrington writes, "With all the uncertainties in life, Brazilians say, it's better to enjoy what you have right now" (Herrington, 30). Among other things, this makes Brazilians notoriously spontaneous, hence somewhat unreliable when it comes to keeping appointments and respecting schedules.

Some readers may wonder if we are not asking the wrong question, that we should worry less about the Brazilians' elastic sense of time and ask instead why Americans are so obsessed with it. Fair enough. Americans are obsessed with time because they are the can-do people, the culture in which achievements account for more of a person's sense of self-worth than in almost any other country. And what does that have to do with time? Easy: achievements = effort + time. If time is one half of achievement, and achievement is a paramount cultural value, then time is a Very Big Deal. And wasting time, which is what happens when people are late or a deadline is missed, is a cultural affront of the first order.

33

Does this mean, then, that Americans have no sense of fatalism and don't care about family? A resounding yes to the first observation and a qualified no to the second. Let's start with fatalism: Americans have none. They are the can-do people, as noted above, who believe that anything is possible, that nothing is outside their control and nothing happens in life that must just be accepted. Even Americans acknowledge that some things happen *to* you, things you did not cause. But you can always do something about them if you so choose. You *may* accept them, in other words, but you never *have* to. Needless to say, if you're in charge of your circumstances like this, there would never be any excuse for being late.

As for how Americans regard the family: Family is paramount for many Americans, too, but it does not always prevail in the competition against work. Americans struggle mightily with work-life balance. Whenever someone leaves a high-profile position in the United States, the reason they inevitably give is so that "I can spend more time with my family," and everyone understands. In those cases where work does not prevail over family, it is usually a very close second; in Brazil, work is usually a more distant second.

Moreover, because the line between work and family is often blurred in Brazil, Brazilians see taking care of the family as a way of serving the business, while Americans see taking care of business is a way of protecting the family. George, in short, would be very unlikely to take two days off from work to show his in-laws around San Francisco, and if he did, most of his colleagues would not understand.

The Fix

Americans must accept that they cannot change the Brazilian attitude toward time. More accurately, you will not convince Brazilians to start caring less about family and friends or to suddenly feel in control of their external circumstances. In a Brazilian work environment, you should build some flexibility into your schedules and also devise an early warning system whereby you can become aware of threatened deadlines much sooner. Finally, explain to your Brazilian counterparts how serious the consequences of missed deadlines are in the American business context. Some Brazilians will assume that tardiness is as acceptable in the U.S. as it is in Brazil, but when they learn otherwise, they may make a special effort to stay on schedule. Herrington advises that if "a deadline is crucial it is best to inform all of the parties involved of that fact. Set up progressive steps that can be checked along the way to ensure that the deadline will be met, and be sure you check those steps as things progress" (60, 61).

Brazilians working in an American context must understand that there are relatively few acceptable justifications for missing a deadline—and far more serious consequences. You may want to set deadlines that give you more flexibility; if you think you can be finished by Wednesday, make the deadline Friday. And let Americans know immediately, not two days out, when there is any chance a deadline may be slipping. Do not expect Americans to understand, meanwhile, when you put family ahead of business; putting family first is only justifiable to Americans in extraordinary circumstances.

8. PHASE II

MIKE: Ana Maria, what can I do for you?

ANA MARIA: Hi, Mike. I just wanted to let you know we finished Phase I last Thursday.

MIKE: Great, right on schedule.

ANA MARIA: I sent you an e-mail. I guess you didn't have time to reply yet.

MIKE: Yes, I got that. Thanks. So how's Phase II coming along so far?

ANA MARIA: Phase II?

MIKE: How much is left to do on that?

ANA MARIA: Did you want us to start Phase II?

MIKE: Yes, we went over the implementation schedule last month, and we agreed you'd start on Phase II immediately.

ANA MARIA: Yes, of course. We discussed that last month.

Business culture in Latin America is more hierarchical than in the United States. In many companies, especially smaller ones, the management model is the extended family, where the paterfamilias is the undisputed head of the household and has the last word on all major family decisions—except those that affect the running of the household, where men have almost no say. In Brazil, Volker Poelzl writes, "family-owned businesses often have a hierarchical structure that offers few responsibilities to employees, leaving the decision-making to the founder or owner of the company" (253). In such cultures, power and authority are concentrated at the top and not readily shared.

Power is unequally distributed in all cultures, of course, even in America; what differs from culture to culture is how comfortable people are with their power and how free they feel to exercise it. As it happens, there is probably more research and data available on cultural attitudes toward power and hierarchy than any other topic in this book. The most famous comes from Geert Hofstede, who coined the term "power distance" and was one of the first to measure cultural differences regarding power. Via survey responses from participants in fifty-two countries and three regions, Hofstede ranked cultures by how readily people accepted the unequal distribution of power. Below are the results for the eleven countries covered in this book; the higher the number, the more comfortable people are with power gaps:

Russia	95	France	68
Mexico	81	Japan	54
Arab countries	80	United States	40
China	80	Germany	35
India	77	Great Britain	35
Brazil	69		

Hofstede considers a difference of ten points between any two countries to be significant, implying numerous differences in common business behaviors and attitudes. The twenty-nine-point difference between the U.S. and Brazil suggests rude awakenings are just around the corner whenever Brazilians and Americans do business together.

More-recent work, such as the comprehensive research survey conducted by Robert J. House et al. of sixty-one countries, supports Hofstede's original findings. Here in numerical order are the House rankings of power distance for ten of our countries; there are no data for Arab countries as such, although Morocco (at 61) had the highest comfort level of all with power gaps, while Denmark (at 1) had the lowest.

Russia	48	Mexico	32
India	46	England	26
Brazil	38	Japan	23
France	34	China	21
Germany	33	United States	13

In this study, we see that Brazil is the third most tolerant country of power distance in our eleven-country pantheon, and the U.S. was the least tolerant. In low-power-distance cultures such as the U.S., managers tend to be more hands-off; in Brazil and other high-power-distance cultures, managers supervise much more closely and are involved even in the most routine decisions.

In other words, one of the many ways more hierarchical business cultures differ from less hierarchical ones is the degree to which subordinates are expected to use their own judgment and make independent decisions, as well as the degree of guidance and supervision managers are supposed to provide. This is the issue the American, Mike, is facing here. Ana Maria is working on a two-phase project for Mike, and apparently she and her team finished Phase I a few days back. We also learn that "last month" they discussed what was supposed to happen at that juncture: Ana Maria and company were supposed to "start on Phase II immediately."

Instead, it appears she promptly notified Mike that they had finished Phase I, and she and her team have been sitting on their hands ever since waiting for his reply, quite possibly setting the project back several days until Mike tells them what to do next. Skye Stephenson has written of "the marked hierarchical configuration" of Latin American business culture. "[T]hose in the lower echelons are accustomed to working under a rather authoritarian and paternalistic type of management and usually wait for specific orders rather than demonstrating initiative" (76, 77).

The question the Mikes of the world would have at this point is why Ana Maria failed to follow "the implementation schedule" as "we agreed." To which the Ana Marias of the world would no doubt reply: We wanted to get your approval first, and why didn't you answer my e-mail? Ana Maria knows she has been given permission to act on her own, but in Brazilian culture most staff, even if only as a courtesy, would check first with their manager to make sure these month-old instructions are still valid, especially at such an important milestone. In other words, most Brazilian bosses would want to be informed at this juncture *even if they had already given their approval to proceed.* After all, many things could have changed since Phase I began, and while an American boss would have kept his staff in the loop, sharing any new developments relevant to the project, Brazilian bosses don't always share information so freely.

Nor do staff members necessarily want to be so well informed; the less they know, the less they can be expected to act on their own, which inevitably comes with some risk in a top-down business culture. "Decision making involves risk," Oliveira observes, "and is not something the Brazilian person takes to aggressively. Most support employees or mid-level managers will be reluctant to make decisions in the workplace, specifically because they want to avoid risk" (55). From a Brazilian perspective, absolutely nothing can be lost by consulting with Mike before proceeding to Phase II, and a great deal can be gained. From Mike's perspective, Ana Maria doesn't want to take responsibility or be held accountable.

Brazilians may have learned respect for and deference to authority in the home, at their father's knee, but it is also all around them in Brazil's strong class system. Class criteria "determine who will be admitted to hotels, restaurants, and most social clubs," Harrison notes,

> *who will get preferential treatment in stores, churches, night-clubs, and travel conveyances; and who will have the best chance among a number of marriage suitors. . . . Interaction between classes is not great. . . . One phrase that is heard frequently in cross-class situations is Voce sabe com quem esta falando (Do you know who you're talking to?), used when the speaker senses a lack of respect. A lower status person (whatever his specific status) may use doutour (doctor) when addressing a person of higher status. The title shows social deference. (4, 5)*

Brazilians, in short, are used to social inequalities, which no doubt helps them accept inequalities in power and authority in the workplace.

Americans, as we've already said, tend to be low-power-distance types. They see inequalities as man-made and largely artificial; while it is sometimes convenient or necessary, it is unnatural for some people to have power over others. Those with power, therefore, mindful of the inherent unfairness, tend to deemphasize it; they try to minimize the differences between themselves and subordinates by delegating responsibility and encouraging ownership. In such cultures, the best organizational charts are the flattest ones, and the best bosses are invisible, flexing their managerial muscle (i.e., drawing attention to their power) only as a last resort. "The traditional guideline for effective American management," two observers write, "has been: Push authority as far down the structure as possible" (Joynt & Warner, 107). American subordinates neither like nor expect close supervision, which has come to be known as micromanagement— and which, incidentally, is expected and normally appreciated in most high-power-distance cultures.

"In egalitarian American culture," Gilles Asselin and Ruth Mastron write,

> power is almost a dirty word, and while people acknowledge the existence of office politics, they regard such maneuvering as slightly distasteful. Companies talk of the participative workplace where employees are empowered to control their own jobs and destinies. The idea of having power over someone, or, worse yet, being under someone's power, makes most Americans vaguely uncomfortable. . . . [In] Latin cultures, power is acknowledged and spoken of openly. High-level people use their power freely, usually to their own advantage, and are respectfully deferred to by those they control. (200)

The Fix

Brazilian staff are quite capable of accepting responsibility and using their own judgment but in many cases have had little practice. Their default mode, in short, is to assume that bosses want to be kept in the loop and consulted before even routine actions are taken. Inaction and approval seeking are risk-free options in the Brazilian workplace. If, as an American manager in Brazil, you want to delegate responsibility and empower direct reports, you will have to make your wishes very explicit, spelling out in detail which decisions are being delegated and which are not. If a Brazilian direct report has to guess whether a manager wants her to use her own judgment or check with the boss, she will always check. Even when you do delegate, you would be wise to check in much more regularly with your Brazilian staff (than you would with Americans) to offer guidance and support.

Brazilians working in a predominantly American business context must get comfortable with accepting more autonomy and less guidance from management. You should feel free to approach your manager whenever you need help, but do not expect managers to regularly ask you how things are going or if you need their assistance. That is considered micromanaging in the United States, and Americans bosses would not be comfortable doing that, nor would American direct reports appreciate it. Be careful not to become what Americans call a "high-maintenance" employee, someone who requires a lot the manager's time and attention. Needless to say, if you are managing Americans in their culture, the safest thing is to leave them alone.

9. LET'S HAVE LUNCH

TERESA:	That was a good first meeting. Only two more days to go.
AL:	Yes, now we know each other's positions. I'm sorry, by the way, that I couldn't join you for dinner last night. Thank you for your invitation.
TERESA:	Did you have a pleasant day?

AL: I did, thanks. I had to do some shopping for my wife and kids; it was my only chance.

TERESA: Of course. Why don't we have breakfast tomorrow morning?

AL: I'm afraid I've got to prepare for the next session all morning.

TERESA: How about lunch, then? Even Americans have to eat.

AL: I've got a conference call with my staff back home from 12:00 to 1:00. But I've got a better idea. Why don't we go to dinner tomorrow night, when we can relax a bit?

TERESA: After the negotiations, you mean?

Brazilians do business with people; Americans do business with companies. Or as one Brazil-watcher has succinctly observed: "The importance of establishing good personal relationships in business cannot be overemphasized" (Herrington, 57). To which we would add the sooner these relationships are established, the better. If at all possible, they should be established *before* doing business, or at least developed simultaneously with and alongside business meetings and negotiations. The bottom line is that Brazilians want to do business with people they can trust, and how can they trust someone they don't know? "Establishing a relationship *and thereby trust* takes a great deal of time and lots of socializing," Jacqueline Oliveira writes (italics added). "This is accomplished through low-key interactions in restaurants and clubs and joining your counterpart at sporting or cultural events. By participating in social events such as these, you are showing your colleagues that you are committed to the relationship" (47).

Al, who barely has enough time to go gift shopping, is probably not joining Teresa anytime soon at the soccer stadium or the samba club. We have to give Teresa credit for trying, which she does in her very first remarks: "Only two more days to go," meaning there is not much time left for them to get to know each other. In Al's next statement ("Thank you for your invitation"), we learn that Teresa has already tried to meet with him socially and been rebuffed. When she subtly probes to find out why ("Did you have a nice day?"), she learns to her surprise and disappointment that Al could easily have met with her the day before, either during the day (it doesn't take eight hours to gift shop) or, if not, then certainly for dinner. Teresa cannot be blamed for wondering if Al is actually serious about doing business with her company.

Any doubts she might have had about Al are soon confirmed when he's too busy for breakfast and likewise can't meet for lunch, ignoring a very pointed hint ("Even Americans have to eat") and offering an embarrassingly amateur excuse: a conference call with his staff back home. They are people he just left and will see again in two days. Is it really more important to connect with them in the short time remaining than to get to know Teresa? Al's suggestion they have dinner together two-thirds of the way through a three-day set of meetings is not—how to put it?—confidence building. In the end, Teresa and her colleagues may still decide to do business with Al, but it will mean venturing into the unknown, and they would much prefer to be on firmer footing.

The key to understanding the importance of good personal relations when doing business with Brazilians ultimately goes back to the centrality of family in Brazilian life. (See Dialogue 7, "First Visit.") In the end, Brazilians would prefer never to do business with anyone outside the ingroup of their immediate and extended family—plus a few honorary family members such as schoolmates, lifetime friends, and friends of lifetime friends. This would take the lion's share of the risk out of doing business and likewise minimize much of the standard unpleasantness:

competitiveness, disagreements, contention, backbiting, suspicion, deceit, and various other frustrations. Ingroup and family members can be difficult, too, of course, but they can be trusted, by and large. And while we always have considerable leverage over our extended family, we have none over all the strangers comprising the outgroup.

And that's the point: Somehow in business we must convert strangers into family, into people we can implicitly trust and over whom we can exert influence. And there's simply no way to do that other than spending time with them and getting to know them. Hence, Teresa's brave and ultimately unsuccessful crusade to give Al the chance to join the family.

Having looked at (and trashed) Al through Brazilian eyes, we need to add the American perspective. Americans are happy to get to know their business partners, and they likewise recognize the importance of establishing good personal relations. But none of this has to happen before doing business—*and especially not as some precondition for working together.* Americans, like Brazilians, also want to work with people they can trust, but in America trust is extended freely—Americans assume people can be trusted until they prove otherwise. Meanwhile, in Brazil, trust extends only as far as the ingroup; everyone else must prove they can be trusted. Americans don't even use the vocabulary of ingroups and outgroups because they don't make such distinctions; strangers are just so many friends we haven't met yet. Tomorrow night at dinner is soon enough.

We might add one more word about trust: *Everyone* likes to do business with people they can trust, Americans as well as Brazilians, but Americans can afford to worry less about trust because they live in a universalist culture. (See Dialogue 6.) In universalist cultures, the system is fair; if it turns out some folks cannot be trusted, the system will always protect you.

44

The Fix

Americans distinguish between business and pleasure; for Brazilians, business is pleasure and pleasure is likewise business. There is no easy work-around for this cultural difference; you will just have to bite the bullet and relax. As a practical matter, that means scheduling an extra day or two when first meeting Brazilian counterparts, being open to long lunches and even longer dinners, and acknowledging that time spent outside the workplace is just as or even more important than time spent in official interactions.

Brazilians coming to America should be prepared to focus more on the deal and less on the dealers. Americans might invite you to dinner, but it would not be for the purpose of deciding if you are acceptable business partners; it would be for the purpose of eating. Knowing this, you might want to put more thinking and detail into your business proposal, since it will count for much more in America than it would in Brazil. Meanwhile, don't interpret any lack of socializing as a signal that the negotiations aren't going well. If Americans seem uninterested in getting to know you better, it's just because it's not essential in their view for a successful business relationship. As Americans would say: "It's icing on the cake."

45

10. MUTUAL UNDERSTANDING

DEBBIE:	João, I just got your e-mail.
JOÃO:	Good.
DEBBIE:	But I had a couple of questions. In the meeting this morning, you said you thought you could finish that project in one week.

JOÃO: I believe you said it would be great if we
               could do it in a week. And then you asked
               me if that was possible.

DEBBIE: Right. And you also said Francisco could
               most likely head the team.

JOÃO: You were obviously very keen to have
               Francisco.

DEBBIE: Yes, I was. But now your e-mail says the
               project is going to take two weeks and
               Francisco isn't available.

JOÃO: Yes. I just wanted to be sure we understood
               each other.

Life is short. Why have arguments, disagreements—unpleasant-ness—when we can all get along? It depends on circumstances and how well people know each other, but there is a strong tendency in Brazilian culture to avoid conflict and confrontation, especially in public, as at a meeting. If this means bending the truth ever so slightly, is it not worth it? Is honesty really the best policy in a culture where harmony and getting along are core values?

"To preserve a sense of harmony," Skye Stephenson writes, South Americans

> *are usually quite careful in their conversations not to bring up anything that might be construed by another as personally offensive or hurtful in order to avoid a potentially explosive situation, even if such avoidance leads to greater complications later. When potentially controversial topics must be brought up at all, they are usually touched on indirectly and often metaphorically. This more circuitous*

communication style is often hard for [North Americans],
with their preferences for clarity and directness. (63)

This dialogue recalls a meeting earlier in the day between
João, Debbie, and others, during which João had to decide
whether to engage in a public spat with Debbie. As a Brazilian,
he is naturally predisposed against confrontation, but even then
he might have stood his ground had Debbie not come on quite so
strong. The first mistake Debbie made was to declare in the meeting that she would be very pleased ("It would be great") if João
and company could complete a certain project in one week. Only
then, after this prelude, did she ask João if that was possible.
João now knows that saying no to Debbie will cause her deep
disappointment, and, accordingly, he must choose between publicly upsetting her (telling her the project will take two weeks)
or momentarily fudging the truth and clarifying things at the
first opportunity. For many Brazilians, this is an easy decision:
whatever the negative consequences could be from temporarily
misleading Debbie, they could never be as great as the potential
embarrassment of a public disagreement. Stephenson calls this
"the approach of emphasizing the positive at the expense of
accuracy" and notes that it "often holds true in the business
realm" (99).

Debbie then compounded her initial mistake by going on at
some length ("You were obviously very keen") about selecting a
certain person, Francisco, to head the project team before asking
João if that was possible. At this point, João (who must wonder if
Debbie ever asks anything other than rhetorical questions) must
choose again between risking a scene—since he knows Francisco
is not available—or temporarily misleading Debbie in the name
of peace and harmony. Having already opted for the "positive"
over the "accurate," João sticks to his strategy and implies that

Francisco is available. To his credit, he only said that Francisco could "most likely" lead the team, a conditional response that would raise eyebrows and trigger a follow-up inquiry from a Brazilian.

While we were not there to read João's body language, chances are when João verbally acquiesced to Debbie's requests, his non-verbal communication and the discomfort of his colleagues told a very different story. Chances also are that Debbie, like most Americans, paid more attention to João's words than to his body language.

Americans don't seek out disagreements or confrontations; indeed, they actively try to avoid argument in certain situations. At the same time, disagreements, even public ones, hold no special horrors for Americans because the value they threaten—social harmony—is simply not stressed in American culture. As individualists, Americans do not cultivate strong group relations and accordingly do not rely on the group for support or well-being. In such a scheme, disagreeing with or disappointing others comes with very few risks. Where harmony does not flourish, it cannot be disturbed.

This individualist streak also explains why Americans favor a more direct style of communication. Indeed, in most cases directness is essential for successful communication. If people don't know each other very well, lacking the shared experiences common in more collective cultures, then mutual understanding requires people to say what they are thinking, to quite literally speak one's mind. In a collectivist culture like Brazil, group members are on such intimate terms that they already know each other's mind.

"Americans value directness," Phyllis Harrison writes,

whereas Latin Americans, because of the value placed on human relations and comfortable interaction, often approach a subject or problem indirectly, working toward a solution by degrees.

This concern for smoothing things over marks daily life, meaning that business deals, job recommendations, or the asking of a favor might all be approached slowly and indirectly.

Brazilians regard an indirect approach as gracious and as a way of sparing the other's feelings, a way to avoid putting the other person on the spot in a potentially awkward situation. The American regards the same approach as inefficient and as a way of evading the issue. The American is frustrated by the Brazilian lack of concern and sees it as a refusal to face facts. The Brazilian is hurt and dismayed by the American's bluntness and perceives it as a disregard for the human being involved with those facts. (17, 18)

49

The Fix

The first thing Americans in Brazil should understand is that meetings are not the place for a frank exchange of views. When Brazilians see a disagreement coming—and they can see it coming from much further off than Americans can—they change the subject or become so vague that what they say can be interpreted however the listener wants. Contentious issues should be taken up one-on-one, not in front of others. Another piece of advice is to be very careful of rhetorical questions, questions that contain the answer you are looking for, in a culture like Brazil where people are already predisposed to saying what others want to hear. Finally, if Brazilians are going to be reluctant to confront or disappoint during a meeting, only offering the bad news later, then it makes no sense to leave a meeting and immediately act on what you heard. Wait for the rest of the story.

For their part, Brazilians should not worry so much about disappointing or disagreeing with Americans in meetings. Americans do not consider this rude or embarrassing. But it is considered rude—not to mention extremely frustrating—when you say one thing in a meeting, to be polite, and then say something else later. In most cases Americans would prefer to have a disagreement or even a confrontation during a meeting, where everyone is present and the contentious issue can be thoroughly vetted, than to save the issue for later to avoid any possible embarrassment. That's just the point: public disagreement and even polite confrontation are usually not embarrassing in American business culture.

3

China

> "The meaning of person is *ren*." Embedded in this phrase is a universe of meaning that reveals how the Chinese regard themselves and their relationship with others. . . . The character for *ren* is composed of the characters for "two" and "person." This etymology suggests that in the Chinese context, no person exists except in relationship to another.
>
> —Ming-Jer Chen

No one who writes about Chinese culture gets very far before mentioning three fundamental concepts: face, harmony, and the group. The first two of these resonate hardly at all with Americans; they know the words, of course, but face and harmony would never appear on any list of key American values, nor do they play any role in the American worldview. And as for the third concept, group, it typically refers to China's collectivist or, more accurately, relationship-driven culture, the exact opposite of America's individualist culture. Surely it says something about the size of the Sino-American cultural gulf that three of the bedrock values of Chinese society have very little meaning for most Americans.

If you are wondering what that has to do with business, consider this from Ming-Jer Chen in his book *Inside Chinese Business*:

> *Just as the structures of Western corporations stem from the political and military models of Old World Europe, modern-day Chinese business structures have their origins in ancient Chinese culture and philosophy. The works of Sun Tzu, Confucius, Lao Tzu, and other thinkers are more than simply texts to the Chinese; they represent an integrated worldview. To do business with the Chinese, it is therefore essential to acquaint oneself with this worldview. (xii)*

If you're all caught up on the works of Sun Tzu and Lao Tzu, then you're good to go. If it's been a while since you opened your *Collected Works of Confucius*, this chapter is for you.

11. SUGGESTIONS

MS. CHOU: Before we go, thank you all for the comments you sent me on the draft proposal.

PAUL: Actually, Ms. Chou, I only read it last night, when I got back from Singapore.

MS. CHOU: Of course. Perhaps we can talk right after this meeting.

PAUL: We could, but I only have a couple of suggestions.

MS. CHOU: Suggestions?

PAUL:	You know, little ways to improve the proposal.
MS. CHOU:	I do know, yes.
PAUL:	It will just take a minute, honest.
MS. CHOU:	No doubt.

This dialogue is about feedback, which means it's inevitably about face. And face is probably the best place to start any discussion of Sino-American cultural differences. The best place because face is one of two or three core values of Chinese culture (and of the Pacific Rim as a whole) and because Americans, as it happens, understand very little about face. They think they do, incidentally, equating loss of face with embarrassment or shame, but that's a very American definition. "The difference in Chinese and American concepts of face," Hu and Grove write in *Encountering the Chinese*,

> *is that face simply has greater social significance for the Chinese. In the United States concern for face exists but remains largely out of most people's awareness. In the People's Republic everyone is conscious of face all the time. An oft-repeated Chinese proverb puts it thus: "A person needs face as a tree needs bark." (121)*

Face is a combination of personal pride or dignity, the kind of face Americans can relate to, and the esteem in which one is held by the group; in effect, one's social reputation. And since individuals in collective cultures derive the lion's share of their personal identity from group membership, that dimension of face is especially strong. It would be no exaggeration to say that in collective cultures the regard of the group is the ultimate foundation of one's self-esteem and self-respect. To lose face, therefore, to lose the high regard of the group or cause someone else to lose face, is deeply troubling in China. "In the Chinese context," Chen writes, "causing someone to lose face is a mode of personal assault that can do serious damage to the relationship as well as to business opportunities. The maintenance of face is so important that people will sometimes lie to preserve it" (73).

And that is the dynamic playing out in "Suggestions," where the American Paul systematically drags Ms. Chou ever closer to the brink of embarrassment. Ms. Chou circulated a proposal to her team and solicited their input, like good managers the world over. But she conspicuously asked them to send their comments to her ahead of time, which all have done except for Paul. Ms. Chou did this because feedback must be handled carefully in Chinese culture, especially "suggestions," which by their very nature imply some kind of criticism, that what has been proposed could be improved. To put it another way, as Ms. Chou's proposal presumably contains her best thinking on the matter, then any comments inevitably imply that her best thoughts are not as good as they could be.

In a face-saving culture, such comments would rarely be communicated in public lest they embarrass the presenter. "The Chinese are acutely sensitive to the regard in which they are held by others," Scott Seligman writes, "or the light in which they appear, and it is very important to be aware of the concept of *mianzi* [face] if only to head off situations in which you cause someone to lose it" (47). It is this deep concern for the face of *others* that distinguishes the Asian concept from the Western concept, where one's own face is the primary concern.

All of which brings Paul's behavior into sharper focus. If he is new to China or simply not very observant, he would not be aware of the sensitivity around feedback and instinctively fall back on his American cultural conditioning, which has taught him that offering suggestions to one's boss at a meeting is well within the bounds of propriety. That said, Paul really should have picked up on the several clues Ms. Chou gives him as she becomes increasingly alarmed at the direction in which he's obviously heading. In fact, it's entirely possible that her very first statement (thanking staff for sending their comments) is a preemptive strike aimed directly at Paul. Knowing he hasn't sent her his comments, aware of his limited cultural acumen, and sensing he's about to speak up—Miss Chou may be signaling that now is not the time and this is not the place for giving feedback.

Ms. Chou's next remark ("Perhaps we can talk right after the meeting") removes any doubt that she knows Paul is about to transgress, and she generously tries to prevent him from embarrassing himself. He misses this clue and mentions "a couple of suggestions" he'd like to make. If she wanted these suggestions, surely Ms. Chou would ask for them at this point, but all she can do is repeat the word "suggestions," accompanied, no doubt, by body language signifying great incredulity. If this is the best Ms. Chou can manage, then clearly she's not in the mood.

Paul merely thinks she misunderstands the word ("You know, little ways to improve the proposal") and gets ready to let loose. Ms. Chou's icy-cold "I do know, yes," should stop even Paul in his tracks, but this is one determined guy. Out of respect for Paul, we shall pull away from the conversation at this point, but it would be irresponsible not to make one final observation: By their nature, dialogues cannot portray body language, but if we could see the look on Ms. Chou's face—and especially the exquisite discomfort of the other Chinese at this meeting—we would notice even bigger clues the hapless Paul is missing.

There are at least two reasons why face matters so much to the Chinese. One is the collective nature of the culture, which can in part be explained by the relative lack of geographic mobility in traditional Chinese society. "People have had little opportunity to move away from the locality of their birth," Grove and Hu observe,

> *and each [person] tends to spend his or her entire life in the company of the same friends, neighbors, and relatives. When one is attached for life to a given group of people, maintaining harmonious relationships among all its members becomes of paramount importance. Consequently, face-saving behaviors take on great significance. (122)*

This aspect of Chinese culture has begun to change rapidly in recent years. Millions of Chinese have moved (at least temporarily) to large urban areas to find work, with consequences as yet unknown for the collective nature of the society.

A related factor that contributes to collectivism is poverty and lack of economic opportunity. In circumstances where individuals cannot survive on their own, groups are a splendid idea. Not surprisingly, the relative degree of collectivism and individualism in societies correlates very strongly with GDP.

The other main support for the importance of face can be traced back, like so much else in Chinese culture, to the teachings of Confucius. To simplify somewhat, Confucius taught that society consists of a series of interlocking relationships, necessarily unequal in nature, with obligations running in both directions. The key to the successful functioning of society is for everyone to act with decorum, recognize their place in the hierarchy, and discharge their obligations, a set of values known as *li*, usually translated as "right conduct in maintaining one's place in the hierarchical order." Hu and Grove write that

> *social harmony is preserved when all parties in a situation behave in a decorous manner. One important way to*

be decorous is to accept and respect each person's need to maintain his or her face. . . . Criticism of another person, especially of a superior, is fraught with danger. Loss of face is not merely a matter of personal embarrassment; it also threatens to disrupt the integrity of the group. (123)

This sensitivity to hierarchy explains another dimension of face on display in this dialogue—the imperative for subordinates to protect the face of their superiors, another norm Paul is on the verge of transgressing. After all, Paul is not simply threatening to undermine the face of a mere colleague, *but that of his boss.* An American M.B.A. student whose family owned a jewelry business once told me about the time the family first began contracting with craftsmen in China. Her mother traveled to China and spent several weeks training the Chinese how to make various pieces. Later the daughter went to China and noticed that while most of the Chinese were right-handed, they were all making jewelry primarily with their left hand. When she asked them why, they said this was how her mother had taught them. The student's mother was left-handed, and apparently none of the Chinese was comfortable asking the founder and owner of the company if it was okay to use their right hand. If *that* could potentially cause the boss to lose face, what does that say about making "suggestions"?

Why don't Americans *get* face? For one thing, the group was never destined to thrive in American culture. The standard explanation, that Americans are individualists, only begs the question. Why are Americans so individualistic? Part of the answer lies with the types of people who were attracted to the New World: nonconformists, religious dissenters, and "go-getters," people who felt especially oppressed by rigid class systems that thwarted personal ambition, independent types who thought

57

for themselves. Many of them either came alone to the New World—the son who was sent off to make his fortune—or with just their nuclear family, quickly learning to survive without the support of others.

Many of these immigrants were forever changing their circumstances: moving on, starting over, and reinventing themselves. Stability was the exception, and mobility became the norm. "Life in the United States has been mobile virtually from the earliest days of European colonization," Hu and Grove write:

> Colonial peoples did not hesitate to move on if life in a certain locality did not suit them. Thus the composition of one's community and friendship groups changed often during one's lifetime. . . . Given the constant shifting of group membership, attention increasingly focused on individuals instead of on groups or collectives. As a result, the maintenance of group integrity and harmony rarely attained the significance for Americans that it customarily did for the Chinese. (122)

The deep egalitarian streak in American culture, a reaction to the tyranny of privilege that prevailed in Europe, is another support for American individualism. Egalitarianism made it highly unlikely that Americans would ever create a culture where sensitivity to rank was going to be valued or where hierarchy stood much chance of gaining a foothold.

The Fix

When Americans work with Chinese colleagues—and especially under a Chinese manager—they must be careful when communicating "harmless suggestions." Any negative feedback should be given indirectly and preferably one-on-one. Regardless of your position vis-à-vis Chinese colleagues, be especially careful during meetings not to cause loss of face. A good rule is to observe body language closely because Chinese often communicate their true feelings through nonverbal cues. When managing Chinese employees, you should not expect to receive completely honest (or at least direct) feedback during meetings; wait until after the meeting for any details that could not be said publicly. The general advice for Americans in the Pacific Rim is to dial back on their directness. Here is a chart to guide both cultures:

When **Americans** are	the **Chinese** consider this
Indirect	Direct
Direct	Blunt
Blunt	Rude

When **Chinese** are	the **Americans** consider this
Indirect	Meaningless
Direct	Indirect
Blunt	Direct

Chinese working with Americans will have to be more direct if they want to be understood. Remember that what you think of as "direct" is very often vague and unclear to Americans, and when you think you're actually being rude, Americans only see that as direct. If you find yourself in an American work environment, accept that they understand very little about face and worry more about being honest than about hurting other people's feelings. You will be expected to say what you think in meetings and not simply what you think others want to hear.

12. NO VISITORS

SARAH: How is the proposal for the procurement group at China Mobile coming along, Minwen?

MINWEN: In the end, we decided not to submit a bid.

SARAH: Really. Why?

MINWEN: It turns out my uncle doesn't work there anymore. He retired a few months ago.

SARAH: OK.

MINWEN: My mother said he's not well, and unfortunately he's not receiving any visitors at the present time.

SARAH: I'm sorry. But don't worry; nobody can beat our price.

MINWEN: You're probably right.

SARAH: And even if they could, we've got more experience than almost anyone.

MINWEN: I know.

SARAH: So we stand a very good chance.

MINWEN: Maybe if my uncle gets better.

No book about Chinese culture gets very far before mentioning *guanxi*, variously translated as relationships, connections, or networks. Like face, *guanxi* is an inevitable byproduct of a collectivist culture. It is best understood as a series of personal relationships that create a system of reciprocity and mutual obligation, sustained and strengthened through the trading of favors. Americans would call it cronyism or favoritism, and while there is a certain you-scratch-my-back-I'll-scratch-yours mentality, *guanxi* goes much deeper than cronyism.

"[A]ll business cultures depend on informal networking," Ming-Jer Chen writes, to provide

> *members of their group with a measure of confidence and trust necessary to underpin business transactions. Guanxi differs from these both in its pervasiveness and in its heavy emphasis on family ties and shared experiences.*
>
> *Guanxi . . . has been perceived as emanating from an innate fear and distrust of others. . . . The concept traces its roots back to ancient Chinese social customs wherein reciprocity and other modes of social exchange were used to build and maintain interpersonal relationships through-out society. . . . Since the Chinese in general prefer to do business with people they know or with friends of friends, they devote a substantial amount of time and energy to establishing relationships with people they find respectable. It is this commitment of time to building relationships with others that truly defines guanxi. (47, 48)*

Which brings us to Sarah and Minwen. It appears they work for a company that has an opportunity to bid on a contract to do some work for another company, China Mobile. The decision to pursue this opportunity comes down to whether they can truly be competitive in bidding on this contract. Is it worth their while to develop and submit a proposal? The answer depends on how each culture defines "competitive" and which factors determine the selection of the winning bidder. While it may be simplistic to say that in China it all comes down to *guanxi*, certainly *guanxi* is one of the factors, and quite possibly the most influential. "[H]aving connections with the appropriate individuals and authorities," Rosalie Tung writes, "is often more crucial than having the right product and/or price" (Joynt, 239).

Hence Minwen's reference to her uncle, who would have been a perfect connection if he had not just retired. While this piece of information would explain a lot to other Chinese, including why Minwen has decided not to pursue the contract, it means next to nothing to Sarah. What does Minwen's uncle, retired or not, have to do with anything? "A North American's first response when faced with a difficult task or a troubling problem," Mary Margaret Wang observes in *Turning Bricks into Jade*, "is to think 'What can I do to accomplish what I need?' Whereas the Chinese person's first response tends to be, 'Who do I know who can help me accomplish this?'" (33)

We can tell by Sarah's tepid "OK" that she's waiting for the rest of the story, for the explanation of what part Minwen's uncle could possibly play in this scenario. Alas, Minwen's reply ("My mother said he's not well, and unfortunately he's not receiving any visitors at the present time") is not especially helpful. What Minwen means, although Sarah has no way to access this logic, is that even in retirement her uncle could exercise his influence, activating his network at China Mobile and thereby greatly increase prospects for Minwen's bid. But as he is unwell and "not receiving visitors at the present time," there's no way Minwen can prevail upon him to do her a favor.

At this point, Sarah, understandably from an American perspective, gives up trying to understand Minwen's thinking and proceeds to explain her own: No one can beat their company on price or experience, so they "stand a very good chance" to win this contract. Odds are good that Minwen's reply ("Maybe if my uncle gets better") might just drive Sarah mad.

So does this really mean China Mobile would overlook price and experience and award a contract just because someone on the vendor side has a connection? This is where the American and Chinese concepts of connections part company. China Mobile will not overlook price and experience to pay exclusive attention to *guanxi*; rather, it will weigh all three (along with any other relevant factors) before coming to a decision. But it's a good bet that *guanxi* would count for much more than price and experience combined.

Here's how this would normally work if Minwen's uncle still worked at China Mobile. When the person on the vendor side calls in a favor, both parties know what this means: If Minwen's uncle manages to swing the contract to her company, Minwen is thereby obliged (by the reciprocity dimension of *guanxi*) to return the favor and do everything in her power to assure this relationship goes smoothly, lest her uncle lose considerable face. The first thing Minwen would have to do, incidentally, is address any inconvenient price differences. If a competing bid came in at a lower price, Minwen knows very well that she must get her superior, Sarah, to either meet that price or, failing that, match it as closely as possible.

Minwen would next be expected to address the experience issue. If the staff of a competing vendor are more experienced in executing the tasks in this contract, Minwen would have to compensate somehow. More experience, after all, means greater competence, higher quality, and greater efficiency—and China Mobile cannot be expected to forgo those advantages in the name of *guanxi*. Perhaps Minwen and her superiors could hire additional expertise, steal staff away from the competitor who lost the bid, or hire experts from the competitor's staff as trainers and consultants (a kind of consolation prize). In short, the mutual obligations inherent in *guanxi*—and most especially the enormous loss of face involved if she proves unworthy of her uncle's trust—effectively guarantee that Minwen will make sure no one at China Mobile ever regrets selecting her company.

While Sarah cannot be expected to know about *guanxi*, all she needed to do here was stop for a moment and think about what she was hearing. Surely this persistent mention of Minwen's uncle must mean something. Sarah doesn't need to know *what* it means, only that it might not mean what she thinks. Is it really likely that Minwen fails to grasp the competitive advantage of a lower price and higher quality? Is Minwen going on about her uncle because she's completely lost? All very unlikely, but this is what Sarah has to believe if she thinks she understands this conversation.

Clearly, *guanxi* is much more than what Americans understand as networking. Americans use every arrow in their quiver when doing business, too, but the nature of their connections is more superficial and, consequently, much less binding. A connection may get you a foot in the door, as Americans say, but it does not win the business. Connections in China come with all the obligations and benefits of a deeply collectivist, group-oriented society; connections in America are almost accidental in comparison. "It is important not to confuse *guanxi* with concepts more familiar to [Westerners], such as networking," Wang observes. "Networking tends to be comparatively superficial and goal-oriented. *Guanxi* is forever" (33).

The Fix

Americans should never assume that price, experience, quality, or production details will win the day in business interactions with the Chinese. While these all certainly matter, always take *guanxi* into account in whatever way you can. You should stress your own connections (in the U.S. and also in China, if you have any) when making your pitches to the Chinese. Partner with other Chinese companies to leverage their influence. As American companies develop and improve their technical expertise, they should likewise make every effort to develop their *guanxi*.

Giving and accepting favors and hospitality are two common

features of *guanxi*. "Banquets, excursions, and gift-giving are popular ways of establishing *guanxi* in China," Wang writes. "If a guest attends banquets and accepts gifts, presumably *guanxi* has been established. And once *guanxi* has been established, the relationship is considered to be a long-term one. The *parties involved are expected to fulfill their obligations* if called upon to do so" (italics added, 169). Americans should take special note of this reciprocal dimension; if you do not want to become beholden or indebted to Chinese colleagues, you must find polite ways to refuse gifts and other favors. Indeed, U.S. government regulations make it illegal to accept the kind of "favors" that are often at the heart of *guanxi*.

Moreover, as Grove and Hu point out,

> the Chinese tend to assume that something similar to the *guanxi* system operates in the United States and that you are part of it. . . . They [may] assume that if you are influential enough to have a respectable, well-paying job, then you must be influential enough to pull the strings necessary to bring about whatever they desire. (65)

For their part, Chinese pitching their business to potential American buyers should expect *guanxi* to count for less and emphasize price, quality, and the other criteria that Americans value. You should also be aware that trying to build *guanxi* via some of the common methods, such as giving gifts and hosting elaborate meals, could easily be misinterpreted as bribery. At the end of the day, you do not need *guanxi* to be successful in the American business context, nor do you have to stress your connections to impress Americans. Indeed, too much emphasis on *guanxi* may give Americans the impression you are not confident you can do the job on your own.

13. DOING OUR BEST

MR. SMITH: Mr. Wang, thank you for coming in.

MR. WANG: It's my honor.

MR. SMITH: We see your company has forty years of experience.

MR. WANG: We know a little, but we can always learn more.

MR. SMITH: Everyone we contacted spoke very highly of you.

MR. WANG: Our friends are very kind.

MR. SMITH: They believe nobody is better than you.

MR. WANG: I wouldn't like to say that.

MR. SMITH: But you do think you can do this job?

MR. WANG: We will do our best.

A famous Chinese proverb contends that "Wisdom springs from being humble." In his book *Inside Chinese Business*, Ming-Jer Chen tells a cross-cultural joke about chefs. "World class chefs from different countries are asked to critique their own food," he writes.

> The American chef boasts, "My cooking is so good it tastes as if it were made by the best chef in France." The French cook allows that his cooking is "exquisite. Only a Frenchman could make something so perfect." The British chef admits, "We don't know how to cook. I recommend serving this meal with five or more warm beers." Finally, the Chinese chef evaluates his performance: "I am a terrible cook. People honor me by being willing to eat something so mediocre." (110)

The Chinese are a proud people; it's important not to criticize anyone or otherwise impugn their reputation in public. At the same time, personal humility is also a cultural touchstone. While boasting and chest beating are clearly beyond the pale, even simply accepting praise is difficult for the Chinese. "You may find the way in which the Chinese deal with compliments rather curious," Scott Seligman writes.

> *Accepting them outright is not considered good etiquette; a Chinese is expected to deflect compliments and pretend he or she is unworthy of receiving them. The Chinese use a number of phrases when flattered but one of the most common . . . is nali, a word with the literal meaning of the interrogative "where" that has come to mean something like "it was nothing." It's as if to say the kind words you have just uttered couldn't possibly be directed at me; where is the person to whom you are referring? (19)*

The cultural prescription to be humble results in routine self-effacement and personal modesty, which Americans inevitably misinterpret as a lack of confidence. That dynamic is on display in this dialogue, where the American Mr. Smith has invited Mr. Wang to discuss an impending business partnership. Mr. Smith has done his due diligence and is obviously ready to begin working with Mr. Wang's company. This meeting is pro forma, in short, a chance for the two executives to meet before signing a contract. At least that's how it begins, but before long Mr. Smith starts to wonder if Mr. Wang really is the man for the job.

The first concern arises when Mr. Wang says that his forty-year-old company knows "a little but . . . can always learn more." While this remark may sound a bit odd to Mr. Smith, he's probably not too worried at this point. Even Americans, with no particular cultural prohibition against blowing their own horn, routinely brush off effusive praise early on in such a conversation. The difference is that when the other party insists on handing out compliments, Americans eventually relent and start accepting them. It's Mr. Wang's persistent modesty that ultimately begins to worry Mr. Smith.

"Our friends are very kind" is likewise probably not too modest for Mr. Smith, but the next exchange raises a red flag: When Mr. Wang remarks that he "wouldn't like to say" that his company is the best, the American interprets this to mean that Mr. Wang disagrees with that assessment. Actually, all Mr. Wang means by this carefully worded reply is that while no company may be better, it's not his place to say such a thing. He would not "like" to say this because it would sound too boastful, and that would be embarrassing.

Clearly Mr. Smith is now beginning to have doubts and tries to reassure himself ("But you do think you can do this job?"), only to be met with a very disappointing "We'll do our best." Alas, that's just the problem: Mr. Wang's "best" is now very much in question, and this pro forma meeting has suddenly turned into something else. "Selling oneself is necessary to some extent anywhere in the world," Hu and Grove explain, "in order to make a sale or land a desirable assignment. But how one competes and how one sells oneself differs from culture to culture. Traditional Chinese values require that a person who wishes to make a favorable impression avoid being self-congratulatory" (56).

It's not difficult to discover the origins of Chinese humility. Self-effacing behavior is virtually automatic in a culture where the collective is paramount. "Valuing humility is part of centuries-old Chinese tradition," Hu and Grove observe.

A series of honorifics and self-deprecating terms [have been] in use for more than two thousand years. When these terms are translated into English, some sound so self-disparaging that they make Americans uncomfortable. . . . One is "my immature opinion is" which is often a preamble for someone's proposal even though that proposal may be very well thought out. To enhance harmony and avoid friction, the Chinese are taught at an early age to keep themselves in check. (56, 57)

Indeed, in Chinese culture, humility is not just modesty or politeness; it's self-preservation. Anyone who promotes the self over the group risks alienation, which is among every Chinese person's worst fears. Another danger of self-promotion in a collectivist culture is that standing out inevitably makes one a target, and targets get a lot of attention. Many Chinese sayings capture the dangers of being too conspicuous: "No one butchers a small pig." "The tallest trees dread the thunder."

The relative lack of modesty or humility among Americans is likewise easy to explain: America is among the most individualist and least group-oriented of all cultures. Anything that affirms, supports, or strengthens the self is valued in America, where individuals must be able to survive on their own. Modesty and self-effacement are not utterly unknown in America; the more successful the individual, in fact, the more she is expected to deflect praise. But the limits of self-effacing behavior are reached much sooner in America than in China, which inevitably makes Americans come across as boastful and perhaps even insecure. Why would you have to talk so much about your achievements if you are so confident?

To which most Americans would answer: If *we* don't talk about them, who will? Part of the fallout from being individualists is that Americans cannot automatically rely on other group members for support and validation. Hence, if an American is too modest, he gives the impression of lacking self-esteem. In China, individuals don't have to say anything about their achievements because everyone else in the collective will. (Remember, "Our friends are very kind.") It is ironic that in America too much modesty is interpreted as a lack of confidence, while in China too little modesty is interpreted the same way. "In *The Book of Means*," Chen observes, "Confucius promotes modesty as a way to achieve personal growth: 'The superior man acts in a way such that he conceals himself, yet every day gains in stature. The inferior man shows himself and every day loses stature'" (104). We might add, finally, that the Chinese appreciate compliments as much as anyone; they just can't accept them.

The Fix

"Whenever you deal with the Chinese," Hu and Grove advise, "we suggest that you do everything possible to ensure that your own speech and writing convey a sense of humility" (57). To avoid appearing haughty or boastful, do not blow your own horn too loudly and likewise deflect most praise that comes your way. In job interviews in China, it's common for the applicant to use "we" rather than "I" in talking about his or her experience; this is not simply because the Chinese identify more closely with the group or team but also done to convey humility. If you want to impress a potential Chinese customer, be sure to put them in touch with "friends" who can do your boasting for you. Whatever you do, be careful not to denigrate others, which will inevitably be interpreted as immoral and a sign of weakness.

For their part, Chinese should be wary of excessive humility in dealing with Americans. While Americans will understand a certain amount of pro forma modesty, if you persist in turning compliments away, they will believe you and start worrying. You should also remember that Americans are unlikely to consult your "friends" for an assessment of your expertise, and they will, accordingly, expect you to make a case for yourself. If you don't, then the case may never be made. Finally, if you think Americans are too boastful, remember that it is more acceptable in their culture to praise oneself—and even more acceptable to accept praise from others. It does not signify arrogance or immodesty.

14. THE PRICE OF TEA IN CHINA

ZHI: It's good to talk with you again, Barbara.

BARBARA: Thanks, Zhi, for taking my call. We're worried about the price of your tea. It's just not selling well at that price.

ZHI: Of course. It's been two months, hasn't it, since we made our first shipment?

BARBARA: My point, exactly.

ZHI: Americans are always in such a hurry. Besides, our tea is something new for them, isn't it?

BARBARA: It's the first time our stores have ever carried this brand.

ZHI: Of course.

BARBARA: Do you think you could lower your price?

ZHI: We could certainly discuss that if it ever becomes a problem.

In the Western mind, one of the qualities most often associated with Asians is patience. It's no surprise that Westerners—and especially Americans—single out this quality, as it stands in such stark contrast to that bedrock American value of action. Patience is about waiting, about letting things happen; Americans are about doing, about making things happen.

Americans are notoriously *im*patient. And why not? If you believe deeply in your ability to make things happen, then waiting makes no sense. One of the consequences of impatience is on display in "The Price of Tea in China": the short-term orientation of most American businesspeople and especially their expectation of immediate results. Barbara's company has recently signed with a new Chinese vendor to sell their tea in her food stores, and apparently the vendor's price means she must charge more to make a profit. And Americans aren't buying. Barbara assumes all she has to do is make Zhi aware of this, and he'll see the need to lower his price.

Zhi's initial response ("Of course. It's been two months, hasn't it, since we made our first shipment?") is music to Barbara's ears ("My point, exactly"). She is no doubt relieved that what could have been a difficult conversation is apparently going quite smoothly. Granted, Barbara's not altogether sure where Zhi is headed with his next remark. ("Americans are always in such a hurry. Besides, our tea is something new for them, isn't it?") But she still thinks they are on the same page and does not hesitate to ask him to lower his price. His response catches Barbara completely by surprise: "We could discuss that if it ever becomes a problem." "Ever becomes?" Barbara is thinking. "It's *already* a problem!" And she may even wonder if she needs to find a new supplier or perhaps just give up on this expensive tea.

The Chinese, like most cultures of the Pacific Rim, have a long-term orientation to business. While Americans think one quarter, at most two, should be enough time to get results, the Chinese think in terms of one or even two years, especially with a new product. They neither expect nor require immediate profit to feel that a business venture is achieving results. We will examine why in a moment, but let's reexamine Zhi's remarks in this light, beginning with "Of course. It's been two months, hasn't it, since we made our first shipment?" "Of course" could mean: Of course Americans aren't buying yet; my tea has *only* been in your stores for two months, hardly long enough for people even to notice the product, much less buy it, much less decide if they like it, regardless of the price. (Hence "Americans are always in such a hurry.") If Zhi's tea is "something new," then all the more reason to wait and see what happens. In short, two months is not nearly enough time to determine whether or not there's a problem with the price of Zhi's tea, and certainly not enough time to evaluate the soundness of this brand-new business partnership.

None of this is to say that the Chinese don't care about profit and results, or that they somehow feel they can't make things happen or otherwise influence the outcome of a business venture. The difference here is not that Americans worship results and the Chinese are indifferent; both cultures wants results, but they achieve and even define results in different ways. The Chinese conduct business primarily through building and cultivating relationships, that *guanxi* that is the subject of Dialogue 12, and there's no question that accounting for the interests, needs, and sensibilities of a group takes time. Trust must be built, disagreements must be surfaced and then resolved, compromises must be hammered out, and consensus must be reached—all while ensuring no one loses face. The Chinese often speak of *yan jiu* (研究, 研究/), which literally means something very close to "research," but which has the broader sense of waiting for events to transpire that will indicate whether potential business partners are trustworthy. If the Chinese are patient and have a long-term orientation, it's partly because decision-making, which must precede any action, is inevitably a much slower process in a collectivist, relationship-based culture. "Cultures [like China] that view time in a more . . . open-ended fashion," Chen writes, "tend to be more group-oriented, stressing the development of relationships over task accomplishment" (95).

Another, related reason the Chinese are willing to wait longer for results is because they see business as much more than an opportunistic arrangement between buyer and seller. They see it, rather, as a long-lasting partnership that will be in place for years and only deepen and mature over time. We may begin with tea, but who knows how broad our mutual interests will turn out to be? Who knows what part of my network I may one day introduce you to and which part of yours you may connect me with? Only time will tell. If you conceive of profit as accruing year after year for decades and quite possibly growing through embarking on additional ventures with your partner—if this is what profit means to you, then two months is insignificant.

"From the Chinese point of view," Wang et al.* observe,

a business relationship is a type of friendship; trust must be established and a "lifetime" of mutual benefits and obligations pursued. To Americans, a business relationship is primarily an opportunity for profits. If there is no profit within a reasonable amount of time, it makes sense for the relationship to end. There is a noticeable cultural difference in what constitutes "a reasonable amount of time" in which to show a profit. Americans have far less patience with an initially unprofitable venture than do the Chinese. [An American] probably has shareholders to answer to and needs to show profits every quarter. In a sense, [they] don't have the leisure to develop long-term markets that the Chinese [have]. (166)

Another Sino-American difference in the ultimate priorities of the two business cultures helps explain the short-term/long-term dichotomy, as Robert Burns observes about Asian business:

This difference in attitude toward time showed up in a study of the managerial goals of business. The U.S. managers rated

---

* An incident in *Turning Bricks into Jade* inspired this dialogue.

*"return on investment" and "stockholder gains" as the two
most important goals—short-term ones. [Asians] both rated
"market share" as their top goal—a long-term one—while
"stockholder gains" was rated last. (21)*

In this context we might also point out that state-owned
enterprises, to say nothing of family-owned businesses, aren't
compelled to appear before their investors every few months and
give glowing reports about how well they're doing.

We've suggested that their can-do mentality, their deep belief
in their ability to make things happen, explains American impatience for results and their overall short-term orientation. But
Americans do not merely crave results; they depend on them for
a large measure of their self-esteem. As individualists, Americans
do not derive their identity from group membership or regard;
they don't have a group. They tend to identify with their achievements, with what they have accomplished, which creates some
urgency around results. "If self-respect and the respect of others come in large part from one's achievements," I have written
elsewhere, "then there is a certain built-in pressure to see those
achievements sooner rather than later. Americans don't like to
wait very long for results, in short, because there is so much at
stake" (2004, 72).

75

The Fix

Americans should adjust their short-term expectations when they
do business with the Chinese. You can try explaining why you
can't wait a year to see improvement, but in the long run it will
make little difference; the Chinese system just isn't designed
to produce or even value immediate results. Your best bet is
to explain in advance to the people in your organization what

they are getting into when they enter partnerships with the Chinese. If *they* are uncomfortable with waiting, then you should think twice before proceeding. At the same time, Chinese business culture is evolving, and many Chinese have a lot of experience working with Western companies. For those who have been exposed to the short-term orientation, there may be room for compromise. Meanwhile, if you can learn to think of "results" in a much broader sense than immediate return on investment, your dealings with the Chinese will cause you less heartburn.

For their part, the Chinese would do well to explain to Americans why a strong relationship is the only result that truly matters. Be as specific and concrete as you can about the benefits and advantages. Once Americans buy the concept that relationships are key to doing business in China—and that *will* take some selling—they will be open to waiting longer for results.

15. LEAVING EARLY

MR. BROWN: Mr. Chin, it's so nice to finally meet you.

MR. CHIN: Our pleasure, Mr. Brown. How was your flight?

MR. BROWN: It was fine, thanks.

MR. CHIN: When do you fly back?

MR. BROWN: Probably on Friday, but it depends on how our meetings go. If we finish early, we might change our reservations and go back on Thursday.

MR. CHIN: A day early?

MR. BROWN: Right, so we can spend the weekend at home with our families. We travel a lot.

MR. CHIN: I see.

The Chinese are famous for asking foreigners when they're going home; that lets Chinese negotiators know how long they can hold out for better terms. While that may be a factor here, the more meaningful behavior from the Chinese point of view is that Mr. Brown and friends are apparently planning to leave "early" if they can conclude their business ahead of time. The Americans make two assumptions here that would appear odd to many Chinese: that business is conducted primarily through meetings and that once the meetings are concluded, there would be no reason to stay on in Beijing.

All other things being equal, the relationship-oriented Chinese always prefer to do business with people they know and can trust, which means family, extended family, and people with whom they have a long-standing relationship. Where none of this is possible, such as when doing business with foreigners, the Chinese will feel a strong need to get to know potential partners before formalizing the relationship. Meetings can help, of course, but they are usually about the deal, the terms, the proposal—all the details that must be agreed upon. And while conduct during meetings reveals a few things about character, personality, and trustworthiness, it's unlikely Mr. Chin and friends will feel they know Mr. Brown and his team solely through these formal interactions. "In meeting Western business people," Ming-Jer Chen writes, the Chinese "will want to become acquainted with the individual and not simply the businessperson. In fact, the notion of knowing a business associate only through the business relationship can seem incomplete and unsatisfactory to the Chinese" (71).

To get a more complete understanding of Mr. Brown and build the trust that will give the Chinese the confidence to move forward, Mr. Chin and his team will need to interact with the Americans in unofficial, informal settings where business is not usually discussed. The perfect opportunity, of course, would be on the weekend, when the Chinese can show the Americans around Beijing, take them out for a nice dinner or two, perhaps introduce them to a few family members, and generally learn more about them as individuals and not just as potential business partners. But if all goes well, Mr. Brown will be spending the weekend at home, washing his car and mowing his lawn.

Why would Americans miss all this? Part of the explanation is that Americans don't make business decisions primarily on the basis of how they feel about potential business partners or if they think they can trust them; on the basis, in short, of personal relationships. When it comes to trust; Americans tend to extend a general trust to everyone, assuming people can be trusted until they prove otherwise. The Chinese, by contrast, withhold trust until strangers prove they *can* be trusted. The Chinese need to find out if they can trust, in other words, whereas the Americans simply assume they can. From an American perspective, then, there is no need to spend much time with people to determine their trustworthiness. "Americans are hardly averse to good social relationships," Hu and Grove observe, "but [they] rarely see the building of a permanent partnership as one of their principal goals. . . . Americans are more inclined than any other group of national businesspeople to rush headlong into making a deal, seemingly with little concern about the level of trust established with their counterparts" (102).

Moreover, it is the terms of the proposal rather than the character of the proposers that ultimately determines who wins the business in the United States. If Americans are inclined to "rush headlong into making a deal" without worrying about building personal relationships—if they focus on the what and not on the who—it is also because they don't have to worry about such things. They believe in the immutability, hence the protection, of contracts and in the power of the laws and lawyers that lie behind them. In the unlikely event it turns out a partner was not trustworthy, what difference does it make? A contract is a contract.

This is a core belief in universalist cultures like the United States, where "the system works," that is, where the rule of law prevails, where there is an independent judiciary, and where regulations and policies are applied impartially. In universalist societies, people trust the system because it is perceived to be fair. What does it matter whether or not you can trust others? The system will protect you.

China is closer to what we have called a particularist society (see Dialogues 6 and 42), where there is definitely a system in place—a set of regulations, policies, and procedures, along with bureaucrats to enforce them—but where laws are not always applied impartially. Outcomes often depend more on who you are and whom you know than on the rightness or wrongness of your position. Is it any wonder that strong personal relationships and the preference for dealing with "family" would loom so large in a particularist world? Or that contracts need not be so specific?

Grove and Hu describe certain

differences in what each side sees as the nature and purpose of a contract. From an American point of view, a contract focuses in great detail on the specific rights and responsibilities of the two parties. A major purpose of a contract is to compel each side to do, within a limited span of time, everything it has promised to do. Another purpose is to deal in advance with the possibility of worst-case scenarios such as a breakdown in contractual relations.

The Chinese think the principal purpose of a contract is to establish a positive relationship between the two parties, one that focuses generally on shared interests and will continue indefinitely. The notion that the two parties could come into serious conflict is not entertained. The idea that the two parties should write out in great detail what each will and will not do is not seen as necessary. (105, 106)

Not necessary, of course, because we know each other so well we don't need a piece of paper to compel us to behave honorably.

The Fix

Mr. Brown and his negotiating team should plan to stay longer in Beijing and accept any social invitations they receive. Americans should also realize that it is not only at the negotiating table that the Chinese are taking your measure. Indeed, the Chinese glean information they find valuable from informal, unofficial interactions, and you should always conduct yourself with that in mind. When Chinese visit the United States, build social events into the schedule to give them a chance to sound out personalities and build relationships.

Chinese visiting the U.S. should not be offended if Americans spend little time with them outside the meetings or other official contacts. Americans will be good hosts, but their idea of hosting leaves you on your own much more than would be the case in Beijing. Remember that the more specific and detailed the terms of your proposals, the happier Americans will be. Finally, be aware that Americans will push for contracts that are much more precise and restrictive—much less general—than what you are used to. Do not interpret this as an insult or that Americans don't trust you; they tend to trust everyone. It simply means they want to protect themselves just to be safe.

4

England

Three things to fear: the horns of a bull, the heels of a stallion, the smile of an Englishman.

—Irish proverb

Many American readers are bound to wonder why there would be a chapter on the English in a book about cultural differences. In the case of England, we are them, aren't we? And they are us. What cultural differences?

It's a fair question, especially when you consider America was once a British colony, the two countries share a common language, and more Americans are of British descent (though not English) than any other background. But who Americans used to be is not the point. More than three centuries have passed since they left the Old World—plenty of time to have become something else.

And they did, almost immediately and out of sheer necessity, adjusting to a world utterly unlike anything any of them had ever known, "so incredibly filled with unpredictabilities," Howard

Jones writes, "one wonders how the Europeans survived" (391). John McElroy agrees:

> *To understand American culture, one must always bear in mind that it developed from the situation of civilized men and women living in a Stone Age wilderness. Almost nothing in the cultural memory of the initial European settlers on the Atlantic coastal plain of North America prepared them for living in such a place. (17)*

The earliest European visitors to America, coming no more than fifty years after the founding, remarked on how different Americans were from their Old World forebears. There is plenty of scope, in short, for a chapter about U.S.-English cultural differences.

That said, we should acknowledge that if America is not exactly an English culture, it is still in many ways a European one—and therefore culturally closer to the three European countries described in this book. For that reason, Americans tend to assume more similarities than there actually are, especially with the English. Precisely because they have so much in common, Americans and the English are especially vulnerable when genuine differences unexpectedly surface. That is, Americans are often more taken aback when they encounter differences between themselves and the English than with the Chinese, say, or the Brazilians. They know better than to assume the Chinese are like them, and they are more psychologically prepared for confusion, frustration, and misunderstanding. But with their English "cousins" (as they call them), they're often caught off guard. Paradoxically, the closer two cultures are, the greater the impact of cultural differences when their two peoples interact. In short, if you're from America or England and you think you can skip this chapter, think again.

We've taken some care to use the word "English" here and not "British." "Great Britain" (and its adjective, "British") refers to England, Scotland, and Wales, and while these three regions form a single political entity, they are quite different culturally. The observations we make about the English here do not necessarily apply to the Welsh or the Scots.

And while we're making distinctions, we might also say a word about social class. While the English are not of one mind on the subject—some say that class is no longer a potent factor in English society—most non-English observers agree that social class is still alive and well. In writing about "the English," therefore, it becomes necessary to specify *which* English one has in mind. In this chapter, the cultural characteristics identified are most closely associated with the English upper and upper middle classes and would not necessarily be true of the lower middle and working class sectors of the population. Indeed, in some ways the gulf between the English working class and the English upper class is nearly as wide as that between the English and Americans.

16. A LOT OF EFFORT

PAUL: So did you guys get a chance to look at our proposal?

ROWAN: We did, actually.

PAUL: Great.

ROWAN: Yes.

PAUL: So what did you think?

ROWAN: Well, there were one or two points we need to take a second look at.

PAUL: Just a couple? So you liked it, then?

| ROWAN: | You certainly put a lot of effort into it. |
| PAUL: | Thank you. |

Poor Paul. He's just not equipped, culturally speaking, to realize that every time Rowan speaks he's putting one more nail in the coffin that now contains Paul's proposal. When he finally does realize this, Paul will understand why it's been called "perfidious Albion" (treacherous England) by so many foreigners, and why the English have the dubious reputation of being untrustworthy. When England still had its colonial empire, the English were quite proud of the fact that "the sun never sets on the British empire," to which many of their subjects were wont to reply that that was largely because "God doesn't trust the British in the dark."

"Perfidy" is certainly too strong a word for what has happened to Paul here, but as an American he can perhaps be forgiven for feeling manipulated and even misled. Paul's mistake is assuming Rowan means what he says. Americans mean what they say, but the English, more often than not, mean what they *don't* say. Or, as G. K. Chesterton so aptly puts it: "The English always [say] a thing in such a way that it could mean something different" (Yapp, 247).

And that's the way to understand each statement Rowan makes in this conversation. His first remark, "We did, actually," is conspicuous for what's missing: any positive comments. If Rowan liked the proposal, this would be the obvious place to say so. The fact that he refrains is no oversight; it's deliberate. Rowan hasn't forgotten to offer praise, in other words; he's withholding it. And it's not because he wants to keep Paul in suspense; he's not offering praise because he doesn't have any.

Any lingering doubt about Rowan's response is wiped out in the next exchange. Paul says, "Great," waiting for the only conceivable response at this juncture: Rowan's opinion of the proposal (positive or negative). Instead he gets a mere "Yes," followed by silence. While it's possible that Rowan simply forgot to add how much he liked the proposal in his first statement, there's no way "Yes" followed by *nothing* could be construed as anything but bad news. Rowan might forget to offer praise once, but he'd never forget twice.

Paul's "So what did you think?" must utterly confuse Rowan, but he soldiers on and now drops all pretense: "There were one or two points we need to take a second look at." It doesn't look good, in other words. But Rowan still doesn't get through to Paul ("Just a couple?") and makes one last attempt to achieve clarity: "You certainly put a lot of effort into it." Alas, like all the others this comment is immediately misinterpreted. What Rowan means, of course, is that while unable to praise the result, he can at least be polite and praise the effort. And surely Paul can fill in the blanks.

85

But Paul can't. For one thing, Americans don't leave any blanks when they speak, and neither do they read between the lines, read *into* what other people say, or send hidden messages. Why would you hide a message if you wanted someone to receive it? Americans, in short, are one of the most literal of all nationalities when it comes to communication. Words mean what the dictionary says they mean; if words meant different things to different people, where would we be?

The English feeling is that language is too crude and primitive an instrument to be trusted with communication. Oh, words are adequate enough for certain mundane tasks—talking about the weather or discussing football—but they're something of a blunt instrument when it comes to conversing about anything the least bit delicate or awkward. Words have their limits, in short, and when those limits are reached, the English resort to understatement (words that mean more than what they appear to), communication by omission (words that are not said), and what we might call anti-statements (words that mean the opposite of what they say). As soon as English speech enters these rarefied realms, literalists like Paul are simply unable to follow.

Some time ago, the Dutch working at the European Court of Justice in Brussels put up this notice to explain the meaning of a few common British expressions:

WHAT THEY SAY	WHAT THEY MEAN
Correct me if I'm wrong:	Please don't contradict me.
I'll bear that in mind:	You're joking, right?
By the way:	This is my main point.
I hear what you say:	Let's not talk about it anymore.
With the greatest respect:	You're an idiot.
Up to a point:	Not at all.

In his travel classic *In Trouble Again*, the English naturalist Redmond O'Hanlon recalls an exchange he had with his guide Juan as they prepared to undertake a journey in remote Venezuela. "'I too have a terrible temper,' Juan remarks. 'I feel it inside all the time. Perhaps it is something in our character, a mix of the Spaniard and the Indian. But you, you are very English, dishonest. You never show your feelings'" (43). How extraordinary that the English reputation for dissembling could penetrate to the deepest reaches of the Amazon and the very edge of civilization.

The English habit of understatement derives in large part from the great English instinct for fairness, here in the form of implicitly acknowledging the right of everyone to their opinion and to make it known to others. But to insist or otherwise be too forceful in one's statements could be taken for trying to squelch other views or intimidating others into meekness. You will notice, in this regard, how English conversation is littered with expressions that acknowledge the other person's point without quite agreeing: "I take your meaning, but . . ." "That's well said, but . . ." "I can agree with you—up to a point."

Another part of the explanation for English subtlety (as Americans would call it) surely lies in the legacy of feudalism. In highly stratified societies, survival depended in large part on the continued good will and sufferance of one's betters. In such circumstances, people quickly learn to be circumspect in their speech, to say what they think other people want to hear, and—as Rowan demonstrates above—to find ways to avoid saying what others might object to. If curbing your tongue keeps a roof over your head and mutton in the stewpot, then you learn the art of understatement.

For their part, Americans associate plain speaking with liberty, and being unafraid to say what you think is perhaps the ultimate expression of individual freedom. It is, moreover, a symbol of equality, that no one is beholden or subservient to anyone else. "Rank of birth is not recognized," an early German visitor to America writes, and "is resisted with a total force. . . . People think, act, and speak here precisely as it prompts them" (Degler, 106). American directness may also be related to the fact that there was so much opportunity in the New World. What did it matter if you spoke your mind and caused offense? You could always move somewhere else and start your life over.

The Fix

If Americans are going to work with the English, they need to listen harder for what's not being said and pay closer attention to tone and body language, which is where the English often put the bad news. Look out for any mildly critical statements, and multiply their intensity by two to get closer to the real message. When you're the one passing out criticism, say half of what you might have said in the States, and the English will understand.

English who want to make themselves understood to Americans will have to be less subtle, closer to what you might consider blunt but what Americans would only perceive as direct. Similarly, try not to be offended when Americans come on a bit strong. Here it must be said that once in a while, when you are tired or need amusement, you often lapse into deliberate doublespeak and enjoy watching Yanks struggle with English subtlety. You may think you're paying them back for throwing off the Empire, but let's be honest: it's just self-indulgence. You're better than that.

17. CARRIED AWAY

ARABELLA: How do you think it went in there?

CARL: Pretty good, I'd say.

ARABELLA: Do you think they'll sign?

CARL: I do. I made it clear there's no way they'll get better terms if they wait.

ARABELLA: Yes, you really emphasized that.

CARL: Maybe I got a little carried away, but they didn't seem to understand.

ARABELLA: I think they understood.

It's no accident that even today the classic cliché of the stiff upper lip continues to define the essence of Englishness. The upper lip that never trembles is of course shorthand for emotional self-control, and there are very few things as important to the English as keeping the emotions in check.

Which is why Carl is in trouble. He and Arabella have apparently just come from a pitch meeting with a group of English businesspeople. And during the meeting, Carl, by his own admission, "got a little carried away" when the clients could not seem to grasp what good terms they were being offered. Carl may or may not lose the deal because of this, but Arabella clearly thinks the meeting could have gone better. She doesn't say so in so many words (she's English, after all), but she makes it clear that Carl came on quite strong: "You really emphasized that," and "I think they understood." Indeed, merely by asking Carl how he thinks the meeting went, Arabella—who is *from* the culture and therefore *knows* how it went—isn't asking Carl for his opinion; she's giving him hers. If she thought it had gone well, she wouldn't be asking him these questions.

People who can't control their emotions frighten the English; there's always a chance they could make a scene or cause a confrontation, both of which are anathema in a country where civility reigns supreme. "This reticence [to show emotion] may be connected to the shyness of the British," Peter Collett writes, "but it probably has more to do with that cardinal rule which says that one must not make a scene in public. This desire not to cause any trouble is a very powerful motivating force in British life—one which sometimes threatens to be more important than life itself" (Hill, 1995, 67).

The desire not to cause trouble surely owes something to the great British tradition of stoicism, of suffering in silence and cheerfully coping with adversity. If you believe, as the English do, that life is a struggle (the creed of the stoic), then clearly we all have to be tough. We can't very well fall apart every time there's a setback, for example, as there are going to be rather a lot of them along the way. If we can't change the human condition, in other words, then we must endure it graciously. "Women in other countries seem to go to bed when they feel unwell," an English friend tells the American expat Muriel Beadle in *These Ruins Are Inhabited*, her classic account of a year spent at Oxford. "We Englishwomen go for a brisk walk with the dogs" (132).

That great observer of European culture Luigi Barzini thinks that the English brand of stoicism is an inevitable byproduct of the harsh conditions and hard living that comprised their daily lot for centuries. It is, he says, the quality:

> of sailors on sailing ships who face raging seas and hurricanes or wait weeks for the windless calm to end; [of] farmers on inhospitable land, resigned to the unpredictable weather; [of] fishermen in the stormy and fog-bound seas of the North; [of] lonely shepherds on deserted moors. . . . Surely it was their hard life that taught the British to be brave, resourceful, far-seeing, self-controlled, or to act as if they were. In one word, they are stoics.
>
> Most of them were stoics to begin with long ago. . . . Later most of them still behaved like stoics, whether they were or not, because that was the way to be and it was inconceivable to be anything else. (61, 62)

The emotional restraint at the core of stoicism is a great enabler of understatement—minimizing difficulties, downplaying misfortune, and generally never getting carried away. "The reasons for our prolific understating," Kate Fox observes,

> are not hard to discover: our strict prohibitions on earnestness, gushing, emoting and boasting require almost constant use of understatement. Rather than risk exhibiting any hint of forbidden solemnity, unseemly emotion or excessive zeal, we go to the opposite extreme and feign dry, deadpan indifference. The understatement rule means that debilitating and painful chronic illness must be described as "a bit of a nuisance"; a truly horrific experience is "well, not exactly what I would have chosen." (66, 67)

The American writer Bill Bryson, an expat who lives in England, notes how the contrast of British restraint and American enthusiasm is especially obvious in the realm of advertising. The same product

has to be sold in an entirely different way. An advertisement in Britain for a cold relief capsule, for instance, would promise no more than that it might make you feel a little better. You would still have a red nose and be in your pajamas, but you would be smiling again, if wanly. A commercial for the selfsame product in America, however, would guarantee total, instantaneous relief. A person on the American side of the Atlantic who took this miracle compound would not only throw off his pj's and get back to work at once, he would feel better than he had for years and finish the day having the time of his life at a bowling alley." (1999, 11)

In America, the idea of controlling one's emotions in public has little cachet; indeed, the very idea of emotional self-control is seen as something of an oxymoron. To begin with, emotions are a natural, spontaneous phenomenon—they just happen—and Americans inherently trust what is natural. For Americans, then, emotions aren't necessarily bad or dangerous, as they seem to be with the English, though Americans do accept that excessive venting is bad in certain circumstances. Americans realize that what is natural may not always be civil, in other words, but they believe strongly that civility purchased at the price of concealment and dishonesty is a dubious achievement. Not surprisingly, Americans don't trust people who don't show any emotions, and they are especially critical of people who feel one emotion and display another, finding such behavior wily and calculating.

Americans tend to regard emotional self-control as a check on their independence, an infringement on their God-given right of self-expression. The freedom to express how one feels is almost as fundamental as the right to feel that way in the first place. This doesn't mean Americans lack self-control or never hold their tongues—as the English often accuse them of—but they are much more inclined to trust their feelings. They believe in the end that any unfortunate consequences of too much self-expression are still preferable to the consequences of excessive self-restraint. "Civility cannot be purchased from Americans on any terms," one nineteenth-century English visitor remarked. "They seem to think it is incompatible with freedom."

The Fix

Americans who want to impress the English need to exhibit self-discipline and emotional restraint. You will not be seen as a good business partner if there's a chance you might lose self-control and embarrass your colleagues and yourself. Expressing perhaps half the emotion you actually feel should suffice to get your message across. At the same time, you should multiply by two (at a minimum) the intensity publicly exhibited by the English to arrive at how they actually feel. Also, try not to interpret English reserve as dishonesty, an attempt to deceive or otherwise hide their true feelings; in their view, it's just good manners.

For their part, the English working in an American context should loosen up now and then and get carried away just a tad. Americans tend not to trust people who are so self-controlled. How are we supposed to know what you're thinking, Americans often ask, if you English are so buttoned up all the time? Meanwhile, you should not be alarmed by mild emotional displays on the part of Americans and assume the person is on the brink of running amok; they're just being sincere and well within the limits of what they consider propriety.

18. CLOSING TIME

AL: Adrian, good. You're still here. Got a minute?

ADRIAN: Just leaving, actually.

AL: It'll just take a second.

ADRIAN: Walk with me to the lift.

AL: I think we finally found a source for that additive, an outfit in Singapore.

ADRIAN: Do we know them?

AL: I thought I'd make some calls.

ADRIAN: Now?

AL: I might get one or two people. It took so long to find this that I don't want someone to get in ahead of us.

ADRIAN: Right. First thing tomorrow, then.

93

Americans have a sense of urgency that is rarely shared by other cultures, certainly not by the English; hence, the wall Al comes up against in this dialogue. Al gets plenty of cues that Adrian does not share his excitement, but he misses them all. The first and most significant is when Adrian answers "Just leaving" without even asking what news the breathless Al has rushed in to report. In other words, there's no need to find out what this is all about at this point because nothing can be that urgent. Al persists ("It'll just take a second") and gets another brush-off ("Walk with me to the lift"). Adrian's not going to let this delay his departure, but if Al can explain it before the lift comes, Adrian may just humor him.

When Al reveals the source of his excitement, Adrian asks an important question: "Do we know them?" There are at least two messages here. First things first, we're not going to close a deal with a company we know nothing about, certainly not this evening. The other is that since we *do* need to check up on this outfit, nothing can happen before tomorrow morning, so let's all go home.

But Al can't let go ("I thought I'd make some calls"), which prompts Adrian ("Now?") to wonder who might still be at work at midnight in Singapore or after business hours here in the U.K. Al's final try ("I don't want someone to get in ahead of us") is pretty lame even for Al; if no one else has found this supplier in all these months, do we really have to act tonight? At this point, Adrian descends with relief to the lobby, leaving a very frustrated Al in his wake.

Al may be a bit worked up in this example, even for an American, but there's no denying that Americans can be very driven: they want to act—often without much planning or thinking, apparently confident that everything will work out for the best. Or, if it does not, then there's no harm done.

There's an awful lot for the typical English person to object to in those last two sentences. Let's start with being driven and impatient; to the English this smacks of being enthusiastic, and enthusiasm is "problematic" (as the English might say) because it's a short step from being enthusiastic to being emotional. At the very least it's not being entirely rational, which is the preferred English way of handling most situations. The next problem with driven people is they often act without planning or even thinking—in a word, spontaneously—which the English equate with being carried away by one's emotions, which can only ever end badly. Then there is the annoying American assumption that everything always works out for the best, to which the English would reply: In which universe, exactly? And finally there's the extremely dangerous assumption that even if things do go badly, it doesn't usually cause any lasting harm. By what twisted logic is that true?

How to explain the English affinity for caution and their aversion to acting on impulse? In part it is all of a piece with the idea that reason, not emotion, should govern behavior. People should act after thinking, not after feeling. Important issues in particular should be decided after careful reflection and analysis, when everyone has calmed down. This instinct for emotional detachment in turn derives at least in part from the deeply held English conviction that we live in a world of finite possibilities. There are limits, you see, on what can happen in life; no matter what we do—how long and hard we work, whether or not we hear the latest development before we reach the lift—things only change within a certain limited range of possibilities. While we should of course remain alert and be ready to exploit opportunities, we should not fool ourselves; we are tinkering at the margins here, not at the core.

95

Needless to say, this worldview takes the urgency out of most undertakings. If what you do will never make *that* much difference, then does it really matter whether you do it tonight or tomorrow morning?

Americans come from a very different world, a world of *unlim-*ited possibilities, where the only restraints are those you impose on yourself. Anything is possible if you want it bad enough and are willing to work hard enough. In a world where anything can happen, there's never any excuse to accept things the way they are; there's always the chance—a good chance, in fact—that timely action can make a difference. Under the circumstances, not to act always carries with it the possibility of some kind of loss. Waiting until tomorrow to look into this new supplier might be too late. "[T]ravelers from abroad," Luigi Barzini writes, "have invariably recorded and still record today the same impression: Why this American impatience? Where was and is the fire? What is the deadline each American is trying to beat?" (239) To which most Americans would reply: The fire is all around us.

The Fix

Americans should realize that the English (and most other Europeans) find them impatient and reckless. You don't need to stop being driven, but in cases where immediate action is necessary, you may have to justify the urgency to English colleagues. You should also try to save your enthusiasm for truly rare opportunities and not just run-of-the-mill possibilities. Otherwise, you will just alarm the English and lose most of your credibility. Meanwhile, if the English come across to you as cautious, timid, or even just lazy, try to get to the bottom of their concerns; you may think little of their reasons for inaction, but they will *have* reasons.

For their part, the English should give more credit to Americans for their ingenuity; in many cases they actually have made a real difference in situations where all you have seen is limited returns. If you think Americans are being impatient and reckless, call them on it. Ask for their reasons when they see a golden opportunity where all you see is the faintest signs of possibility. Also remember that if Americans want to take what you consider unacceptable risks, it's not just because they are reckless or naive; it is also because they are supremely confident in their ability to handle any and all setbacks. If they're willing to shoulder the blame, where's the harm?

19. WE'LL HAVE A GO*

SHARON: Hi, Nigel. Did you get my e-mail?

NIGEL: We did.

SHARON: How does that request look to you?

NIGEL: We'll have a go.

SHARON: But this *is* your area, isn't it? Or should we
           have sent this somewhere else?

NIGEL: No, no. This is what we do. We're not too
           bad, either, for amateurs.

SHARON: Excuse me?

NIGEL: We'll do our best.

SHARON: So you'll let us know, then, if it doesn't work
           out?

NIGEL: Sorry?

There is understatement, as shown in Dialogue 16, saying less than what you mean, and then there is anti-statement (aka irony), meaning the opposite of what you say. The English excel at both. Americans struggle mightily with the former, with occasional success, but irony defeats them entirely. Indeed, they're not even aware that there's *been* a struggle, much less that they have lost it.

In this dialogue, we see what can happen when Americans, with their tendency towards chest beating, and the English, with a deep instinct for self-deprecation, have a brief conversation about competence. Kate Fox, in her book *Watching the English*, explains quite succinctly what Sharon needs to know:

---

* British English for "We'll try." Or, as Americans would say, "We'll take a stab at it."

Our famous self-deprecation is a form of irony, saying the opposite of what we intend people to understand, or using deliberate understatement. It's a kind of code: everyone knows that a self-deprecating statement probably means roughly the opposite of what is said, or involves a significant degree of understatement, and we are duly impressed, both by the speaker's achievements or abilities and by his/her reluctance to trumpet them. (408)

Everyone knows? Not quite, especially not Americans. In this dialogue, the "code" has caused a first-class misunderstanding and left Sharon with the exact opposite of the reassurance she was looking for from Nigel. She has made a request of Nigel, whom she has reason to believe possesses the expertise she's looking for. Things go south almost immediately with Nigel's "We'll have a go," which sounds very cavalier to Sharon, almost as if he's never done anything quite like this before but there's a first time for everything. For his part, Nigel is deliberately sending (so he thinks) the opposite message: that nothing could be easier for a pro like him.

Sharon, nervous now, tries to confirm she's got the right Nigel: "But this *is* your area, isn't it?" Nigel confirms this, but then his modesty reflex kicks in, and he can't help adding the requisite "We're not too bad, either, for amateurs" to reassure Sharon that he's the right man for the job. This backfires, of course, and it's Nigel's turn to be confused when, for some odd reason, Sharon now appears to have doubts about him: "So you'll let us know, then, if it doesn't work out?"

"Problems arise," Fox continues, "when the English try to play this rather silly game with foreigners who do not understand the ironic code and tend to take our self-deprecating remarks at face value" (409).

Problems indeed.

As it happens, "face value" is a big part of the problem here. While Nigel might have gotten away with speaking in his ironic code if Sharon were Japanese or Chinese, who have similar codes of their own, she's an American, hence a member of one of the most literal of all cultures. Americans don't do irony. If someone says to an American "We'll have a go," or "We're not bad for amateurs," or "We'll do our best," what the person must mean is, respectively, they will try, they're somewhat inexperienced, and they'll do the best they can but there are no guarantees.

By itself, the ironic vs. literal cultural difference is more than enough to derail this exchange, but there is a deeper confusion at the heart of this dialogue: the value placed on personal modesty in these two cultures. It is highly valued among the English who are, accordingly, somewhat uncomfortable with recognition. As is so often the case with the English, this is as much a matter of appearances as of reality. The English take pride in a job well done, but it's decidedly bad form to *appear* proud. They likewise expect and appreciate praise when it is deserved, but they know better than to *act* as if it's deserved.

The English instinct toward self-deprecation is probably more fallout from the stoicism syndrome. If life is a struggle where only the tough prevail, then shrugging off compliments is simply proof of your toughness. Life is supposed to be hard, after all, and we shouldn't expect that our efforts will be appreciated; you do something because it's the right thing, not because it will be recognized or rewarded. In such a world, people who need praise, or, more precisely, people who *appear* to need praise (we all need it, even the English), will be seen as weak. Luigi Barzini describes how

> stoic were the sober newspaper comments on the brilliant, skillful, and daring Falklands war . . . a highly pragmatic

operation undertaken in defense of international law and morality and surely not for gain. I will quote only one comment, Alexander Chancellor's in the Spectator after the victory. It began, "A little rejoicing is now in order, but only a little. We may rejoice that the Falklands war did not end in a bloodbath at Port Stanley. . . . We may rejoice at the performance of our armed forces who have conducted themselves with great skill and with as much humanity as is possible in war." It is clearly inconceivable for anybody not a Briton to write so soberly after such a brilliant and risky military performance. (63)

Surely another factor behind English self-deprecation is the cultural attitude toward work. Work is important, of course; you should do a good job—your best, in fact—and generally take work seriously but not too seriously. It's all part of that general English distrust of any kind of earnestness or of anyone who is "too keen." "If your work is interesting," Fox writes,

you are allowed to be interested in it—even to the point of being a bit of a workaholic, but if you are too much of a workaholic . . . you will be regarded as "sad" and pathetic.

Our instinctive avoidance of earnestness results in a way of conducting business or work-related discussions that the uninitiated foreigner finds quite disturbing: a sort of offhand, dispassionate, detached manner—always giving the impression . . . of being rather underwhelmed by the whole thing, including [our]selves and the product [we] are supposed to be selling. It is not done to get too excited about one's product or services—one must not be seen to care too much, however desperate one might in fact be to close a deal. (180, 181)

In a world where you're not supposed to care too much about work, it's generally "not done" to accept work-related compliments.

Americans value humility, too, and even have their own version of self-effacement—"Oh, it was nothing"—but it is not a religion with them. They are more comfortable with personal recognition and with having attention drawn to their achievements. Indeed, they tend to hand out compliments indiscriminately (and quite insincerely as far as the English are concerned), as if they were candy bars. While Americans think it bad form to solicit or revel in praise, they see no need to run from it so long as it's earned. In fact, to Americans too much self-deprecation sounds phony—false modesty, they call it—and may even suggest a lack of self-confidence. In the end, it is the tenacity with which Nigel insists on his averageness that worries and confuses Sharon.

101

The Fix

Americans need to be aware of the English instinct for self-deprecation and be careful not to misread English modesty and humility as expressions of self-doubt or a lack of confidence. Nor should you stop complimenting the English just because they refuse to accept it; they need and appreciate praise as much as any people. Meanwhile, you might want to deflect at least some of the praise that comes your way, so as not to appear immodest or proud, and likewise desist from praising yourself too much. The less you say about your achievements, the more impressed the English are when they eventually find out about you.

For their part, the English need to understand that a little humility goes a long way with Americans. Yanks understand and practice token modesty, but excessive modesty puts them off; you either must be fishing for compliments or genuinely lacking in confidence. Meanwhile, if Americans come across as boastful, don't interpret this as covering up for insecurity—although there may be a little of that, especially when Americans are dealing with Europeans—or just plain egotism; It's only what Americans consider healthy self-respect.

20. GOOD NEWS

TOM:	How's everything going with that data recovery?
AMANDA:	We've tried everything we can think of.
TOM:	So it's not going to be a quick fix, I guess?
AMANDA:	And we couldn't find anybody who's ever done that kind of recovery.
TOM:	Well, at least there's some good news.
AMANDA:	What's that?
TOM:	You can have as much time as you need.
AMANDA:	But we don't need any more time.
TOM:	I don't understand.

On occasion, the Anglo-American cultural divide narrows just enough to appear bridgeable; on others, it opens so wide that mutual understanding seems impossible. In this dialogue, Amanda and Tom are standing on opposite sides of a yawning chasm.

Not to put too fine a point on it, but Americans like Tom often drive the English crazy (along with most other Europeans) with their bedrock belief that anything is possible. From an English perspective, this is much worse than optimism ("Just wait, everything will turn out OK"), that other annoying American national disease. Despite their hopeless naïveté, you can at least reason with optimists and temper their wilder flights of euphoria with a few cold facts. You will probably be accused of being cynical and pessimistic—and Americans will feel bad that you live in such a disappointing world—but by and large you won't be dismissed out of hand.

Americans are not very objective when it comes to their can-do mentality. While even they can laugh sometimes at their optimism, Americans are not amused when people challenge the core belief that all things are possible. Pessimism is annoying, but defeatism is deeply frustrating.

Charged with recovering some lost data, Amanda and her team have been working very hard. They are, as they see it, near the end of their efforts, having tried "everything we can think of." But for Tom ("So it's not going to be a quick fix?"), the message is not that recovery is impossible but only that it might take longer than everyone thought. Amanda doubles down and points out that no one else has ever thought of a way to do this either. The problem isn't lack of trying, in short; it's that this recovery just isn't doable.

Since total defeat is inconceivable in Tom's world, he happily offers what he assumes Amanda must be asking for and the obvious solution to this problem: more time. When Amanda says she doesn't need any more time, meaning this job is simply not possible, Tom is culturally incapable of processing this information—if she doesn't need more time, then what *does* she need?

Americans epitomize the can-do mentality, the notion that there are no givens in life, no limits on what people can achieve if they want something bad enough and are willing to try hard enough. Hence, the corresponding belief that if people fail to accomplish something, it is never because it is impossible but only because they can't be bothered. And why shouldn't Americans believe this? The American story is all about rejecting and transcending limits, pushing the frontier across the country and into the Pacific Ocean—and then going to the moon. Moreover, the sheer size of the country and the abundance of its resources likewise made it virtually impossible for any notion of limits to get a foothold in the American character. One only had to look around to see there was no such thing as limits. Richard Pells observes

> that the disparities between the United States and Europe were obvious. In small countries like Britain, Switzerland, or Italy, spatial restrictions led to . . . a sense of limited possibilities. In America, Harold Laski asserted, the horizons were infinite and so too were the opportunities. There were few obstacles to economic or social ascent. In Laski's view, "the element of spaciousness in American life" resulted in a dynamism that was the opposite of European "rigidity." (169)

104

Accordingly, there's no real tradition in America of resigning oneself to the facts. For people like Tom, however things *may* be, they can always be changed. All problems have solutions if you work on them long enough. If there are no real limits, then people who don't achieve what they set out to do just didn't want it badly enough. Amanda *could* go on, in other words, but for some reason she's decided not to. In a word, she's a quitter.

Here's hoping Tom never uses that word around Amanda, for he will be roundly—and rightly—abused. The English national experience has taught them that there will be reverses in life (the loss of empire) as well as advances. It has taught them that there are circumstances over which we have no control and which must therefore be accepted. This doesn't mean the English passively bow to the inevitable; it means, rather, that they are an eminently practical people, given to cold, objective analysis and not afraid to cut their losses. They will try their best—they're not slackers or quitters—but there comes a point beyond which trying is no longer a virtue. For the English and most other

Europeans, there's such a thing as giving up gracefully, admitting defeat, and moving on. This is not considered failure, by the way—failure is stopping before you've made your best effort—but resignation, the mark of a mature people. "Europe has what we do not have yet," James Baldwin observes, "a sense of the mysterious and inexorable limits of life, a sense in a word, of tragedy. And we have what they sorely need: a new sense of life's possibilities" (Pells, 140).

The Fix

There are times when English people inevitably come across as giving up too soon and when Americans inevitably come across as unreasonable. The best each side can do in these situations is to mitigate the name-calling. If Americans want the English to go on trying after they've tried everything they can think of, no problem: you simply must point out what the English have not thought of yet. If you can't do that, then simply saying, "There has to be a way," (while offering no suggestions) will not prove especially motivating. You should be willing to offer resources and any other support the English might need if you insist they make more effort.

For their part, the English should not be too hasty to brand Americans as hopelessly naïve and walk away from seemingly intractable problems. Naïve Americans may be, but sometimes their incredibly annoying persistence pays off. If you really feel you have gone the extra mile (as Americans put it) and exhausted all possibilities, then explain this and ask what they would do in your place. If the Americans don't have an answer, you can rest your case. If they simply say, "There has to be a way," ask them what it is.

105

5

France

Americans have no capacity for abstract thought and make bad coffee.

—Georges Clemenceau

While we cannot be sure which flaw he considered more serious, Clemenceau did manage to touch pithily on two matters that mean a great deal to the French—and very little to most Americans. Americans are enthusiastically unintellectual (though not *anti*-intellectual, as the French sometimes think) and somewhat puritanical (taking a dim view of sensual indulgence, for example). Meanwhile, the French lionize great thinkers and practically invented *joie de vivre*. If Clemenceau had permitted an American rejoinder, it would no doubt have gone something like this: "The French think too much and are obsessed with food."

Franco-American relations are unquestionably more fraught than either Anglo- or German-American relations. Americans can sometimes see themselves in the English and the Germans, but they hardly ever identify with the French. That is probably because the United States is most distinctly influenced by *northern* European culture—and France is a decidedly Latin, southern European nation. Indeed, the English and the Germans have as hard a time understanding the French—and vice versa—as the Americans do.

We hasten to add that most Americans love France (if not the French). They realize the French condescend to and patronize them, normally two of the worst things you can do to an American, but they somehow accept this behavior—probably because they are not singled out in this regard. Americans find the French terribly sophisticated and, knowing they are almost boorish by comparison, they cheerfully accept their inferior status. They forgive all manner of offensive traits in the French because of their terrific sense of style. "When they die," the American writer Henry James observes, "good Americans go to Paris"—a sentiment later embellished by Oscar Wilde, who observes (in *The Picture of Dorian Gray*) that when *bad* Americans die, they go to America (James, 8). Admire them though they may, Americans aren't fooled by the French and know better than to trust them. The French may have good taste, but they are incorrigible opportunists (as they would be among the first to admit).

The French, meanwhile, are greatly amused by Americans—when they aren't totally exasperated by them. They resent American power and influence, of course—it takes the spotlight away from where it rightly belongs—but they find Americans endlessly engaging and admire their spirit. The French wouldn't stoop to be jealous of Americans (or anyone else), but they do envy all the attention they get.

21. GLOOM

JENNIFER: Did you see the fourth-quarter sales figures yet?

JEAN-CLAUDE:	Yes. Rather bad; down a third from last year.
JENNIFER:	We really took a beating.
JEAN-CLAUDE:	Yes. We did very poorly.
JENNIFER:	Oh, well. We might as well look on the bright side; things can only go up from here.
JEAN-CLAUDE:	I'm not so sure. I think the figures could go either way.
JENNIFER:	Well, no point in being gloomy though, is there?
JEAN-CLAUDE:	What do you mean?

If you asked European businesspeople for their biggest complaint about Americans, you would hear a lot about their optimism. If you asked Americans the same question about Europeans, you'd get an earful about how negative and pessimistic they are.

Even optimistic Americans must admit that Jean-Claude's question at the end of "Gloom" is completely legitimate: What does Jennifer mean by accusing him of being gloomy? Nothing in the conversation justifies that conclusion. The facts are that the group had a bad fourth quarter ("down a third from last year"); Jean-Claude says exactly that ("We did very poorly"); and Jennifer agrees ("We really took a beating"). So far, so objective.

Then Jennifer betrays her Americanness with "We might as well look on the bright side; things can only go up from here." Assuming she has no more information about the future than Jean-Claude does, there is nothing to support this statement. The only thing that can be said for sure is that the figures could go up or they could go down. Hence, Jean-Claude's remark that "the figures could go either way" is the only realistic assessment that can be made at this time.

And that's just the problem: Jennifer, being a good American, is actually not in touch with reality nor in any hurry to be brought closer. She would rather stay in her world—the world of "the bright side," where things are always better than they look. From that perspective, Jean-Claude's realism naturally comes across as pessimism.

We can understand, then, why Jennifer would accuse Jean-Claude of being gloomy and why Jean-Claude would be surprised ("What do you mean?"). But where does this unstoppable American optimism comes from? There are in fact several sources; a prominent one is what we might call the "land-of-opportunity" trope, which comprises a large part of the foundation story of the New World. Relative to the crowded, opportunity-poor world they came from, European settlers found America impossibly empty and endless. "For centuries," Carl Degler writes,

> the problem in Europe had been that of securing enough land for the people, but in the New World the elements in the equation were reversed. . . . The possibility of exaggeration should not hide the undeniable fact that in early America, and through most of the nineteenth century, too, land was available to an extent that could appear only fabulous to land-starved Europeans. (2)

One such land-starved European described the fabulous American countryside thus on a trip down the Mississippi:

> Here, magnificently grand eternal forests, in appearance as interminable as the universe . . . constitute the scenery for thousands of miles contiguous to this matchless stream.

As to the river itself, I shall not attempt a description of it. What has already been said proves its magnitude to be immensely great; even some of its branches, as the Ohio and the Missouri, are said to be classed among the largest rivers in the world. (Hutner, 44)

In the midst of such bounty, only the churlish could fail to be optimistic. "Unlimited space [is] not just an attribute of the American continent," Pells writes, "it is a key to the American psyche" (169).

Abundance also supports another deep American belief: the idea that you are the author of your destiny, the so-called self-made man. In a world of plenty, there is nothing stopping you from achieving your goals, and if you are likewise self-made, then anything else that might make you, such as any number of external factors, can always be overcome. People who believe that what happens in life is ultimately up to them would never have any excuse not to be positive and optimistic. In America, setbacks are nothing more than brief interludes during which you plan how you're going to prevail.

A Chinese man once told me a fascinating story. He was working at an American university as part of a three-man team—the other two were an American and an Iranian—overseeing the development of a new drug for a major pharmaceutical company. The Chinese man accompanied his two colleagues to a meeting with the client and took notes. The client asked the American for his assessment of the project and whether they were still on schedule to start the drug trials. The American answered that everything was going fine, there were no major obstacles, and he was confident the trials could start on schedule. Asked the same question, the Iranian man replied that there was still much work to be done and it was too early to tell if the trials could start on time.

Later the Chinese man, curious about the discrepancy, asked the American how sure he was the team would complete its work on schedule. The American said 25 percent. When the Chinese man asked his Iranian colleague how sure he was, he said 85 percent. But it was the American, the one with serious reservations, who gave the rosy prediction.

We can understand, then, why the American national instinct is to be optimistic, but what explains the deep French (and European) instinct toward realism? Surely Jean-Claude comes by his worldview as legitimately as Jennifer comes by hers. In his classic *Understanding Europeans*, Stuart Miller provides some clues. "[In] general," he writes,

> *the European exists in an inner world where things won't get better and life is not very good to begin with. Psychologically, this view shelters him from some of the shocks and disappointments of existence. Practically, such an attitude leads to the caution necessary for confronting what experience has shown to be a dangerous and intractable universe. (32)*

In looking for the origins of this somewhat bleak "inner world," Miller explains how European history is a "tale of a world painful and unsafe" (5). For the last 2,500 years, he notes,

> *one year in five is a year of armed conflict [and] war is a normal condition. . . .*
>
> *Only by plunging ourselves into a sense of the enormous weight of historic violence can we begin to understand the European soul. We must think of a vast South Bronx of a continent, repeatedly devastated not for ten or twenty years but, as men experience time, forever. . . . The background of collective violence, combined with other historical forces like*

memories of massive poverty, makes the European [see the world] in ways that are typically un-American. (17)

The Fix

No matter how hard they try, Americans will always come across as naïve and unrealistic to the French. And that means they will view you with suspicion. But at least let them have their say. Don't simply dismiss French misgivings out of hand if they sound defeatist; hear them out. If their concerns are unsupported by the facts, point this out; otherwise accept them. Meanwhile, curb any unjustified enthusiasm and make an attempt to be realistic. If the French feel you're at least trying to see things as they are, they are more likely to trust you.

The French must accept that objectivity comes across as negative to Americans. It's not accurate, of course—you're only being realistic—but that's the perception you've got to live with and must try to mitigate. Remember that Americans think when you are being negative, even if the facts are on your side, that you are just making excuses for doing nothing. So you need to explain why you see things the way you do; Americans will listen. Meanwhile, try to be positive wherever there is obvious justification. If Americans see you're trying to be fair, being positive where it's warranted and realistic where it's not, you will become more credible. Also remember that one of the reasons Americans are so optimistic is their great faith in their ability to cope if things do not work out. You take fewer risks than you think by "looking on the bright side."

113

22. LET'S MOVE ON

MARTHA: We thought we would leave behind Provision 2 for now and move on to talk about Provision 3.

THÉRÈSE: But we had such interesting discussions.

MARTHA: Yes, but we don't agree on anything in that provision.

THÉRÈSE: No, of course not. We argued a lot.

MARTHA: We just weren't getting anywhere.

THÉRÈSE: No, not really.

MARTHA: So perhaps we can agree to disagree and move on.

THÉRÈSE: Or we could just continue to disagree and keep talking.

Americans don't like to argue. While that seems at odds with their direct style of communication, there are limits to directness. They don't mind discussion, but if the conversation starts to get heated, Americans back off until "cooler heads prevail." Indeed, in most discussions Americans look for what they call "common ground," points everyone can agree on, as if staying on good terms were the most important outcome of any exchange. After a contentious exchange, it's not uncommon for Americans to ask, only half-jokingly: "But we can still be friends, right?"

The French have no qualms about arguing; they relish it. Nor can they imagine how a heated exchange could ever threaten a true friendship. "Americans tend to like people who agree with them," it has been noted, whereas

French people are more likely to be interested in a person who disagrees with them. . . . A conversation where disagreements are exchanged [is] stimulating [to] a Frenchman, while an American is likely to be embarrassed. It is not uncommon to see two Frenchmen arguing with each other, their faces reddened with what seems to be anger, exchanging lively, heated and irreconcilable arguments. Then, later,

they shake hands and [say], "That was a good discussion.
Let's do it again sometime." (Harris, 449.)

Therein lies the confusion in the earlier part of "Let's Move
On." Obviously there was a lively discussion about Provision 2
the day before, with no agreement anywhere in sight. It appears,
in fact, that the conversation got very close to an argument,
which was music to Thérèse's ears, perhaps, but enough for Martha to conclude that they should leave the provision alone until
everyone calms down. Thérèse naturally wonders where the fun
is in that.

Another cultural difference on display here comes via Martha's remark, "We just weren't getting anywhere." Reaching a
concrete agreement—in short, accomplishing something—might
be very important to Americans, but for the French the discussion is just as important, and certainly more enjoyable, than the
eventual outcome. When Thérèse answers, "No, not really," she's
agreeing the two sides didn't get anywhere, but she's certainly
not disappointed. Indeed, if the two sides *had* gotten somewhere,
then the lovely discussion would now be over.

The French take their discussions seriously, not merely as
means to an end but as a kind of beautiful end in themselves.
Conversation is an art in France, after all, valuable in its own
right, and the people who do it best are widely admired. An
eloquent defense of a bad idea is almost as acceptable as a halt-
ing defense of a good one. Repartee, one of the cornerstones of
sophisticated conversation, is a French invention and it is much
appreciated. Besides, through a heated and lively exchange, we
can stimulate each other's best thinking and achieve a better
end result.

"French business people [view] conflict and dissonance as
bringing hidden contradictions to light," Erin Meyer writes, "and

stimulating fresh thinking." She goes on to quote a French colleague who observes, "[W]e make our points passionately. We like to disagree openly. We like to say things that shock. With confrontation, you reach excellence, you have more creativity, and you eliminate risk" (200). To people who like to disagree openly, Martha's final remark ("Perhaps we can agree to disagree") is a solution to a nonexistent problem.

Why do Americans prefer to avoid argument? Because they have a strong need to be liked. "[I]n America," Stuart Miller writes "it is important to be popular. . . . People want to be loved, so they must learn to agree with others" (23). As to why that should be, surely it has something to do with American individualism. Self-reliant, independent people who are raised to stand on their own two feet are not inclined to nor very good at relying on others. And yet we all need other people from time to time, even individualists, but since Americans are not raised to forge close ties to others, since they cannot automatically depend on the support of the group, they must inspire that support by being nice to people. If you alienate people by arguing with them, you will not be able to rely on them in times of need.

Another, related reason may be that because Americans are such a mobile people, they regularly find themselves in new environments with few connections. One of the quickest ways to make friends—and there is some urgency here, what with all the relocating going on—is by being pleasant, agreeable, and easy to get along with.

Whether or not the French want to be liked—most would say they prefer to be respected—they don't have to worry about arguments coming between friends. French friendships are decades old, often lifelong; they go through a lot together over the years, and nothing as trivial as an argument is going to undermine a relationship. "French friends do not seek to maintain harmony," Asselin and Mastron observe,

116

but rather to cultivate distinction and avoid boredom. They expect to disagree, to criticize, even to argue. A friend may be very direct, even frankly critical. . . . French people find it tedious to always be in agreement and for this reason may be attracted to friends who are quite different from themselves. Since the relationship is not based on agreement, it is not threatened by disagreement, and French friends expect one another to comment honestly on their actions and choices. Support can be expressed in confrontation as well as by acquiescence. The bond between friends is not fragile and can stand up to this tension, even be strengthened and deepened by it. (89)

Most American friendships, as we've already noted, are not very deep nor especially robust. One argument might not cause a rupture, but why take the chance?

The Fix

Americans should not be afraid to openly disagree with or strongly object to anything their French colleagues say. When those same colleagues attack your proposals, you should vigorously defend yourself. Otherwise, the French will be disappointed and not take you seriously; they are very suspicious of anyone who agrees with them too quickly. Finally, you should realize that the French love to prolong discussion; be patient and do not force them to make decisions before they are ready. If the French feel a suggestion or proposal has not been sufficiently probed, they will be reluctant to make a decision and even less enthusiastic about implementing it.

For their part, the French should not interpret American reluctance to argue as a lack of conviction; they're just trying to be polite. If Americans grow impatient with discussion, it's not because they don't want to be thorough but only because they do not believe in discussion for its own sake. If Americans want to act before you are ready, you can always express your reservations, thereby absolving yourself of any responsibility, and let the Americans get on with it. If it turns out they acted prematurely, they will happily take the blame.

23. HELPING JEAN

GAIL: Jean is late with his report.

FRANÇOIS: He should have started two weeks ago. I told him. Now it won't be ready for the big meeting.

GAIL: Distracted by his new baby, I guess. Michel won't be happy about that.

FRANÇOIS: Our division chief? No.

GAIL: Makes your division look bad. I guess you're pretty busy right now, too?

FRANÇOIS: Me?

GAIL: So you can't help Jean, I mean?

FRANÇOIS: Help Jean?

Americans may be known for their individualism, but they are practically team players compared to the French. However, the two cultures practice very different kinds of individualism. The American kind is based on the values of self-reliance and independence in the service and pursuit of personal freedom. It is not at all incompatible with a concern for others and pulling together when necessary for the common good. American individualism is not compromised by self-sacrifice.

The French version of individualism is very close to conceit and self-centeredness (*egoisme* in French). It can be summed up in the phrase *amour-propre*: literally "self-love" but usually translated as "self-regard" or "self-esteem." And as for the common good, the French recognize no good greater than the individual. "The French have a visceral need to assert their individuality," Richard Hill observes. "Most self-respecting French people are short on modesty, even disarmingly conceited about their intellectual prowess. I say 'disarmingly' because they are quite happy to admit it; an American publishing friend of mine had one of his [French] employees concede, straight-faced, that 'We French are full of ourselves, and justifiably so'" (1995, 56). *Egoisme* is no doubt the origin of the charges of arrogance and superiority that have stuck stubbornly to the French for centuries.

French self-centeredness is on graphic, insistent display in this dialogue. No matter what (American) argument Gail tries, she is utterly unable to evoke any sympathy for the hapless Jean. She starts, in all innocence, with the simple observation that "Jean is late with his report," assuming, naively, that this should be enough to rouse François to action, especially since Jean works in his division and is thus a close colleague. We learn immediately that not only is François well aware of the situation, but that is in fact quite serious ("Now it won't be ready for the big meeting"). At this point, Gail should probably stop and ask herself: If François knows all this, why isn't he already helping Jean?

For his part, meanwhile, François feels he has explained himself more than adequately by noting that he told Jean two weeks ago to start writing his report. François was under absolutely no obligation to do this, of course—to interest himself in a colleague's work and even to offer a helpful suggestion—and no doubt feels he has been uncommonly kind. Indeed, François is probably patting himself on the back for not taking advantage of Jean's predicament, as many French would, to enhance his own position in the division. "Professional relationships between colleagues are founded more on rivalry than collaboration," John Mole notes. "This begins in the highly competitive school environment which is based on getting over a series of ever higher hurdles. Learning to collaborate to solve problems is not an educational goal. Far from refreshing, people find it disconcerting when others do not compete" (20).

Gail now tries two other tactics to bring François around: She suggests that it is not entirely Jean's fault that he's behind ("Distracted by his new baby, I guess"), suggesting that he deserves some help in this particular instance. And just in case that doesn't rouse François, she adds that the division chief, Michel, won't be happy, implying, we can assume, that he will be angry with François for letting Jean flounder. These might be compelling arguments in the U.S. workplace, but not here in France. Who doesn't have a new baby at some time or other? But that's hardly justification for poor performance on the job. And Michel *will* probably be unhappy, but not with François. Indeed, if he had wanted François to help Jean, Michel would have asked him. (We should add here that if Michel has not asked François to help, that doesn't mean he'll accept Jean's unfinished report; more likely he has asked someone else or will even finish the report himself.)

Gail then tries to appeal to François's loyalty to his division, an entity bigger than himself ("Makes your division look bad"), which of course is a complete nonstarter to the French. When Gail finally comes out and asks directly if he can help, François is naturally quite surprised.

None of the above should be construed to mean the French cannot rise to the occasion when necessary or unite to save an enterprise—that they believe it's better to let the ship sink than step in and help an incompetent captain. But the circumstances must be quite dire before the French are willing to sacrifice their *amour-propre* for the sake of the cause. Collaboration and coopera-tion are not completely foreign to the French, but they are by no means instinctive. "The French may display complete disregard for the welfare of those around them," Asselin and Mastron write. "There is little sense of civic responsibility in relation to common property. In some cases the need to *défendre son bifteck* (defend one's own steak) can be more important than high flown notions of solidarity and unity" (19, 20).

As to why the French are like this, one explanation might be the relative lack of social and professional mobility in their soci-ety. Historically, one was born into one's station in life, and you were as likely to change it as you were to suddenly grow another arm. There was no idea that you "did something" with your life, as in America, only that you resigned yourself to it. Unable to take any particular pride in their occupation or accomplishments, the French cultivated instead an intense pride in who they are, in their personal identity, something which they *have* had the chance to shape.

"Pride is very close to the self-esteem that has helped the European deal with his difficult world," Miller observes.

> [I]n societies where life has been as hard as it has in Europe, the individual is driven to feed on the primal energy of his own individual existence and affirm it.
>
> Hence, the French peasant who has not enough money to buy even a horse, who has barely enough food to eat, can wilfully assert his sense of personal being and worth. . . .This kind of defiance of circumstance and all other [people] is common in Europe.
>
> Because the European comes from a tradition much more closed to opportunity, the farmer, the working man, even the middle-class person, inherits centuries of institutionalized

121

*difficulty in social mobility. Against the ceiling on his prog-
ress, he cultivates his pride in himself. (62, 63)*

The American experience was much different. From the very
beginning of the republic, Americans learned that if they didn't
work together, they might very well perish—and would almost
certainly not prosper. "During the formative period of American
culture," John McElroy writes,

> *to improve one's lot in life—and at times just to survive—
> demanded . . . forming organizations that would not only
> benefit the lives of individuals directly but also strengthen
> communities, and in that way indirectly benefit individuals.*
>
> *In places where few people live—such as a frontier or the
> rural communities and small towns that replace a frontier—
> mutual reliance is as practical as self-reliance; and extending
> a helping hand to one's neighbor is no less important than
> taking responsibility for one's own well being. (94, 95)*

There is no room in such a scheme to let self-love stand in
the way of getting the job done.

The Fix

Americans should never automatically rely on the French for help
or assume that an appeal to mutual advantage will always carry
the day. The French will examine the advantages very carefully
and then decide. This doesn't mean they will never extend a hand
but rather that you must offer very good arguments for why they
should. For other Americans, a good argument is simply that
you need help; for the French, you'll have to dig deeper, ideally
explaining how helping you will mostly help them. And as for

appealing to the greater good, a good greater than the self, that is, that's always going to be a bit tricky. It's not that the French cannot conceive of a good greater than the self, but you need to make a very strong case for it. And part of that case, of course, should include an appeal to the individual's *amour-propre*.

It would be wise if the French could learn to trust Americans more. They aren't out to get you, take advantage of your good will, or use your kindness against you. They are willing to give their unconditional help, and you should, too. To be sure, Americans are very competitive, but that does not extend as far as letting you flounder so they will look better, especially if a common good hangs in the balance. They *are* individualists looking out for their own welfare, but rarely will it be at the expense of yours. The way they see it, there's plenty of welfare to go around.   123

24. A GOOD FEELING

YVETTE: What did you think of Ecotek's presentation?

BARBARA: They're very nice people. I have a good feeling about them.

YVETTE: And the presentation?

BARBARA: It was a very good overview, I thought.

YVETTE: A bit lacking in details. We still don't know what their assets are.

BARBARA: They were probably rushed. I'm sure they'll send details if we ask for them.

YVETTE: I thought their timetable, from design to manufacture, was very ambitious.

BARBARA: Maybe a little. But I'm sure they know what they're doing.

YVETTE: We'll see.

One of the most common characterizations the French apply to Americans is that they are naïve. It's okay to be naïve, of course, and it can even be charming at times, but you'd be crazy to go into business with a naïf. Business is for clear-thinking realists, people with both eyes open, both feet on the ground, skeptical, and with no illusions about human nature—a set of characteristics no one would ever apply to an American.

Hence, Yvette's growing frustration in this dialogue. She and Barbara have just sat through a business pitch to their company by Ecotek, a potential supplier. When Yvette wonders what Barbara thought of the presentation, she is surprised at Barbara's reply, "They're very nice people." Even if that *were* relevant, which it's not, it's a remarkably low bar. Who isn't on their best behavior when making a business pitch? And what does that have to do with the presentation? If Yvette is concerned about Barbara's judgment, her next remark ("I have a good feeling about them") removes all doubt: This woman is using some very curious metrics to evaluate a potential supplier.

Yvette, overlooking these alarming signs for the moment, persists ("And the presentation?") and gets another troubling glimpse of Barbara's thinking: "It was a very good overview." Barbara is apparently ready to make up her mind based on vague, incomplete information. From Yvette's perspective, any potential supplier who would come to a presentation so unprepared, assuming a potential client would actually be satisfied with an overview—such a supplier is probably not serious about getting Yvette's business.

The rest of the dialogue is increasingly painful for Yvette, who tries to convince Barbara why she should be concerned. They don't know about Ecotek's assets in any detail, for example, to which Barbara responds that Ecotek may have been rushed and they could get the details if they asked for them. Yvette doesn't say this, but surely she's wondering why they should have to ask a potential supplier for information they should have known enough to bring in the first place. Indeed, Yvette, whose professional responsibility it is to be skeptical in these situations, is probably thinking Ecotek has something to hide. How else to explain the curious lack of details? And as for pointing out that Ecotek may have felt rushed, Yvette's courage surely starts to fail at this point; not only is Barbara putting the most positive spin possible on this supplier's behavior, now she's covering for them.

Yvette's final attempt to get Barbara to see reason—Ecotek's ambitious, hence unrealistic timetable—is met with her crowning display of naïveté: "I'm sure they know what they're doing." They might very well, but one thing is certain: that is something Barbara could not possibly know and certainly not anything Ecotek has demonstrated so far.

We should point out that both these women sat through the same presentation and have exactly the same information about Ecotek, including the same unknowns. Neither knows what the asset details will reveal and neither knows for sure if Ecotek can meet its time line. What distinguishes these two women is how they feel about the unknown, specifically what they see when they look into the future. Barbara assumes everything will turn out okay, while Yvette is deeply skeptical. But these sentiments are not the end of the story; they are merely manifestations of a much deeper cultural difference at the heart of this dialogue and, truth be told, at the heart of many frustrating and unsuccessful Franco-American business relationships: how people view human nature.

Americans have a very positive view of human nature; they believe people are naturally good and trustworthy until they prove otherwise. All things being equal, people can be relied upon to do the right thing and, accordingly, should be given the benefit of the doubt. People may on occasion turn out to be bad, of course, but no one starts out that way. Bad actors are a perversion of the norm; they are not a category of normal.

Notice how when someone does something genuinely evil—a word Americans rarely use because the concept is so unthinkable—Americans immediately and somewhat desperately start looking for the explanation. There *has* to be an explanation, you see, because such behavior clearly defies the logic that people are naturally good. For the naturally good to suddenly turn perverse, something must have gone terribly wrong somewhere. "You don't expect to come [across] pure evil," the American journalist Roy Gutman observes. "I've never used the term in my writing. It's hard to bring yourself to utter the word evil" (Hendrickson).

If worldly journalists are uncomfortable with the concept of evil, what does that say about the average American? The French sociologist Michael Crozier calls it "the American disease," this refusal to acknowledge the darker side of human nature. It is "America's essence," Crozier observes, "to be optimistically confident in the goodness of man, which was a stimulating attitude when the frontier was still open, but which is useless in coping with the modern world. America's disease is a result of not having enough sense of the evil in man" (Zeldin, 506).

Not to worry, though; there are folks who do know about evil, or at least accept that human beings are somewhat flawed creations. Yvette is among them, along with most Europeans (including the English and the Germans). Yvette doesn't believe that people are naturally *anything*; they can be good, but they can also disappoint. There is no historical evidence for assuming people can be trusted or relied upon to do what is right. On the contrary, much of what Europeans have seen of humanity over the millennia has not been encouraging: a war somewhere on the continent every five years (as noted above), two world wars, and when there wasn't a war to worry about, there was often the plague. France may have had its moments of hopefulness—surely the French Revolution was one—but hope has never really prevailed. We might recall that Voltaire's great hero Candide, he of the best of all possible worlds, was a comic figure. If Yvette instinctively assumes people cannot be trusted, who can blame her?

The American national experience, by and large, has been much less checkered and almost always trending positive (excepting the Civil War and assuming one is not a Native American). America was a new Eden, after all, a place to fix what the Old World had bungled, "a giant political and economic laboratory," as one observer noted, "in which the libertarian and egalitarian ideals of the eighteenth-century revolutions could be . . . improved and implemented" (Pells, 5). If that is more myth than reality, as it surely is for some segments of the population, it's a strangely enduring sentiment. Another European observer of the American scene in the years just before World War II writes of how "Americans seemed indecently optimistic, a country that believed itself to be immune from most human ill" (Pells, 11). In a land where the humans are free from most ills, why would you not trust them?

By and large, there has never been a "winners and losers" mentality in America; there were enough resources and opportunities for everyone to be a winner, a dynamic that captures the essence of the great European-American cultural divide. While the French are pleasantly surprised when things work out for the best, Americans are quite upset if they do not. "When things are not as they should be," Luigi Barzini writes, "when injustice prevails, when failure crowns your efforts, when, in spite of all hopes, man shows himself as he always has been, Americans are . . . surprised and maddened—more so than any other people because they are so defenseless and so ignorant of the lessons of the past" (Pells, 172). The lessons of the European past, perhaps, but not necessarily of American history.

Looked at in this way, it becomes quite difficult to support the enduring European belief that Americans are naïve. It *would* be naïve to believe in something contrary to one's own personal experience, to adopt an attitude that flies in the face of reality. But in a land where more often than not things work out for the better—where life has been good—assuming the best about other people is nothing more than trusting in your own experience.

The Fix

Naïveté unnerves the French. From their perspective, trusting others without any proof is risky at best and unrealistic to boot. The French don't want a business partner who's out of touch with reality. Accordingly, you might want to curb your enthusiasm in dealing with the French. There's nothing to be lost, after all, in withholding trust, and if the French turn out to be right, *tant mieux*. (And you can secretly be enthusiastic, meanwhile, without having to show it.) When you do feel very positive about a potential partner or business deal, try to have some facts to support your case. The French are open to persuasion, but you will need to use logic, not emotion.

In dealing with Americans, the French might want to conceal their instinct to assume people cannot be trusted. To Americans, being reflexively suspicious is no more justifiable than being reflexively trusting. If Americans act naively, meanwhile, call them on it. If Yvette were to ask Barbara why she is so "sure Ecotek know[s] what they're doing," the ensuing discussion might be illuminating to both parties.

25. WHAT DOES PERFUME MEAN?

MONIQUE: How did your meeting with Alain and his team go?

MARCIA: We didn't accomplish very much. There's a recent hire who has a new theory about print advertising. We mostly just talked about her ideas.

MONIQUE: That sounds very interesting. What did she say?

MARCIA: To be honest, I didn't pay that much attention. I kept asking to see some text, but they haven't written a single line of ad copy yet.

MONIQUE: Still discussing ideas, I guess?

MARCIA: Alain said they had to decide what the new fragrance *means*. I said it was just perfume; it doesn't *mean* anything.

MONIQUE: What did he say?

MARCIA: He didn't answer me, but the new woman said they needed to figure out how people process a new scent. I said, "That's easy; they smell it."

In their excellent book *Au Contraire: Figuring Out the French*, Gilles Asselin and Ruth Mastron contrast two iconic works of art: the painting *American Gothic* by Grant Wood and the French sculpture *The Thinker* by Auguste Rodin. The painting depicts a farmer and his wife or daughter, the former holding a pitchfork, suggesting "these people clearly have work to do and are serious about it."

The Rodin sculpture depicts "a man sitting—and thinking." As the authors observe, "French society values thought and ideas for their own sake" (40). To which we would merely add that America, "the pitchfork" society, values thoughts and ideas much less—and never just for their own sake.

In "What Does Perfume Mean?" we see what happens when the doing culture meets the thinking culture—and it's not a pretty picture. Marcia needs Alain and his ad team to produce some copy to help launch a new fragrance. Accordingly, she attends a meeting to see how things are going, only to learn that from her perspective things aren't going anywhere. ("They haven't written a single line of ad copy yet.") Moreover, the meeting apparently "didn't accomplish anything" because all the attendees did was discuss some new hire's theories of print advertising. Clearly, Marcia's notion of an accomplishment does not extend as far as a spirited discussion of ideas. Accomplishments are concrete things you can quantify or point to. An idea may be the germ of an accomplishment, the starting point, but it should not be confused with the genuine article. Nor, to be honest, is it worth much before then.

Monique is immediately intrigued to hear there was a lengthy discussion of ideas at the meeting and wants more details from Marcia. After all, if this new hire's ideas are at all novel or untraditional—she might be young and hence a recent graduate of design school, in touch with the latest trends—they could have implications for all ad campaigns going forward. And even if none of that is true, a spirited exchange of views is always beneficial to any work process; when people are forced to defend their ideas, which is what happens in most French discussions, it focuses their thinking and sharpens their intellect. And the accomplishments that come from *that* can be considerable indeed. The French are not indifferent to accomplishments, in other words; they just have much more respect for their parentage.

Alas, Marcia is not much help to Monique ("I didn't pay that much attention"). Indeed, not only did she ignore the discussion (a huge lost opportunity from Monique's perspective), she apparently kept trying to cut it off (to the great surprise and annoyance of the team, no doubt) and steer the conversation back to the "point"—lines of ad copy. Talk is all well and good, but at some point the team needs to come up with something concrete. Even Alain and Monique would agree, of course—they know they can't *just* talk—but the point at which talk turns to action, when ideas morph into results, comes later for the French than it does for Americans. From the French perspective, Americans don't think enough before they act; from the American perspective, the French are all talk and no action.

"The French are doomed to be abstract," D. H. Lawrence wrote. "Talking to them is like trying to have a relationship with the letter 'x' in algebra" (Hill, 1995, 78). The French love ideas—and everything associated with ideas: philosophy and philosophers, of course, but also books of any kind (*Apostrophes*, one of the most popular TV shows in France, was all about the latest books), serious conversation, and anything else that comes under the general heading of intellectual. We should remember that it was a Frenchman, after all, the great Descartes, who said, "I think; therefore, I am," and another French philosopher, Pascal, who defined man as *un roseau pensant*, a thinking reed. Being an intellectual comes closer to an actual profession in France than in practically any other country, and one of the greatest compliments you can pay a French person is to call him or her an intellectual. As Lynn Payer writes: "One must understand that the French, more than just about any other nationality, value thinking as an activity in itself" (37).

This does not make the French very good at actually getting things done. Indeed, as soon as an idea begins to migrate away from being a concept toward some kind of actual application, away from the abstract toward the more concrete, the French lose interest. After all, what is a sordid and imperfect application next to a beautiful theory? Delivering on their wonderful concepts, in other words, just doesn't engage the French quite as much as formulating them in the first place. Analysis, discussion, theorizing of any kind—these intrigue the French greatly; implementation merely bores them. "Implementation is not a French strength," Lawrence and Edwards observe. "[I]t is an unprogrammable, messy, hands-on, compromise-driven enterprise best delegated to somebody more junior" (44).

When a French company has a vacancy to fill, especially in management, they want a thinker, not the so-called "people person" Americans often recruit for. "People who run big enterprises must above all else be clever," Jean-Louis Barsoux and Peter Lawrence write. "The emphasis on cleverness shows up even in executive recruiting advertisements. They hardly mention the drive or initiative looked for in Anglo-Saxon recruits; rather they call for more cerebral qualities—an analytical mind, independence, intellectual rigor, an ability to synthesize information" (60).

Americans are a different breed altogether. They never have had any particular interest in abstract things in general—and no interest whatsoever in ideas for their own sake. The pragmatic streak runs so deep in the national psyche that anything that is not patently utilitarian is almost automatically suspect. Thus, you will get an American's attention if you show him or her the practical application of an idea or how to make money from it, but otherwise ideas have very little cachet.

And as for being an intellectual, it's something Americans might whisper to trusted comrades, but it is nothing like the badge of honor it is in France. Indeed, Americans can be somewhat anti-intellectual. How else to explain the dismissive tone in the United States toward academics, those much-maligned denizens of the Ivory Tower whose only real failing seems to be that they don't *do* anything—except, of course, think and write? The United States, we should not forget, is the country where "those who can, do," and where "those who can't, teach." Little wonder, then, that there has never been a great American philosopher—except perhaps for William James, whose contribution to the field, tellingly, is the theory of pragmatism.

In their defense, Americans never had much time for thinking; there was always so much to *do*. Thinking, after all, is a luxury for those who have already created their country, but in the New World there wasn't time for thinking; indeed, there was barely time for all the doing that had to be done. "[T]he need to master the wilderness and extract its natural resources," Pells notes,

> *to construct great cities and develop a modern industrial nation, had required a practical, problem-solving cast of mind. Consequently, Americans preferred the "man of action" to the theorist, the person who rejected absolutes in favor of concrete solutions that worked in the particular instance. The classic American hero was the inventor, the engineer, the technological wizard, not the artist or academic. (178, 179)*

Americans barely have time to apply a fragrance, much less to figure out what it means.

There may be an even deeper strain of the American character at work here, and that is the deep-seated faith in empiricism, in accepting as true and real only that which has been personally experienced. The only ideas that matter, in other words, are those that have come from the school of life. And the only philosophers who dispense such reliable ideas are those with practical experience, men and women of action. Intellectuals, in short, need not apply. "[T]he person who discovered something in the 'school of hard knocks' through 'hands-on learning'," McElroy observes, "or who created something new and useful as a result of what he had learned on his own by trial-and-error experimentation or independent study, was more greatly respected and admired than the man of book learning" (102).

The Fix

Americans should just relax whenever the French engage in spirited intellectual exchanges. If that builds French confidence in what is ultimately decided, everyone wins. Of course if you want to jump in and join the fun, all the better. But losing patience, showing frustration, and especially trying to cut off the discussion will only annoy the French, and may even alarm them if they think you're in too much of a hurry. If you listen to them, they just might return the favor (on occasion) and listen to you.

134

The French should know that Americans will get impatient if discussion goes on too long and may very well stop paying attention. In cases where a lengthy discussion is in fact warranted, you should explain the stakes and why so much back-and-forth is necessary. But to prolong a discussion that clearly isn't "going anywhere" (as Americans like to say) will annoy Americans and may cause them to stop taking you seriously.

6

Germany

In Germany one breathes in love of order with the air;
even the babies beat time with their rattles.

—Jerome K. Jerome

Most experienced international observers would agree that Americans are culturally more like the Germans than they are like any other nationality in this book. Germans are direct communicators (to a fault, Americans would say); they are more egalitarian than hierarchical; they are individualists (though less than folks in the U.S. or England); and they are universalists (the "system" is fair) rather than particularists (it's who you know)—all qualities they share with Americans.* John Ardagh, in *Germany and the Germans*, writes that Americans and Germans "may differ greatly in their degree of social formality, but they share something of the same business ethos, the same liking for thoroughness, efficiency and modernism, and the same fondness for litigation" (569).

---

* See Dialogues 6 and 42 for discussion of universalism and particularism.

In this context, we might note that more American surnames are of German origin than any other nationality and that over 50 million Americans, close to one out of six, can claim at least partial German heritage, making Germans the single largest ethnic group in the United States.* If they were forced to live among and get along with Germans, Americans would manage to adapt in a matter of months.

None of which is to suggest that Americans don't drive Germans mad from time to time, and vice versa. Indeed, very few Americans consider themselves to be anything like Germans and would be surprised to learn otherwise. They do not assume any cultural sameness (as they do with the English), before they are therefore not terribly surprised when they encounter differences. Americans often speak of their English "cousins," for example, but they would never speak that way about Germans.

If the two cultures are close, there are enough differences to fill this chapter. The German passion for order that Jerome cites above and related preoccupations with clarity, structure, and planning—not to mention a deep fear of uncertainty and ambiguity—are cultural touchstones that do not resonate with most Americans and thereby set the stage for plenty of German-American misunderstanding.

26. ON SCHEDULE

SHARON: Hi, Hans, good to see you. Actually, I was just about to call you to find out if the analysis will be finished this afternoon.

---

* The enduring legend that German failed by one vote to become the official language of the United States is not true; the United States has no official language, and there was no such vote.

HANS: Yes, it will be ready by 3:00.

SHARON: That's excellent, Hans, right on schedule. I really appreciate that.

HANS: Sure. It *was* due at 3:00 today, right?

SHARON: Yes. Why?

HANS: Oh, nothing.

This might just be the purest dialogue in this entire book, a completely innocuous exchange that still manages to illustrate a major U.S.-European business culture difference. The difference has to do with the degree of positive feedback—appreciation, praise, expressions of gratitude—Americans and Europeans routinely give out. In a word, Americans dispense a lot and Germans, along with most other Europeans, relatively little, a difference that can easily undermine good working relations.

I was once asked to do some training for an American company that had been acquired by the German pharmaceutical giant Bayer. I asked the two groups what cultural issues they were having, and one that came up in both camps was the question of praise. Some of the Americans now being managed by Germans said their German bosses didn't appreciate them. When I asked why, they said, "Because they never tell us we're doing a good job." Later I asked the Germans how they felt about working with Americans, and a few who were working under American managers claimed their bosses were patronizing and condescending. When I asked why, they said, "Because they're always telling us what a good job we're doing." The Germans explained that in their culture (but this is also true in general throughout northern Europe), people are expected—and get paid—to do their best. To thank or praise people for doing what you pay them for is almost to suggest you weren't sure they were going to do their job. You do expect to hear from your boss, on the other hand, if you exceed expectations or if your performance is subpar. If you're not getting any feedback, then all is well.

People from many other cultures—and not just Europeans—regularly remark on how much positive feedback American bosses give their workers. Americans are taught to do this in management training seminars and business school as a way to motivate staff to do their best work. Thus we find Sharon thanking Hans for turning in his analysis on schedule, while Hans ("It *was* due at 3:00 today, right?") wonders what he's done to merit such appreciation. Aren't people supposed to meet their deadlines? Maybe if he'd turned it in early . . .

Compared to Germans, Americans are quite liberal, even indiscriminate, with their praise (a charge, in fact, which Germans often level against them). While Germans reserve compliments for exceptional achievements, Americans lavish them on the most ordinary accomplishments. A worker doesn't have to exceed or even meet expectations to be given a word of encouragement. On the contrary, Americans will compliment workers merely for making a good effort, whatever the result, or in some cases just for having a positive attitude! The role of praise in America, in short, is not so much to recognize excellence as to provide reassurance and build confidence. To put it another way, Americans need encouragement in a way Germans do not. A German will continue to turn in his or her best with or without recognition, but Americans become disheartened and even resentful if they are not recognized. Not surprisingly, Germans find American compliments empty and insincere.

For Americans, the need for recognition is partly a result of a certain national insecurity. They lack confidence in themselves in a way seldom seen among Europeans and require regular reassurance of their worth. On the surface, this might seem surprising given their opportunity, wealth, and international preeminence—Americans more or less saved Europe from Hitler, after all (with help from the Brits), and then rebuilt it. Americans ought to be *more* confident than Europeans, not less. In a perverse sort of way, however, it may be their very success that causes Americans to doubt themselves. When success comes easily, when there is no real limit to what you can accomplish and nothing external holding you back, then there's bound to be some doubt that whatever you have achieved, you could always have achieved more. If the only limits to success are those within yourself, then in a perverse way the very act of achieving a certain degree of success only reminds you of your inadequacies. "In America," Miller observes, "it is especially hard nowadays to have personal pride. The doors of opportunity in our country are, supposedly, open to all. Therefore, one is always inclined to question oneself and ask why one isn't rich and famous, or richer and *more* famous" (62).

Another part of the explanation may be that in highly individualist cultures such as the United States, where people cannot automatically rely on the goodwill of others—where mutual support is not built into the culture as in group-oriented societies—people must actively cultivate and consciously pursue the support of others. Hence, the need to ingratiate oneself by dispensing praise and expressing appreciation.

Finally, it's possible that egalitarianism also plays a role. In a deeply egalitarian culture like the United States, there is a feeling that as we are all equal, no one *has* to do anything for anyone else. People may *choose* to do things for other people, but there is no fundamental obligation; expressing appreciation, therefore, is merely recognizing that fact. But won't workers lose their jobs, the reader asks, if they don't perform? True enough, but even that does not mean they *have* to perform if they choose not to. In a culture where no one is beholden to anyone else, it's only proper to thank people for doing the decent thing *anyway*.

The German attitude toward compliments, or any kind of encouragement for that matter, is in large part a function of their perfectionism. Germans are especially intolerant of inefficiency—errors, mistakes, or snafus—anything that suggests a lack of discipline or vigilance. An untidy workspace, for example, or a leaking tap in the cafeteria, or an improperly completed time sheet—all of these would be noted and possibly even commented on. There is never an excuse for sloppiness, whether physical or mental. The Germans pride themselves on the efficiency of their systems—and, not surprisingly, they have systems for virtually everything. They spend more time and effort on worker training than any country in Europe. Needless to say, in a country where people expect perfection more or less as a matter of course, the threshold for handing out compliments will be rather high. To put it another way, if you're not getting complimented, it probably means you're doing a good job.

Perfectionism aside, there is another factor at work here, the notion that the motivation to do a good job should come from within, that you shouldn't have to be encouraged or recognized by someone else to do your best. You should naturally want to do your best, and your reward is the satisfaction you feel for having done so. "Praise of performance is rarely used to motivate employees [in Germany]," Greg Nees observes,

> as is typical in the United States. Because of their thorough educational and vocational training, combined with their strong sense of accountability, Germans have internalized performance criteria and are highly self-directed. . . . The more emotional motivational strategies used by American managers are viewed as unnecessary "hand-holding."
>
> Both employees and managers take the old Swabian saying, "Net g'schimpft isch Lob g'nug" (If you weren't criticized, that's praise enough") quite literally. (105, 106)

The Fix

Germans simply do not appreciate praise for anything less than greatly exceeding common workplace expectations. You should cut back on the number of routine "thank-yous" and "good jobs" without worrying that Germans will think their work is unappreciated. Too many compliments will either make you sound phony or cause Germans to think you're trying to shame them into doing a better job. On the other hand, when Germans excel they expect and appreciate praise as much as anyone. Meanwhile, if you do not get regular praise from German colleagues or a German boss, relax; you're doing just fine.

Americans need reassurance in a way most Europeans do not. If you are a German who works in an American business environment, express appreciation more often and be more generous with your praise. This will not come across as condescending or sound insincere to Americans, who are used to routine recognition of even average performance. A dearth of positive feedback, on the other hand, sends the message to Americans that they're not doing as well as they should. Meanwhile, try not to interpret routine, excessive praise from Americans as insincerity or condescension; they think it's motivating. And while they might praise almost everyone, that doesn't mean they can't distinguish between who is performing well and who is slacking off. Average performance gets mild praise; exceptional performance gets considerably more.

27. RUNNING LATE

DAN: Horst, where are you going?

HORST: It's 4:00.*

---

* Four o'clock is quitting time in many German companies.

DAN:	I know we're running a little late; two people went over their time—Americans, naturally. But your presentation is coming up in just ten minutes.
HORST:	I pick my children up at 4:30.
DAN:	I'm sorry we started late, but I had that trouble with my laptop, as you saw.
HORST:	Yes.
DAN:	Just a few more minutes.
HORST:	Maybe another time.

There are two significant cultural differences at play in this dialogue. The more important one is the different value people in the U.S. and Germany put on their personal or private time, the "life" aspect of the work-life dynamic. Germans place a great deal of importance on their private life and Americans somewhat less. Or, to be more accurate, Americans value their work more highly than Germans do, identifying more closely with what they do and deriving more satisfaction from it. It's not true that Americans have no life outside work, as they are often accused of by Europeans; it is, rather, that they are less bothered on those occasions when work intrudes on their private life. There are very few circumstances that justify staying late or working on a weekend for most Germans, and rather more for the average American. Germans "are not fond of unpaid overtime," John Mole writes, "[they] clockwatch at the end of the day, and rush off home without lingering with their colleagues" (43).

Another story about the pharmaceutical company Bayer (see the preceding dialogue) captures this cultural difference perfectly. An American expatriate in Germany was in charge of a certain division that was getting ready to introduce a new drug to the market. To celebrate this product launch, the American executive planned an elaborate company picnic for all the employees of his division and their families and scheduled the event for a Saturday. When word got out, his German colleagues informed him that Saturday was not a "work day," and he was obliged to move the picnic to Friday afternoon. It's hard to imagine many Americans objecting to attending a company picnic on a Saturday.

"There is a clear demarcation between private and business life," Mole continues.

[Germans] leave work as punctually as they arrive and rarely take work home. They do not like being called at home on business unless there is a very good reason. People at all levels take their full holiday entitlement, and they do not keep in touch with the office when they are away or expect to be called. (39)

143

To protect personal time, some German companies now have a policy whereby work-based e-mail servers are not accessible to employees after working hours.

Another reason Germans feel free to draw such a firm line between work and personal time is the fact that when they are at work, Germans do very little socializing, certainly as compared to Americans. "Germans at all levels . . . happen to be very disciplined," John Ardagh has noted. "[They] do not work such long hours as others—their weekly rate is well below Japan's—but when they *are* at work, they tend to work hard and methodically" (105–06). This explains why Germans always keep their office doors closed so they cannot be easily or casually disturbed. It's safe to say, therefore, that when a German goes home at the end of the day, he/she has given eight full hours to the company. If you have given the company its due, then the company must give you yours. Indeed, when a social event at work, such as a birthday lunch for someone, goes on a bit long, many Germans will stay late to be sure to put in their eight hours.

The protective attitude of Germans toward their home life is the issue illustrated in the dialogue. Dan appears to have organized some sort of event where Horst is scheduled to make a presentation. The event is supposed to finish at quitting time, 4:00. Consequently, when time runs out before his presentation, Horst feels no obligation to remain any longer at work, especially since he has to pick up his children at 4:30. He no doubt feels bad about leaving Dan in the lurch, but it can't be helped. And surely Dan will understand.

But Dan will not. Indeed, Horst's behavior would come across as rigid and inflexible to most Americans, perhaps even unprofessional. To be fair, some Germans might sympathize with Dan, although they would never dispute Horst's *right* to leave at 4:00. However, any sympathy would be mitigated by how poorly Dan managed the whole event, offending two core German values of discipline and efficiency. Dan's first mistake was was not to come in early enough to allow for the possibility of technical problems, which resulted in pushing back the start time. Next, Dan apparently let two speakers exceed their time allotment, for which there is no justification in Horst's world. Speakers should know better than to go over time, and if they do not (they *were* Americans, after all), then the person in charge should immediately cut them off. In short, this meeting has gone over time due to reasons entirely within Dan's control; while even a German might allow work to intrude on personal life if there are extenuating circumstances, simple incompetence and inefficiency are definitely not extenuating.

As noted earlier, Americans are more tolerant when the lines between work and personal life become blurred, perhaps because professional accomplishments comprise more of their identity.

Americans don't exactly live to work, but it is true that they derive much of their sense of self-worth from personal achievements—whether educational, intellectual, artistic, athletic, or professional—and work is certainly among the most potent sources of achievement. Americans would not struggle as much as they do with work-life balance if they were not torn by the pull of work.

Let's give Greg Nees, author of *Germany: Unraveling an Enigma*, the last word here:

> *[W]hen they are at work, [Germans] do indeed work quite effectively and with great focus. But when the workday is finished, so are the workers. Punctuality is apparent, not only in starting times but also at the end of the workday; employees see overtime as an infringement on their private lives. . . . Perhaps because Americans are less protected by a social security net, or perhaps because they socialize more on the job and work less intensely, they are generally less vocal when asked to put in unpaid overtime, often staying until the job is done. (139)*

145

Dienst ist Dienst, the Germans say of the work-life divide, *und Schnaps ist Schnaps*. Duty is duty, and liquor is liquor.

The Fix

Americans working in a largely German business environment should socialize less at work and assume Germans will not stay late except in extraordinary circumstances. If you have to ask someone to stay late or, heaven forbid, come in on a weekend, it must be for a genuine emergency or because something has happened that you could not possibly have foreseen. Even then, you should be sure to offer time off later on to make up for the intrusion into private life. (Germans will appreciate this even though they might not accept your offer.)

Germans working in a U.S. environment should socialize more with colleagues; otherwise you run the risk of being branded as distant, unfriendly, and antisocial. You should understand that Americans are less troubled about staying late (especially in the private sector), and you should be open to the fact that from time to time your life will not be your own. Occasionally, *Dienst* may be *Schnaps*, and *Schnaps* now and then might partake of *Dienst*.

28. A GREAT PLEASURE*

PAUL:	Hello, everyone. It's a great pleasure being on this call with you today.
HELGA:	Hello, Paul.
PAUL:	Hello, Helga. Thanks so much for making time. I know you guys must be very busy.
HELGA:	It's fine. We have a lot to talk about.
PAUL:	Yes, we do. I know we're going to enjoy working with your team very much.
HELGA:	I certainly hope so.

Americans have a somewhat deserved reputation for insincerity, certainly with Europeans. Looked at objectively, which is how Germans tend to look at things, not a single one of Paul's statements is true. Let's take them one by one:

---

* This dialogue was inspired by an anecdote in Erin Meyer's *The Culture Map: Breaking through the Invisible Boundaries of Global Business*.

- "It's a great pleasure . . ." Not really; this is work. Going to a very good concert or having a gourmet meal might be a great pleasure.

- "Thanks so much for making time." Of course Helga has made time; she needs to talk with her new partner.

- "I know you guys must be very busy." Maybe they are; maybe they aren't. But Paul could not possibly know this.

- "I know we're going to enjoy working with your team very much." And how exactly do you know this since we have not yet started working together?

In an exchange of just five lines, Paul has raised a lot of eyebrows over in Berlin. If Helga knows anything about Americans, she will dismiss Paul's missteps for the usual harmless exaggerations they clearly are. But if this is her first time dealing with Americans, she may start to have some reservations about Paul and be on the lookout for other examples of his unreliability. Paul's "enthusiasm" (as Americans would probably call it) is not automatically a deal breaker, but it could very well give Helga pause.

Speaking of objectivity, let's look at Helga's three statements:

- Hello, Paul.
- It's fine. We have a lot to talk about.
- I certainly hope so.

Helga has been perfectly correct—and entirely honest—in her three statements: she says hello and either ignores or does not understand Paul's enthusiasm ("a great pleasure"); she does not respond to Paul's expression of thanks, offering an utterly neutral "it's fine"; and she does not partake at all in Paul's excitement over working together, suggesting in fact that it's too early to say (which it is). You could accuse Helga of a lot of things, but enthusiasm is not one of them. From an American perspective, Helga is quite reserved, verging on cold, even sullen. Paul could be forgiven for thinking this relationship isn't going to be much fun.

So that's it, then: Americans are insincere and phony, and Germans are severe and joyless? It may be how they come across to each other, but naturally it's not how they see themselves. From his perspective, Paul is merely being upbeat, positive, and, yes, enthusiastic. If he doesn't mean exactly what he's saying, neither is he being entirely dishonest. It may not be a *great* plea-sure talking to Helga and her team, but he is genuinely pleased to be starting this new business relationship. And what's wrong with thanking Helga for her time? To be sure, it's in her interest to set this time aside, but she did have to put in some effort to pull her team together for this conference call. And is it so bad to suggest that these folks are hardworking people who probably *are* quite busy? Finally, what's wrong with assuming this is going to be an enjoyable partnership even if, strictly speaking, it does not exist just yet?

And that's just the problem—Paul is not speaking strictly; he's exaggerating. The concern for German (and most other Euro-pean) businesspeople is that anyone who exaggerates is appar-ently choosing not to see things the way they are but as better than they are. In other words, they're not being realistic or objec-tive, and how can you trust the judgment of such people? "To [us] it is all a lot of hogwash," Erin Meyer remembers a European colleague telling her.

All that positive feedback just strikes us as fake and not
in the least bit motivating. I was on a conference call with

an American group yesterday, and the organizer began, "I am absolutely thrilled to be with you this morning." Only an American would begin a meeting like this. Let's face it, everyone in the room knows that she is not truly, honestly thrilled. Thrilled to win the lottery—yes. Thrilled to find out you have just won a free trip to the Caribbean—yes. Thrilled to be the leader of a conference call—highly doubtful.

When my American colleagues begin a communication with all of their "excellents" and "greats," it feels so exaggerated that I find it demeaning. We are adults, here to do our jobs and to do them well. We don't need our colleagues to be cheerleaders. (78)

Why *are* Americans so enthusiastic? Why do they have to exaggerate? Why can't they be happy just describing things the way they are? The short answer is they can't help themselves; they are an exuberant, hopeful, irrepressible people, firm believers in what they call the power of positive thinking. To Americans, exaggeration is not fooling around with the truth but looking on the bright side and putting things in the best possible light. This tendency is all of a piece with their innate optimism and deeply held belief in progress—in the notion that however things may be, they can always be better. In a world where anything is possible—just give us a little more time—and things always seem to get better, one exaggerates almost as a matter of course; today's exaggeration, after all, is almost guaranteed to be tomorrow's reality.

With their exceptionally high regard for accuracy and precision and their virtual obsession with the truth (as Americans see it), Germans have limited patience with American enthusiasm and none whatsoever with their penchant for exaggeration. Exaggeration, after all, is a way of playing fast and loose with the truth, and thus it deeply offends German sensibilities. They mistrust anyone who cannot see—or at least does not describe—things as they are. "In general," Edward and Mildred Hall observe, "Americans are inclined toward overstatement . . . [whereas] Germans avoid it. Germans think Americans blow things out of proportion as if they are afraid they won't receive enough attention unless they indulge in hyperbole" (51). To a German, exaggeration is not merely lying; it's an insult to their intelligence. And as for the power of thinking positively, it makes no more sense than thinking negatively. What's important, of course, is to think *clearly*.

The Fix

In dealing with Germans, Americans must realize that curbing their enthusiasm and cutting back on exaggeration will not be misread as lack of confidence or insufficient optimism. On the contrary, being objective and precise is what impresses and inspires Germans; exaggerations and enthusiasm just alarm them. At the same time, do not interpret German insistence on absolute honesty—eschewing all hyperbole—as anything other than the search for truth. They're not being negative or gloomy. If you must accuse Germans of something, accuse them of being realistic but not of being pessimistic.

For their part, Germans might try to put a bit more enthusiasm into their exchanges with Americans. You don't have to stop being objective and realistic, but you can still sound a little more excited. You will not come across as insincere to Americans or as trying to flatter them. Meanwhile, try not to interpret American exaggeration as dishonesty or phoniness; they're just trying to be positive.

29. PRODUCT LAUNCH

KATHY: Did you hear? CompuTech is launching their product next week.

KLAUS: That's odd. They started on their version the same day we started on ours.

KATHY: I looked at their testing schedule. They do one week less than what we're planning.

KLAUS: That explains it.

KATHY: Should we cut out a week of testing?

KLAUS: Certainly not.

KATHY: So they'll beat us to the market, then?

KLAUS: Yes, but with what?

Several classic German themes are on display in this dialogue, or lurking just beneath the surface: the concern for quality, an aversion for undue haste, dislike of uncertainty, fear of making mistakes, and a general passion for thoroughness. As it happens, Americans have more or less the opposite attitude toward each of these themes.

Let's begin with Klaus' response to Kathy's announcement: "They started on their version the same time we started on ours." In the IT world, there is a standard development cycle for each type of product, which means Klaus knows within a day or two how long it should take for CompuTech to develop and test a product, especially since his company and CompuTech are developing two versions of the same product. In other words, when Klaus says CompuTech started the same day, he means there is no way they could finish an entire week ahead—unless, of course, they are cutting corners. And if they are cutting corners, then there's nothing to worry about. Kathy can relax.

But Kathy is not focused on the product, which she has just been told will be inferior; she's worried about who will get to the market first. When she reveals that CompuTech is cutting their testing time in half, she expects this will light a fire under Klaus and prompt him to act. Klaus may be glad to have

151

an explanation—there had to be one, after all—but it doesn't change the facts: cutting corners, no matter how they are cut, is always bad practice. If anything, this news is reassuring to Klaus. And he's horrified, needless to say, when Kathy suggests they should also cut a week from their own testing process.

Germans attach singular importance to quality—and to its cousin, perfection—and there's no faster route to poor quality than to cut corners. If two weeks of testing is the industry standard, then you can be sure the Germans will do at least two weeks if not more. "Prior to a launch," Roland Flamini observes,

> *market and product testing can sometimes be carried to extremes. At the main Mercedes-Benz plant in Stuttgart, visitors are proudly shown the testing rooms where the doors of a vehicle are hydraulically slammed shut and reopened again and again for days, until the door finally falls of its hinges. The number of openings and closings is meticulously recorded and compared with previous door slammings to ensure that the component has lost none if its toughness. (41)*

There is a story (it may be apocryphal) that when Daimler and Chrysler began their ill-fated merger, there was some discussion about this door-slamming test. Both companies had the same testing machine, which can be set to perform as many slammings as the engineers think is necessary to determine durability; Chrysler set its machine at 3,000 slams, while Daimler set theirs at 5,000. It's interesting to note that nearly all postmortems of the Daimler-Chrysler breakup began with an analysis of the cultural differences between the two companies.

Needless to say, Germans hate mistakes and anything that makes them more likely—such as being in a hurry, taking risks, sloppiness, and taking shortcuts. They are, accordingly, great fans of anything that prevents or minimizes mistakes—such as adhering strictly to procedures, being deliberate and methodical, refusing to rush or compromise, and, above all, being thorough. The appeal of thoroughness, of course, is that it goes a long way toward guaranteeing the high quality and perfection so dear to the German heart.

"There is a pervasive commitment to doing things thoroughly," Richard Lord writes,

> *a quality [foreigners] find, by turns, reassuring and irritating. Foreigners here frequently discover that Germans will come in and put the finishing touches on what [the foreigners] thought they had already completed in a fairly decent manner. Or the Germans will tell them that the job has been done well so far—now complete it. (48, 49)*

153

In short, you never do things by halves in Germany. If you can't do a thing properly, if the only way to finish is to rush, then better not to attempt it at all. If you're not sure your product is as good as you can make it, if you have not checked and rechecked it for flaws or bugs, then you must continue checking, no matter how long it takes, and no one will fault you. On the other hand, if you stop testing before you should—to beat the competition to the market, for example—then you have earned the opprobrium that will surely be heaped upon you.

And then there's the whole matter of risk, which is anathema to most Germans. In many ways, the great value they place on quality and perfection is a manifestation of an even deeper cultural characteristic: the fear of uncertainty. The Germans call it *angst*, anxiety, a kind of general, nonspecific uneasiness that comes from not knowing the future. In the *Globe* study of sixty-one countries mentioned earlier, Germany scored very near the top (57 out of 61) on a quality known as "uncertainty avoidance," a measure of how comfortable people are with the inherent uncertainty of life. In the high-scoring cultures, people go to great lengths either to eliminate risk and uncertainty altogether or, where this is not possible, to minimize their effects and control the consequences.

Americans are neither indifferent to quality nor obsessed with being first in the market, but they do have a somewhat different attitude toward quality and especially toward perfection. Thoroughness and perfection were very often not possible in the New World, where there evolved instead the philosophy of "good enough" or "making do," which has survived to some extent down to the present day. Early immigrants faced numerous tasks they had never faced before in the Old World; for them the question was not whether the job could be done well but whether it could be done at all. When the deadline for planting arrived, for example, you didn't worry about digging up the unsightly stumps in your newly cleared field; either you sprinkled your seeds around the stumps in May or you didn't eat in September. In Germany, by contrast, where the fields have been cleared for centuries, you're free to indulge your passion for perfection. For Americans, then, coming from a culture that has learned to live with less than perfect, a lower-quality product that gets to market first is an enticing proposition.

Part of the Americans' attitude toward quality can be explained by their deep and abiding faith in progress. Experience has shown them that however perfect a product we may have today, it's bound to be eclipsed tomorrow by an even better one. If that's really the case, if quality is relative, then there comes a time when other factors must be weighed in the balance. When that time comes, Americans, unlike Germans, are much more willing to compromise.

Stuart Miller discerns one additional current in the two countries' differing attitudes toward quality:

Americans have been more interested in producing some-
thing expediently than in producing it exquisitely. The roots
of this difference are historically complex. The European
aristocracy monopolized nearly all manufactured products
and set higher and higher standards for them. . . . Though
quality has declined, the demand for it still hangs in the air
and conditions European attitudes toward products.

American democratic tradition worked the other way. A
mass of potential consumers, with little wealth but a normal
human attraction to the showy and the luxurious, created
a market for goods manufactured quickly, cheaply, and in
great numbers and, naturally, of a quality inferior to the
aristocratically grounded crafts of Europe. (179, 180)

155

The Fix

Perfection takes time. In a German work environment, Americans must accept the fact that product development will take longer than in the United States. In most cases, the process will not be rushed to beat a competitor's timetable. You can console yourselves, meanwhile, with the knowledge that in Germany quality always wins out. Germans will gladly pay more for quality, and they will wait to buy a brand of established quality even if a lower-quality brand reaches the market sooner. Perfect is worth the wait.

Germans in the U.S. work environment must accept that while Americans appreciate quality, it is not a religion with them. And as for perfect: even if it were attainable, it's not necessary. Good enough is quite acceptable. Continuous improvement, on the other hand, the idea that a better version of every product is already on someone's drawing board, *is* a religion with Americans. There's no need, in short, to spend too long trying for perfection; chances are what's perfect today will be obsolete in a few months. Do not be upset when Americans cut a few corners; if the risk doesn't pay off, the consequences are much less serious than in German business culture.

30. FIRST DRAFT

BIRGIT:	How did it go with Irmgard?
RICK:	OK, I think.
BIRGIT:	What did you tell her?
RICK:	I told her it was OK for a first draft, but it needed more work.
BIRGIT:	But it wasn't OK.
RICK:	No.
BIRGIT:	And it needs a lot of work.
RICK:	Right.
BIRGIT:	So let's start again, shall we?

We have taken pains throughout this book to establish that Americans are a direct people, certainly compared to most cultures of the Pacific Rim, the Middle East, and Latin America. But it would not be fair to the Germans, or the French for that matter, to let Americans walk off with the honors. While Germans are not the world's most direct culture (that prize goes to Israel) nor even the most direct of European nationalities (that would probably be the Dutch or perhaps the Danes), they are certainly the most direct of the cultures in this book. Americans owe a great debt to the Germans for making them seem diplomatic and tactful. We write these words without any fear of causing offense, as we know Germans are in fact quite proud of their reputation for honesty and bluntness.

Nees writes that in terms of stating facts,

offering criticism, and issuing direct commands, Germans are generally more direct [than Americans]. . . . [D]irectness and honesty are highly valued by Germans and thus among the most telling characteristics of their style of speech. Part of this emphasis on directness is related to their desire for klarheit [clarity] and dislike of ambiguity. (72, 73)

Rick probably thought he was blunt until he met Birgit, who puts American-style straight talk into much-needed perspective. There is, of course, no arguing with anything Birgit says here; indeed, Rick doesn't even bother to defend his pitiful performance with Irmgard. But how to account for it? Why do relatively direct Americans have such a hard time handing out negative feedback?

We took up this question in Dialogue 22, "Let's Move On," where we discussed the other conspicuous exception to American directness: a decided distaste for arguing. The reluctance to argue and give negative feedback both stem in part from the same source: the strong American need to be liked. And we suggested that that need, in turn, comes from the relative loneliness, hence insecurity, of being raised as individualists. Being independent and self-reliant is great—until you need other people, as even individualists do from time to time. But Americans don't have a set of other people (an ingroup) immediately on hand, as people in more family- and group-oriented cultures do, so they must work at cultivating the kind of support that collectivists take for granted. And this need is exacerbated by the fact that Americans move so often, meaning that even the friendships they do manage to develop are not especially robust.

Another problem Americans have with negative feedback is that they define themselves to a large extent by their achievements. In that context, negative feedback, a criticism of someone's performance, is equivalent to an assault on one's self-esteem. For their part, Europeans do not derive nearly as much of their self-worth or identity from their work. Work is what Europeans do; it is not who they are. You can criticize a German's work without destroying his ego; indeed, Germans actually appreciate negative feedback as long as it is warranted.

For Germans, criticism is much more than finding fault; it is a moral duty and a civic responsibility. If the society as a whole is to thrive and prosper, everyone has to do their part. Standards can only be maintained through constant vigilance. "There is a strong sense of community and social conscience," John Mole observes,

> [and] there is no hesitation in pointing out to someone that he or she does not meet acceptable standards of behavior. This may be for something as trivial, in your eyes, as taking off a jacket at a meeting or parking in the wrong place. Policing each other's behavior is not seen as offensive but as a social duty. (40)

While in the United States the good of society is often sacrificed to protect the rights of the individual, in Germany the rights of the individual are often sacrificed for the protection of society. This is an important distinction between American and German individualism.

There is a long and hallowed tradition of philosophical criticism in Germany, in which a phenomenon is examined from all angles to arrive at a more complete understanding. "Part of this legacy," Nees writes, "is that criticism is seen as a right that must be well protected and reaffirmed through continual use. Criticism has a long intellectual pedigree in Germany and is often viewed as something both useful and necessary for the smooth functioning of a business or society." (85)

If Rick doesn't do his duty and hold Irmgard to the highest standards, then the "smooth functioning" of the business is threatened. Although Rick doesn't say this (thank goodness), at least part of his rationale for being indirect with Irmgard was to avoid hurting her feelings. Most Germans would respond first of all by asking what feelings have to do with doing a good job, and secondly why people would not want to hear the truth. We're all grown-ups, aren't we? Surely we can handle the truth. "Because Germans believe that content is more important than style," Flamini writes,

> they can be brutally frank. Rarely is there anything to read between the lines and hardly ever is the conversation so subtle as to be open to more than one interpretation. The plus side of this trait is that they will never tell you something because they think it's what you want to hear. Varnishing the truth isn't a German trait, nor is it a trait they appreciate in others. (69, 70)

159

The Fix

When working with colleagues in Germany, Americans must be considerably more direct when giving negative feedback. And you need not worry about being unpopular; Germans are used to and genuinely appreciate honest criticism. "A number of German acquaintances . . . have told me that they don't really feel comfortable dealing with Americans," Lord observes.

> Why? Because they just can't trust them. What they mean with this put-down is that Americans . . . tend to be altogether more circumspect in their criticisms, that they will pad the truth to protect the other person's feelings. If this is

your way of doing things, be aware that Germans don't see it as any kind of virtue. You are better advised to become a little more blunt in your pronouncements, to drop all the adornments of rhetorical airbrushing and serve up a more point-blank account of what you think and feel. (50)

When you are on the receiving end of feedback, realize that what might seem like "brutal honesty" is merely run-of-the-mill directness from a German perspective. No one is out to get you.

Germans giving negative feedback in an American business context should say half as much as you might in Germany—and realize you still run the risk of devastating an American colleague. When Americans criticize you, multiply by two what they say to arrive at an approximation of their real opinion.

7

India

Whatever you can rightly say about India, the opposite is also true.

—Amartya Sen

In his book *From Midnight to the Millennium*, Shashi Tharoor explains how Winston Churchill once "barked that India is merely a geographical expression. It is no more a single country than the Equator" (xiv). The diversity of India is well established, and while Churchill's and Sen's warnings should probably act as correctives to anyone who dares write about Indian culture, they have obviously not worked in the present instance. That's not because the diversity is not real and fundamental, but only because in these pages we have not set out to write about India, but about a particular subset of Indians—educated urban professionals—who do in fact share certain characteristics and who are more like each other than they are like other Indians. It is possible, in short, to generalize with some accuracy about this "type," even as we hasten to add the standard disclaimer that generalizations only apply to types, but you will never meet a type, only persons.

India is an obvious choice for this book, not just because of the size of its economy but also because more Americans interact with Indians on a regular basis than they do with any other nationality featured in these pages. That's largely because of the growth of outsourcing, of course, which for the last two decades has grown annually at a rate between 6 percent at its slowest and 20 percent at its fastest. At the end of every year for the last twenty years, more Indians and more Westerners were working together than at the end of every previous twelve-month period.

The need for Americans to understand Indians better and vice versa has never been greater. If India is not in your company's past or present, it is almost certainly in its future.

162

31. EXPLANATIONS

KATHY: How are you, Dev?

DEV: Great! And you?

KATHY: I'm fine. Hey, Dev, on this payroll screen—this isn't exactly what I was looking for.

DEV: I'm very sorry.

KATHY: It's probably my fault, but we did go over this last week, and I asked you if you understood.

DEV: Yes, of course.

KATHY: And you said yes.

DEV: Yes.

KATHY: But I guess you didn't really understand?

DEV: Perhaps not. I did ask Raj, but he couldn't help us.

KATHY:	No, his team is not familiar with this screen. But you could have come back to me.
DEV:	Of course.

We start our India chapter with what is probably the number-one challenge Americans face in working with Indians, usually phrased as "Indians never tell us if they don't understand something." We can say number-one challenge with some confidence; I conducted a survey for one of my American clients (of close to a thousand of their employees) in which I asked what was their greatest challenge working with their colleagues offshore in India. And this was the most common response.*

In the dialogue, we learn that last week Kathy explained a task she wanted Dev to perform and then asked him if he understood. And he said yes. But it turns out that he did not understand, and instead of coming back to Kathy to ask for clarification, he asked Raj, one of his colleagues. But Raj couldn't help him, and Dev evidently tried something that was not what Kathy had in mind ("This isn't exactly what I was looking for"). From an American's point of view, there are at least two mysteries here: Why did Dev say he understood Kathy when he did not? And why did he ask Raj for help instead of going back to Kathy?

The answer to both questions has to do with the deep value Indians place on hierarchy and rank in the workplace, especially the imperative for juniors to be respectful to seniors at all times. "Once a hierarchy is established," Jai Sinha writes in his book *Work Culture in the Indian Context*,

> *juniors yield to seniors on every conceivable occasion. They leave their seat for a senior in a crowded bus or train; stand*

163

---

* Actually, this was the most common *cultural* issue; the most common challenge overall, by a large margin, was difficulty understanding spoken Indian English, either on the telephone or in person.

up when he enters the office; open doors for him; refrain from smoking or drinking alcohol in his presence even on social occasions; speak humbly and politely; do not disagree strongly; and would rather withdraw from a situation that is likely to force a confrontation with their senior. Indian teams do not consist of equals; they consist of unequals. (35)

When a boss explains something to an Indian member of staff (let's assume Kathy oversees Dev's team) and then asks if the person understood, many Indians would be reluctant to say no for three reasons: (1) Kathy is a busy person, and they do not want to take too much of her time; (2) it might make the Indians look incompetent; and (3) they might be afraid of insulting Kathy by implying she gave a poor explanation, which could come across as disrespectful in Indian culture. These three reasons explain exactly what Dev did in this situation, which was to tell Kathy yes and then try to get clarification from his colleague Raj.

I have written about this phenomenon in my book *Speaking of India*:

I was once giving a workshop at NIKE in Portland to a mixed group of Americans and Indians, the latter working on teams led by the former. . . . I turned to the Indians [in the room] and asked them: "If your boss asks you to do some coding for a particular software application, and you have no idea what he wants, what do you do?" The Indians looked at each other and laughed. "We talk among ourselves," they said, "to see if any of us understood." "Fine," I replied. "And what if none of you understood?" "Oh," they answered, "then we just try something and hope it's right." I had given the Indians two chances to give the "right" answer—"We go back and ask our manager for clarification"—and it never occurred to them that that was what the Americans were expecting. It goes without saying that the bosses sitting around the table were not amused. (107)

There is a hierarchy of power and authority in all cultures, of course, including the United States, but cultures differ in how much they emphasize the hierarchy, in how comfortable people are with the unequal distribution of power. In the United States, managers are uncomfortable, and the gap between those who have power and those who do not is accordingly deemphasized. Managers know better than to "pull rank" or to "wear their rank on their sleeve," meaning they may have more power than their staff but it is very bad form to act like it.

Why are Americans so uncomfortable with power? Simply stated, it's because the exercise of power involves inequality, which is a very sensitive subject for people who value egalitarianism. In every workplace, someone must give instructions and someone must carry them out; employees must be subordinate to the authority and will of managers. When circumstances oblige Americans to act like they are superior to others—as a manager must on occasion—this behavior feels almost shameful.

In Dialogue 8, we introduced the concept of "power distance," a measure of how comfortable people are in various cultures with the unequal distribution of power and authority and, by inference, the degree to which they are sensitive to rank and hierarchy. We cited two studies, one by Hofstede and one by House, that ranked various countries in terms of power distance from high (tolerant) to low (intolerant). In the House study, India was among the most tolerant of power distance, while the U.S. was among the least tolerant. In the Hofstede study, with scores ranging from a high of 104 for Malaysia to a low of 18 for Denmark, India scored 77 and the U.S. scored 40.

At the end of the day, Kathy had no hesitation asking Dev if he understood her explanation because in her culture there could be no reason why any direct report should have a problem answering this question. Nor, for that matter, did Kathy have any reason to suspect Dev would feel uncomfortable coming directly to her to ask for clarification. If he didn't come to her, then that must have meant he understood her explanation and started work on the assignment.

For readers who are still unconvinced, who wonder if Indians really do exhibit such exquisite sensitivity to their manager's feelings, I offer the following anecdote. I was giving a workshop on cultural differences once to a group of Indians in Bangalore, using many of my dialogues, including this one, to illustrate the main points. The Indians acknowledged that the conversations did in fact accurately portray many common Indian workplace behaviors, but one man objected to one of the lines in this dialogue, saying it sounded inauthentic to him. When I asked him which line, he said, "The one where Dev says, 'Perhaps not.'" I asked him why this did not sound authentic, and he replied, "Because saying 'perhaps not' might hurt Kathy's feelings."

The Fix

In cultures where people are reluctant to say no, asking yes-or-no questions is a nonstarter. Fine (you might be thinking), but then how *is* Kathy supposed to find out if Dev understood her? First, you should learn to ask open questions, questions that cannot be answered with yes or no but require Indians to start talking. Here are a few examples:

- So, Dev, can you walk me through how you're planning to do this?
- How are you going to proceed with this?

- I might not have been clear: Can you summarize your understanding of what we talked about?

Second, do not assume Dev is comfortable asking for help (he is not), and make it clear that you know he must have questions and are more than happy to answer them. For example, you could say, "This is pretty complicated, Dev. I had a lot of questions when I did this the first time, too. You *must* have questions. What are they?"

Finally, be careful *not* to do what Americans almost always do when giving explanations: leave out details on purpose. Many Americans will give general, vague, big-picture explanations, afraid to say too much for fear of insulting the other person's intelligence, tying their hands, or limiting their freedom to do the job in whatever way works best for them. In short, Americans tend to err on the side of giving limited instructions and providing fewer details rather than saying too much. After all, Americans would never hesitate to ask for more information if they needed it—the cultural norm that gets Kathy into so much trouble when she projects it onto her Indian team.

For their part, Indians working with Americans should never hesitate to ask questions. And above all, you should never claim to understand something when you do not. It does not embarrass Americans if you ask for help, and it does not make you look incompetent. Moreover, in most cases Americans would prefer you ask them for clarification rather than asking one of your colleagues.

If you are managing Americans, don't be surprised or hurt if they ask a lot of questions or if they get annoyed if you give them too much guidance. Also remember that American direct reports are much more informal with their bosses; they do not mean any disrespect if they fail to defer to you or treat you as an equal.

32. I'M GLAD YOU CALLED

CARL: Hey, Krishna. I just called to see if we're still on track to fix that bug by the first of next week?

KRISHNA: I'm glad you called. It's going quite well, but there have been one or two unexpected problems.

CARL: Boy, I know how that is.

KRISHNA: I'm glad we understand each other.

Nice try, Krishna, but you and Carl have most definitely not understood each other. For such a short exchange, this dialogue is practically top-heavy with misunderstanding. And it all comes down to the two words "unexpected problems" and the cultural assumptions that lie behind them.

To understand what happened in this dialogue, we need to touch on a concept that lacks an agreed-upon name in the intercultural field. It has been called "locus of control" (by this author) or "human agency," but neither of those terms communicates very much. The issue here is what or who the people in a particular culture believe is responsible for what happens in life. The two camps are usually called "internalists" and "externalists." Internalists believe the individual is responsible for what happens in life, not in the sense that you cause or control everything but that you can manipulate or "do something about" any given set of circumstances. At the core of the internalist mind-set is a strong belief that there is nothing you cannot change and must just accept. There is no such thing as luck—you make your own luck—and nothing you cannot accomplish if you want it badly enough and work at it long enough. There are no limits to what you can do or how far you can go, except those inside your own head. In the internalist's world, every problem has a solution.

Gazing over at internalists across a very wide cultural gap (rolling their eyes and shaking their heads) are the externalists. These folks have a very different take on human agency. They accept limits and believe that some things are beyond anyone's control, all those things (as externalists would phrase it) that are just "not meant to be." Not everything is possible, which doesn't mean you don't try your best, but in some cases your best will not be enough. And that's okay. Not all limits are in your head, and not every problem can be solved. Externalists are not defeatists, though internalists tend to see them that way, but they are certainly realists.

Our dialogue reveals one of the many practical consequences of the difference between internalists and externalists: their attitudes toward deadlines. If you come from an externalist culture, as Krishna does, you can more readily accept that there will sometimes be reasons to change a deadline—namely any one of the many things people in your culture regard as beyond their control—and an "unexpected problem" certainly fits that description. If this is how you think, then you would assume, as Krishna almost certainly does, that you need only refer to "unexpected problems" for Carl to realize—and *accept*—that you're going to miss your deadline. When Carl says, "Boy, I know how that is," that just confirms Krishna's mistaken belief that Carl understands.

But Carl does not understand that Krishna expects to miss the deadline, and he would certainly not accept Krishna's reasoning if he did because Carl is an internalist. In his world—where he is in control, remember—there are very few things that cannot be changed, meaning there are almost no justifiable excuses for missing a deadline. After all, whatever might happen to threaten a deadline, there has to be a work-around, some steps that can be taken to eliminate the threat and keep everything on schedule. Carl is sympathetic ("Boy, I know how that is") not because he accepts that some deadlines just can't be met, but because he feels bad about all the extra work Krishna will have to do to stay on schedule. At the end of the day on Monday, Carl is going to be very upset with Krishna, and Krishna will be completely taken aback.

One of the effects of being able to rely on deadlines—and one of the reasons Carl will be so upset on Monday—is that Americans make a variety of contingency or follow-up plans based on the immutability of deadlines. When a deadline is missed, all of these plans must be changed or in some cases scrapped altogether.

Does this mean Indians don't believe in deadlines? Not exactly. They believe in deadlines and try to meet them, but there is generally more tolerance for missed deadlines in Indian culture than in the West. This is due in part to the fatalistic mindset described above as well as the more mundane infrastructure challenges in India: power outages, traffic jams, and monsoon floods. Simply stated, in a country where people believe there is only so much you can do, once you've done all those things, everybody understands that all bets are off.

The Fix

Americans should not assume that Indians understand the seriousness of missed deadlines in American business culture. You must explain this difference to your Indian colleagues; they may be surprised at first, but when they understand the consequences you face, they will try their best to protect you from such great misfortune. Apart from appealing for sympathy, you might also want to proactively build some flexibility into your timetable. If your actual deadline is Friday, you might want to announce that it is Wednesday. Finally, do keep checking in with your Indian partners on a regular basis to determine if they're still on schedule. If you don't want any last-minute surprises, don't wait until the last minute to become informed. Don't worry, meanwhile, if it doesn't feel quite right to be checking in so often, about coming across as a micromanager; most Indians are quite tolerant of micromanagement.

For their part, Indians working in an American context should realize that there are relatively few acceptable excuses for missing a deadline. Let Americans know immediately, no matter how early in the process and no matter the explanation, whenever you see any signs of a deadline slipping from your grasp. While they are never thrilled about having to change a deadline, Americans are especially unhappy if they have to change one at the last minute. You might also want to give yourself an extra day or two when you set a deadline (in case the proverbial unexpected happens). Finally, remember that Americans are not going to be checking in with you every other day to find out if you're on schedule. It's your responsibility to inform them if you're falling behind.

33. COMPLETION DATE

CARL: Well, I think that's everything, Indira. Thanks for staying late over there.

INDIRA: You're welcome. I was just wondering, before you go, about the completion date on that accounting test.

CARL: Sure. I think that was in an e-mail I sent you. Let me check my sent mail.

INDIRA: I believe you mentioned the end of May.

CARL: Here it is. Right: the end of May.

INDIRA: I see. That's still good for you, I guess?

CARL: Yes. It's fine.

INDIRA: Anyway, we'll have updates every week,
             right?

CARL: If you'd like.

INDIRA: That might be a good idea.

In the survey mentioned earlier, I asked Indians what their biggest cultural challenges were working for Americans. To my surprise, one of the most common responses was that "Americans always ask for things at the last minute." What made this surprising is that Americans usually go to great lengths *not* to do things at the last minute—everyone knows the quality of last-minute work—designing elaborate project plans and scheduling frequent status reports to ensure they know of any problems ahead of time. Why would Indians say this?

Then I realized the answer was right in front of me—in this dialogue, which I have used for more than fifteen years whenever I give workshops on Indian-U.S. cultural differences. It's not that Americans ask for things at the last minute; it is rather, as illustrated in "Completion Date," that Indians let Americans know they're falling behind in ways that are just too subtle for Americans to pick up on. Americans don't hear these periodic cries for help, assuming all is well, and only *realize* at the last minute that Indians are lagging behind. And at that late juncture they often do want very fast turnaround.

This dialogue contains four places where Indira informs Carl that she's falling behind and wonders if the deadline for the accounting test can be moved back. The first is when she says, "I was just wondering . . ." We learn in the next line ("I think that was in an e-mail I sent you") that Indira and Carl had previously agreed on the completion date. What Indira is actually doing here, then, is intentionally bringing up something these two had already decided. In Indian culture, especially in a vendor-client relationship, when a settled issue is again raised for discussion, the implied meaning is that the issue needs to be revisited.

In Indian culture, perhaps, but not in Carl's world. If one American or northern European says, "I was just wondering" to another, the meaning is the speaker has forgotten what was agreed to and needs to be reminded. Which is why Carl replies as he does ("Sure. I think that was in an e-mail I sent you.") and starts searching his emails to find the one where he and Indira agreed on the completion date.

But notice what happens next: before Carl even finds the e-mail, Indira says, "I believe you mentioned the end of May." In other words, she's not wondering what date they agreed on. So she must be "wondering" about something else, and the only thing that could be, of course, is whether it might be possible to change the completion date.

If that's not enough to make her point, what she says next should clear up any doubt: "That's still good for you, I guess?" asking Carl if his deadline is still good for him. If Carl were Indian, he would understand immediately that this gratuitous, unnecessary question—why *wouldn't* his own deadline be good for him?—is in fact a statement: that the deadline is not good for Indira, (albeit a statement that is couched politely in the form of a rhetorical question). But Carl is an American, for whom questions are questions and statements are statements, but questions, even rhetorical ones, are hardly ever statements. So he simply answers the question: "Yes. It's fine." Indira, who has now asked three times for an extension, makes one last try: "Anyway we'll have updates every week, right?" Here her message is this: "I'll inform you every week that I need more time, and one of these weeks you'll understand and extend the due date."

We should add that the great care Indira has taken to be polite in this dialogue, polite in the sense of not coming out and asking for an extension, is most appropriate if Carl is in some way her senior, perhaps a team leader, project manager, or client. If Indira were speaking with a peer, however, she would not have to be nearly so careful; indeed, she would ask quite directly, the same way two Americans would. It's only because of Carl's presumed higher rank that Indira resorts to classic Indian politeness.

Finally, it's important to note that neither party is to blame for the unpleasantness that awaits them at the end of May, when Carl will be very upset to learn Indira is not on schedule (Why didn't you tell me?) and Indira will be very surprised to learn that Carl has misunderstood her weekly updates. Carl was not trying to misread Indira, and Indira was not trying to mislead Carl. They've had the proverbial honest misunderstanding, forgivable, perhaps, for being honest and unintended, but no less of a misunderstanding, complete with all the attendant frustration and bad feelings. Their situation is not something we want to happen even if nobody is at fault.

Sensitivity to rank looms very large in U.S.-Indian interactions and accounts for more misunderstandings than any other cultural difference. Nor should that be surprising: the respect for hierarchy is one of the deepest values in Indian culture, while its exact opposite, egalitarianism, is the pride of American culture. These respective values are so embedded in each society, so completely internalized by the two peoples, that not only do Indians and Americans fail to understand this cultural difference, they are largely unaware of it. Numerous Indians have told me that theirs is not a hierarchical society, and many Americans have said that the American workplace is not all that empowering. Yet when both types are confronted with specific examples, such as the dialogues in this chapter, they readily agree that the behaviors described are accurate.

In *Being Indian* Pavan Varma observes that

> *the caste system began several thousand years ago as a functional categorization . . . [and] the mentality of a stratified society remains very much in evidence in everyday life. The structure of hierarchies may be changing but for an Indian, superior and subordinate relationships have the character of eternal verity and moral imperative—and the automatic reverence for superiors is a nearly universal psycho-social fact. (20)*

By way of contrast, in his book *Out of Our Past*, Carl Degler describes how fundamental the notion of equality was to the new American nation. He quotes first a French traveler: "We must acknowledge that they direct themselves generally by this principle of equality." And then a German: "Rank of birth is not recognized [and] is resisted with a total force. People think, act, and speak here precisely as it prompts them" (106). Degler goes on to observe that

> *during the first half of the nineteenth century . . . the blurring of classes was a fact and a boast. "We have no different estates," Erastus Root told the New York Constitutional Convention of 1821. "We are all of the same estate—commoners." New citizen Achille Murat said "the lines which divide [Americans] are so delicate that they melt into each other; and there are neither castes nor ranks." (159)*

One of the best ways to identify the deepest, most fundamental value in a culture is to look for the behavior that bothers people the most. Hiding beneath that strong reaction is the value that has just been violated. By this standard, egalitarianism is indeed a mighty force in America. There is no quicker or more foolproof way to upset an American than to act superior, as if you were somehow special and should be treated differently from others. This value runs so deep it even extends to people who clearly *are* special, presidents and the like, who therefore must be particularly careful to act like everyone else.

The Fix

Americans need to get better at reading between the lines when communicating with Indian subordinates. The alternative, to encourage Indians to be more direct, is always a possibility, but the journey for Indians from being very polite to being direct (with superiors, that is, not with peers) is going to be much harder and take longer than the journey for you from understanding straight talk to decoding subtlety. Indians would have to start behaving differently; you only have to start interpreting differently. Another fix here is to be careful not to ask Indians if they are on schedule or if they can deliver something by a certain day (a yes-or-no question); instead, ask them where they are in the process or what day they think they'll be finished. Indians have told me that when they're falling behind, a common practice is to send an unsolicited update. The update does not state that they are running behind or ask for an extension, it merely shows where they are on the timetable. The idea is that anyone reading this will see they're not where they should be and offer more time. Finally, if you're an American being managed by Indians, you will probably come across as blunt and even rude on occasion. Try to pull your punches now and then.

For their part, Indian direct reports should try to accept that they really can talk to American managers the way they would talk to their Indian peers. Although this would represent quite a departure for most of you, who are so used to being deferential to seniors, it would prevent more misunderstanding and frustration than almost any other single behavior you could adopt. If you can't bring yourself to be quite as direct as you are with peers, then at least try being more direct. If only you could listen to how subordinates talk to their bosses in an American work environment, you'd realize how much more direct they can be without causing any offense. I have never had Americans tell me that Indians are too direct, but Americans regularly tell me Indians are too polite. Finally, for Indians who manage Americans: If they come across as rude or blunt, don't take it personally; that's just how Americans talk to their bosses.

34. PROBLEMS SOLVED

RALPH: Hey, Anju. What's up?

ANJU: We fixed those two problems with that
            Windows application.

RALPH: Great. Thanks.

ANJU: And we found another problem that needed
            to be fixed.

RALPH: Great. Thanks for fixing that one, too.

ANJU: Did you want us to fix that one?

Many Americans feel that their Indian colleagues dislike taking responsibility or ownership. The "proof" of this, in American eyes, is when Indians routinely check in with their managers to get approval before taking action, *including action on tasks delegated to them*. When I first began hearing this complaint I was puzzled, as I have never actually observed this behavior in the Indian workplace. But I think this dialogue can clear up the confusion.

Ralph has sent Anju off to fix a couple of problems with a Windows application. Anju found the two problems, fixed them, and then found a third problem. In the traditional Indian work environment, Anju has to make a decision: She could fix the third problem, making the product users happy but potentially upsetting her manager by exceeding her authority and stepping on his toes. Or she could not fix the third problem, condemning the users to another day of frustration but avoiding trouble with her manager.

For most Indians, this is not a difficult decision: whatever the consequences of not fixing the third problem, they could never be as serious as the possible negative repercussions of exceeding their authority. Most Indian subordinates are extremely sensitive to their manager's prerogatives and hesitant, as a result, to do anything they have not explicitly been instructed to do. They are not comfortable "interpreting" their instructions, going beyond their instructions, or otherwise reaching any independent conclusions regarding what their boss *might* have meant or *should* have said. To most Indians, then, Anju has done the right thing by going back to Ralph to get his approval. But many Americans will shake their head and see this as just another example of the classic Indian reluctance to accept responsibility.

This is actually a relatively mild illustration. An American manager once told me that one of the Indians she supervised nine and a half hours away in New Delhi always asked her (via e-mail) if it was okay if he went on his dinner break. She laughed and told him he didn't have to ask for her permission, but he insisted that he did "because I'm your subordinate." After some time he did manage to stop asking, but he still routinely e-mailed her when he was going on break and again when he was back at his desk.

The difference at the core of "Problems Solved" is not so much a question of who delegates and who does not—both Indian and American managers delegate to their staff—but rather how each culture defines delegation. In the United States, delegation in most cases means turning over all authority, including the authority to make decisions, exclusively to staff unless otherwise stipulated. Staff then feel free to act without any need to request permission from management or any fear of being second-guessed. Managers might remain aware of decisions made by subordinates, but they would normally not "interfere" with staff's right to act unless specifically asked for their opinion.

In India, direct reports also have the right to make decisions on their own, and they do decide many day-to-day operational matters without consulting higher-ups. At the same time, the deep respect for hierarchy in Indian culture means that in the end juniors will usually consult with their bosses before making decisions of real consequence. "To the Indian way of thinking," I have observed elsewhere,

179

> this is just common courtesy, showing respect by tacitly acknowledging the manager's prerogative to be regularly informed of and approve what subordinates are doing. There is more ritual to this than substance, in that Indian bosses usually just go along with whatever the subordinate was planning to do anyway, but checking in is not entirely pro forma in the sense that an Indian boss would certainly take note (and not a positive note) if a subordinate did not check in. Or, to put it another way, checking in is in fact pro forma, but form and appearance matter almost as much as substance in Indian culture. (2015, 92)

As the reader might expect, when the tables are turned and Americans are working under Indian managers, they do not take kindly to being second-guessed (as they perceive it). The senior vice president of an American steel manufacturer once called me after his company was acquired by an Indian industrialist. The American plant managers were deeply frustrated by the new Indian owner and on the verge of a revolt. The managers, who were accustomed to near complete autonomy in running their plants, were annoyed by probing phone calls, endless and intrusive requests for information, and a regimen of quarterly performance reviews (which had previously been annual).

At the end of the day, the reason Americans feel Indians do not want to accept responsibility is because they mistake classic Indian deference for fear of being held accountable. Indians are not afraid to take ownership, but they *are* afraid of showing disrespect or discourtesy by keeping their managers in the dark.

180

The Fix

If the Ralphs of the world want the Anjus of the world to take responsibility, they must be very explicit about their expectations. If Anju knows you expect her to use her own judgment, she will be happy to do so; you only have to tell her. This may sound like obvious advice, but we hasten to add that it would be unnecessary to spell out your expectations in this manner to most American staff because they come from the same culture and they know what you're expecting. Indeed, a common complaint from Indians about their American colleagues—and this is a direct quote—is, "Our American bosses seem to think we always know what's in their heads." But how could Indians know this? If you were Anju and you had any doubt, wouldn't you go back and ask Ralph? And if this wastes a day, as it often does, wouldn't this be Ralph's fault for not making his intentions clear?

For their part, Indians working under Americans should sit down and have a talk with their bosses, figuring out what decisions they expect you to make on your own and when they want you to check in to get approval. That way you'll never have to guess what an American boss is thinking. Meanwhile, if you manage American subordinates, expect them to take full responsibility for anything you delegate. They will not necessarily see any need to consult with you before acting unless you specifically ask them to. At the same time, they will not enjoy being micromanaged, which they define as any kind of interference into matters you have turned over to them. If you don't want them to use their own judgment in certain circumstances, then don't delegate.

35. TIMING

CAROL: Hi, Anand. We were thinking this batch should take your guys about fifteen hours. How does that sound to you?

ANAND: Fifteen hours?

CAROL: Give or take. What do you think?

ANAND: Sure. So that's your best estimate, then?

CAROL: As near as we can figure it. But you guys know better than us.

ANAND: I see.

CAROL: So what do you say, Anand?

ANAND: That would be very efficient, wouldn't it?

CAROL: Just like you guys always are.

In the company surveys I have conducted, another common complaint Americans make is that "Indians overcommit," that they agree to deadlines they can't possibly meet and take on tasks they really don't have the expertise for. It should be noted that for each of the survey complaints mentioned so far in this chapter, and for this one as well, when I bring up the statements with

Indians, they vigorously protest; they say they *do* tell Americans when they have not understood something (Dialogue 31); they *do* inform Americans when they are falling behind (Dialogue 33); they *are* quite willing to accept responsibility (Dialogue 34); and they *do not* commit to work or time lines they cannot execute (see below). This dialogue explains why Americans think Indians overcommit and why Indians deny doing any such thing.

The problem is that Indians refuse requests so politely that Westerners think the Indians have agreed, hence the charge of overcommitting. "The value orientation of individualism," two cultural analysts note, "propels North Americans to speak their minds freely through direct verbal expression. Individualistic values foster the norms of honesty and openness. Honesty and openness are achieved through the use of precise, straightforward language" (Gudykunst & Ting-Toomey, 102). But in the deeply hierarchy-sensitive Indian workplace, any kind of refusal from a direct report to a superior must be handled with great tact and sensitivity so as not to appear disrespectful. "Indians like to tell you what you want to hear," Gitanjali Kolanad observes, "or, rather, what they think you want to hear. The tailor who says it will be ready by Friday and the person who assures you that the place you are looking for is just ahead are obeying a proverb that says 'it is better to say something pleasant than something true'" (251). Clearly, "precise, straightforward language" is not always the optimum approach in the Indian workplace.

As that more or less rules out using the word "no," Indians have devised several other ways of answering in the negative without using the word. While these methods differ, they all have one thing in common: the complete—and to Indians, *conspicuous*—absence of the word "yes." Note in this dialogue that Carol gives Anand four chances to agree to her request, and he never explicitly does. To be sure, neither does he quite manage to *dis*agree with Carol's request, but to Indians that's beside the point. It is the absence of agreement and *not the presence of disagreement* that Indians listen for, and here that absence is deafening.

We might take a minute to examine more closely just how Anand treats Carol's questions. He not only refuses to answer them, he actually sends both her questions back: "Fifteen hours?" and "So that's your best estimate then?" Carol may think Anand is simply asking for clarification, but when he says, "I see," there can be no doubt that he understands. Nor can there be any doubt, given the completely noncommittal nature of "I see," that Anand cannot agree to this request.

This situation will end in one of two ways, neither of which bodes well for Carol and Anand's relationship. Most probably Anand will assume Carol has understood that fifteen hours is inadequate—he has been very clear about that, after all—and has given him permission to take as long as necessary. Carol has not understood, of course, so when she comes back and finds that Anand is not finished, she will promptly join the ranks of Americans who accuse Indians of not honoring their commitments. The other way this could end is that since Carol does not offer Anand more time, although he has clearly asked for it, he assumes she expects him to do this in fifteen hours. Accordingly, he must now work late, keep his team late, and perhaps even bring people in over the weekend just to meet this American's completely unrealistic timetable. In this scenario, Carol is quite happy—while Anand and his team are burned out and wondering if there might be a more reasonable manager they could work for.

There is another cultural difference at play here, too, which concerns the degree of empowerment practiced in the two cultures. Generally, American bosses delegate a great deal of responsibility to their employees and leave them on their own to get the job done (as discussed in the previous dialogue). These managers, as a result, are somewhat removed from the day-to-day realities of their subordinates and are only aware in a very general way of what staff are up to at any given point in time. In this hands-off model, managers frequently do not have enough information to be giving orders or otherwise making important decisions without first consulting staff. As a result, when a manager mentions a number (say, fifteen hours) or a time frame for any given piece of work, it's always much more of a suggestion than a request; a genuinely hands-off manager simply doesn't know enough to make an astute request. In short, the manager depends on the team to consider the suggestion and let her know if it's workable. If not, it's the team's responsibility to say so, and the manager will either reconsider or simply ask the team for their number.

In Indian culture, managers typically delegate less responsibility and independence, with the result that they stay much more involved in and closer to the work of their team. Consequently, when Indian managers mention a number or a time frame, they have enough information to make a reasonable request—they don't need to ask for an opinion—and accordingly staff regard their manager's number as much closer to a demand. Thus, while Carol believes she is asking Anand for his feedback on her suggestion, Anand assumes she's telling him what she wants. To his credit, Anand does push back against what is clearly an unreasonable number, but he does it so politely that Carol misses the cue.

The Fix

American managers throw out numbers and propose time lines quite casually, for the reasons just described, and expect staff to have the final say. When you manage Indians, either refrain from throwing out any numbers and first ask for *their* number, or, if you do give Indians a specific number, make it clear that it's only a suggestion and you genuinely need their input. You should also realize that when Indians persist in evading certain questions, that's not evasion; it's their answer. If you are working for an Indian manager, you would be wise to assume a number is closer to a request; in those cases where the request is unreasonable, challenge it with some tact.

Indians who work under Americans should realize that when managers suggest a time frame, they are not making a request, although they may indeed be expressing a preference. In either case, it's expected and acceptable for you to challenge anything unreasonable; this is not considered insubordinate. If you manage Americans, you should ask them for their opinion and not assume they interpret proposals as commands. They expect to be consulted first.

8

Japan

> The sense of self grows more intense as we follow the
> setting of the sun, and fades steadily as we advance into
> the dawn. America, Europe, the Levant, India, Japan,
> each is less personal than the one before. We stand at one
> end of the scale, the far Orientals at the other. If with
> us the I seems to be the very essence of the soul, then
> the soul of the Far East may be said to be Impersonality.
> —Percival Lowell, *The Soul of the Far East*

Most observers would agree that Japan is the most culturally different from the United States of the ten countries in this book. In *Doing Business with the Japanese*, the American Mitchell Deutsch observes that Japan's "cultural, social, political, organizational, and even interpersonal dynamics are exceedingly different from our own" (14). That's a lot of difference.

China, the other Pacific Rim culture in these pages, certainly presents challenges, but there is a certain brashness about China, a drive that many Americans can identify with. The Japanese are driven in their way, too, but you could never accuse them of being brash, quite unthinkable in a culture where masking one's true feelings (if they are negative) and controlling one's emotions are two fundamental norms. This leads many Westerners to accuse the Japanese of being devious and calculating, but for the Japanese (and most other East Asians) emotional self-control is essential for maintaining group harmony and protecting face, two dynamics at the very top of the Japanese value system.

Japanese-American cultural differences are fundamental, and they affect every aspect of business and workplace interactions. Dean Barnlund describes the extent of the difference succinctly: "If one were forced to choose only a few words to capture the ethos of these two societies," he writes, "they might be these: Homogeneity, Hierarchy, Collectivity, and Harmony for Japan; Heterogeneity, Equality, Individualism, and Change for the United States" (161). These are not mere differences; they are polar opposites.

The good news here is that the gap between American and Japanese culture is so demonstrably wide that both sides are prepared for surprises and misunderstandings when they do business together. There are not many obvious similarities, in other words, that might mask more subtle differences and thereby lull either side into complacency. Moreover, the differences are not especially subtle.

That's the conventional wisdom anyway, and still accurate for many U.S.-Japanese interactions. But numerous Japan-watchers have observed that today's younger Japanese are more individualistic than their parents' generation and that the gap between American and Japanese cultures may be narrowing in some respects. The dialogues in this chapter should all be read with this caveat in mind.

188

36. THE PRODUCTION SCHEDULE

CHERYL: Good morning, everyone. I've asked your team leader, Masaaki, to brief us all on the production schedule.

MASAAKI: Thank you, Cheryl. As you all know, we signed the contract back in May and began work three weeks later.

CHERYL: Actually, I think it was late April.

MASAAKI: Of course, my mistake. We agreed at the time that Phase I would be completed in three months.

CHERYL: I think we actually said ten weeks, but you guys are ahead of schedule anyway, so it's not important. All of us execs back in Houston are very happy about that, by the way.

MASAAKI: Thank you, Cheryl.

Masaaki may say "Thank you" at the end of this conversation, but he has precious little to be thankful for. This visiting senior executive, Cheryl, has gratuitously embarrassed him twice, and he probably thinks she is very unhappy with him.

Really? All that in six short lines? Short to you, perhaps, but it probably seemed like an eternity to Masaaki. Consider: Masaaki is chairing a meeting with his team in the presence of a bigwig from Houston, and the first thing Cheryl does is correct Masaaki in front of everyone. That's bad enough, but she corrects something so minor, a date, that Masaaki might briefly wonder if there isn't another message here. Then Cheryl corrects Masaaki again—more embarrassment—before adding that "It's not important." If these things are so minor, why is Cheryl so insistent on correcting him, especially she must know this makes Masaaki look bad in front of his team? The only explanation must be that Cheryl is *trying* to embarrass him, seeking out things to criticize in order to send him a message. From Masaaki's perspective, the message might very well be that Cheryl is not pleased with him.

Cheryl *is* sending Masaaki a message: how much she and Houston appreciate the performance of his team. And Americans know it's a message because it's actually something Cheryl *says*. By and large, Americans do not communicate via silence, nor do they say one thing and mean something else. When they want to say something else, Americans say that other thing. When Cheryl says something is unimportant, it means that thing is unimportant. When she corrects the date Masaaki gives, there's no hidden meaning; it's the wrong date. If you wanted somebody to actually *get* a message, why would you hide it?

The cultural difference at the heart of this dialogue has to do with face. Face is inextricably bound up with the Japanese concept of personal identity, which in turn is well on the collectivist side of the great individualism-collectivism divide. The Pacific Rim as a whole is collectivist territory, but Japan might be the poster country for collectivism. In the more individualist West, the words "identity" and "self" are almost interchangeable; indeed, a common synonym for identity is "self-concept." Hence it is difficult for Westerners to imagine any sort of identity not based on the self. In a collectivist culture, however, individuals derive much of their identity from their membership in and close association with a group (the collective), such as family, extended family, and even a clan. At work, employees profoundly identify with their corporation, division, and work team, and they define themselves in terms of their role and place within the larger unit. It would be wrong to say they lack a separate personal identity (especially younger Japanese), but a significant part of their identity derives from something larger than, separate from, and in addition to the individual self.

The link to face is that face is essentially the esteem in which one is held by others, the regard of one's group (although there is a personal pride dimension as well). In a collectivist culture, anything that undermines group regard—such as a potential loss of face—automatically threatens one's identity and overall sense of well-being. "How well one discharges one's responsibility is part of one's *kao* (face)," Edward Hall writes. "*Kao* encompasses pride, self-esteem, and reputation. It is vital to the Japanese. A foreigner should avoid criticizing a Japanese or demeaning him in any way, nor should one disparage his work" (1983, 57).

Which in a nutshell is why Masaaki is probably upset. If Cheryl corrects him in front of his team, and his mistakes thus become known to the group, his credibility is questioned and his public esteem is diminished. He loses face, in short, and his own viability as a group member is compromised. The loss of face is even more painful for being tied to such trivial mistakes. Cheryl's overreach seems completely unjustified to Masaaki.

If Cheryl heard any of this, she might well wonder if she had passed through the looking glass. In what universe do people think like this? From her perspective, Masaaki made a couple of minor misstatements, and she set the record straight, end of story. Cheryl values facts and, moreover, appreciates it when someone points out mistakes. She would probably agree that Masaaki's two misstatements are minor, but in her world that means people would have no qualms whatsoever about being corrected. If Masaaki had made a major mistake, however, that would be different.

The two competing values here are the importance of telling the truth (in this case the admittedly mundane example of getting one's facts straight) and the importance of face. As she is an individualist, very little of Cheryl's identity depends on the good opinion of the group; crudely put, if face is in large measure the esteem of one's collective, then Cheryl doesn't have any because she doesn't identify with any collective. Cheryl's behavior in the meeting must derive from some other value or norm, such as the American love of clarity and directness. In individualist cultures where people are more self-reliant, there's no need to beat around the bush to protect other people's feelings. People appreciate straight talk, even if it is at times sugarcoated and somewhat tactful. And that's what drives Cheryl's behavior in the dialogue: people need the facts, and meetings should be conducted in way that encourages clear communication.

In Masaaki's culture, the facts may indeed be valued, but they do not always prevail in competition with higher values. In this particular situation, face would trump the truth every time. "Westerners consider deception as immoral," Rosalie Tung has written. "In East Asia . . . deception is considered as a neutral concept which should be engaged in if it [leads] to a greater good. From the East-Asian perspective, the 'greater good' embraces the well-being of the nation-state, the clan, the extended family, the nuclear family, the corporation, *and the self*" (italics added, Joynt & Warner, 235, 236). There is no deception in "Production Schedule," of course, but the larger point here is worth emphasizing: in many cultures of the Pacific Rim bending the truth is often acceptable in cases where it prevents significant embarrassment. Westerners might call it lying, but the Japanese see things differently.

We should add, finally, that a Japanese person in Cheryl's place would also correct Masaaki, but only one-on-one after the meeting or during a break. If the mistake needed immediate correction, a Japanese Cheryl would simply state the correct facts without referring to the misstatement. Soon after Masaaki mentions "three months," his Japanese boss might say, "According to that original ten-week schedule . . ." The error is thus corrected without ever being mentioned, hence with minimal embarrassment to all parties.

The Fix

American-style directness could not be a worse match for a culture like Japan, which places so much emphasis on harmony and saving face. The most tactful American is still almost entirely boorish by Japanese standards. The only suggestion we can offer here—and it's not especially helpful—is for you to pay very close attention to how the Japanese handle "difficult" situations (i.e., situations fraught with the risk of causing offense), and try to copy them. We could tell you to be more subtle, to dial back the straight talk, to say as little as possible, to imply rather than state outright, to say half of what you mean when delivering criticism—and to be especially careful in meetings. We could tell you all of these things, and you're still going to make mistakes right and left. The best advice, courtesy of Mitchell Deutsch, is to "apologize for everything" (102).

Japanese working in an American setting will have to grow very thick skins. While it may help to realize that Americans don't deliberately try to cause offense, it still hurts when Americans are too blunt. Just as they can't help being direct, you can't help being offended. Meanwhile, be much more direct with Americans without worrying about causing offense. If you are too indirect, Americans will not understand you. Here we present again the chart from Chapter 2 as a guide to how Asians and Americans interpret each other's communication style:

When **Americans** are	the **Japanese** consider this
Indirect	Direct
Direct	Blunt
Blunt	Rude

When **the Japanese** are	the **Americans** consider this
Indirect	Meaningless
Direct	Indirect
Blunt	Direct

194

37. ANOTHER BRIEFING

MS. BROWN: So my team and I were wondering, Sato-san, if you were ready to sign the agreement?

MR. SATO: Oh, yes. The agreement. It's very good, but we don't completely understand about the timetable.

MS. BROWN: So I guess the documents I sent over yesterday weren't very clear. I was in a hurry.

MR. SATO: No, no. The materials were very clear. Thank you.

MS. BROWN: I would be happy to arrange a briefing for you and your team later today.

MR. SATO: Or you and I could talk after this meeting.

MS. BROWN: Of course, but it might be good for the whole team to hear.

MR. SATO: Of course.

MS. BROWN: And then we can sign the agreement this afternoon?

MR. SATO: Oh, yes. But it's possible we may not understand the briefing.

Different cultures express negative feedback differently, but they all have to deal with it. In the relatively direct cultures of North America and northern Europe, negative feedback takes the form of a negative statement: "I'm not sure about that." "I see a problem with that." "That would never work." In other words, because people in direct cultures are expected to say what they think, if what they think happens to be negative, then their words must sound negative. To be sure, they are often diplomatic in one context and more frank in another—polite with a senior during a meeting, let's say, and blunt with a peer when one-on-one. But even at its most polite, negative feedback in the West almost always explicitly communicates a "problem" of some sort: a disagreement, hesitation, concern, or objection.

Direct negative feedback works fine in a culture where honesty is the best policy, but in cultures where honesty has to compete with other best policies, negative feedback can't always sound so negative. Avoiding confrontation, for example, often trumps honesty in face-saving Japan, and when it does, criticism and objections have to be communicated very carefully. Confrontation can easily disturb harmony, and harmony is the glue that holds collectivist cultures like Japan together. "*Wa* or harmony is one of the oldest and most important Japanese values," two longtime Japan-watchers have written. "In the workplace, a manager's job is to create harmony so that conflicts do not occur. When they do, the Japanese prefer to avoid direct confrontation. In their view, confrontation is likely to cause the people involved to lose . . . face" (Clarke & Lipp, 249).

195

Everything Mr. Sato does in this dialogue has the same purpose: avoiding an open confrontation with Ms. Brown. This is made difficult by the fact that Mr. Sato does in fact have a serious disagreement with her: he cannot accept the timetable she has proposed. The issue for Mr. Sato then becomes how to communicate this without causing a confrontation.

Seen in that light, his every move makes sense. To begin with, he tells her that he and his team "don't completely understand about the timetable." In Japanese culture, saying something is "not understandable" is often code for calling it unacceptable. Ms. Brown can't be expected to know that, of course, but she should realize something is wrong when Mr. Sato claims the additional materials she sent to explain the timetable were "very clear." If they were so clear, Ms. Brown should ask herself, why does he still not understand? The answer, of course, is that he does understand; he just doesn't like the timetable. Not wanting to say as much directly—reluctant, that is, to confront Ms. Brown in front of her team (and in front of his)—Mr. Sato pointedly replies the materials were clear, assuming she'll now realize that lack of clarity must not be the problem, that she will then sense what the real problem is, and finally that she will offer an alternative timetable that is more acceptable.

But Ms. Brown, oblivious to all of Mr. Sato's efforts, instead offers a solution ("to arrange a briefing") to a problem that does not exist. Indeed, this only makes an already awkward situation even more uncomfortable, as Mr. Sato now faces the prospect of having to reject Ms. Brown's timetable a third time (i.e., after the upcoming briefing). He tries to maneuver them both away from this looming showdown by suggesting a one-on-one meeting ("Or you and I could talk after this meeting"), which is a much more acceptable venue for a confrontation in Japanese culture. In such a meeting, he will be able to speak more directly, Ms. Brown will understand, a face-saving compromise will be arranged, and no one will be embarrassed. Alas, this gambit fails, and Mr. Sato is now obliged to be as direct as he dares, making the extraordinary assertion that he will most likely not understand a briefing *that has not yet taken place*. Surely *that* will break the logjam.

Americans just aren't very good at reading between the lines or reading things "into" what other people say. They read the lines (which is where *they* put the message) not between them, and they hear the words people say and would never imagine other words that are not said but which should be inferred. It is striking how many colloquial expressions Americans have to describe their preference for direct communication: they want people to get to the point, tell it like it is, call a spade a spade, face the facts, let the chips fall where they may, and put their cards on the table. And they don't like it when people mince their words, beat around the bush, pull their punches, or hold back. They like the unvarnished truth, plain speech, straight talk.

It goes without saying that direct negative feedback is the norm in such a value set, which explains why Ms. Brown has little hope of understanding Mr. Sato. "Reluctance to emphatically state a negative response," Dean Engel writes, "and the tendency to resort to euphemism ('That would be difficult')—common approaches in Asian cultures—are sources of aggravation to Americans, who are more concerned with knowing the intent of others than with having their feelings spared" (74).

As to why Americans are so direct, several bedrock American values are at play. One is the egalitarian ethos mentioned frequently in these pages. If everyone is the equal of everyone else, there is no need to fear what others think or to edit one's speech to suit the rank or status of the listener. The values of self-reliance and individualism also support being direct; if you do not require the good opinion of others for your success or well-being, you can speak your mind without fear of the consequences. If the "self" is indeed supreme in individualist America, then self-expression, by extension, is a fundamental right.

Not surprisingly, Americans have no particular fear of confrontation since even its worst outcome—a damaged business or personal relationship—is not only less likely in an individualist culture but also not as serious. "For many Americans," Clarke and Lipp write,

> direct confrontation in conflict situations is a commendable course of action. . . . [T]he American belief [is] that the most effective way to resolve a conflict is to confront issues quickly, rationally, and directly. They believe that things said between two people in a confrontation should not necessarily affect their relationship. . . . Americans sometimes accept emotional outbursts as a normal part of the conflict resolution process. This phenomenon of letting off steam allows Americans to vent their frustrations without serious consequences. (252)

The Fix

Americans who sense hesitation on the part of Japanese—if they never quite agree while not exactly disagreeing—should back off and give them a chance to regroup. You will know you have reached agreement when the Japanese start talking about next steps, details, who will do what. If the discussion stays in the realm of generalities, the negotiations are likely going nowhere and specifics are thus irrelevant. Whenever the Japanese say they do not "understand" something, that's usually code for some kind of objection.

Japanese must realize that Americans are quite literal. If you say you do not understand something, Americans assume you need more information, not that you disagree. Polite but open disagreement is acceptable in the American business context, largely because face and harmony are not nearly as important as they are in Japan. Do not hesitate, then, to express disagreement directly; you will not sound rude or cause loss of face. And remember that when Americans are very direct with you, this is not disrespectful or rude in their culture.

38. SORRY

ANDREW: How do you think our meeting with the auditors went yesterday?

KENICHI: Quite well. You discussed all our issues.

ANDREW: I was surprised you didn't tell them your suggestions for the quarterly review.

KENICHI: You mean the observations I went over with you before the meeting?

ANDREW: Right. You heard them ask me about that, but you didn't say anything. I thought you must have changed your mind, so I just changed the subject.

KENICHI: No, I didn't change my mind. I'm very sorry.

ANDREW: So why didn't you say anything?

KENICHI: I didn't find an opportunity.

ANDREW: But you were in the room?

KENICHI: Of course. I'm sorry.

"The aspect of Japanese culture which is probably the most subject to misinterpretation," John Condon writes, "and which provokes the strongest emotional response from Americans is the hierarchical nature of the social structure. The Japanese are extremely status conscious" (1984, 19). Japanese society does indeed pay great attention to rank and status, making Japanese among the most deferential of all peoples. Student defers to teacher, junior defers to senior, and—most importantly—youth always defers to age. In the business environment, direct reports are unerringly polite and deferential to their "superiors," which, tellingly, is the word most Japanese use for those above them in the chain of command.

"Japanese [workers] make an active commitment to preserve harmony," one Japan-watcher notes,

> *through intimate social rituals like gift-giving, bowing to superiors, and using honorific language to show deference.*
> *From the moment two [Japanese] meet, they must move fast to ascertain which of them has to defer to the other. Asians do not believe people are inherently equal, as Westerners typically do. The differing degrees of social stature must be revealed . . . so that both parties will know how to speak to one another and how to behave properly. (Engholm, 44, 80)*

"Sorry" contains several examples of classic Japanese deference to authority. It appears that Andrew and one of his staff, Kenichi, met with the company's auditors yesterday. When Andrew asks Kenichi how he thinks the meeting went, Kenichi sounds positive: "Quite well. You discussed all our issues." Later in the dialogue, however, it emerges that "You discussed all our issues" may in fact have another meaning altogether: Andrew discussed all the issues *including the one Kenichi should have been asked to discuss.* Is this not perhaps a mild rebuke? (We hasten to add that while a Japanese subordinate would never rebuke a Japanese manager in this fashion, Kenichi might feel less inhibited with an American who is not used to deference and who also might benefit from a few cultural hints.)

We learn next that Kenichi had a few suggestions to make to the auditors and that he informed Andrew of these before the meeting. In Japanese culture, there are several reasons Kenichi might do this: the first is that it would be rude to surprise Andrew with these suggestions in the middle of the meeting; the second, related reason would be to give Andrew a chance to consider the suggestions and give his input; and the third reason would be to signal to Andrew that Kenichi should be invited to offer these suggestions at the proper juncture, or, if not, then at the very least Andrew could offer these suggestions himself.

Americans can relate to the first two reasons, perhaps, but the third one does not compute. An American direct report would almost never need an invitation to speak up at a meeting, with the possible exception of a meeting with a very senior person. In American-style meetings, everyone around the table is free to speak if they have something to contribute, *regardless of their rank vis-à-vis the other participants*. In short, what determines if a person speaks is not who they are, but what they have to say. American subordinates are not insensitive to rank, but it counts for much less. Deference to rank, especially to the extent of waiting to be called on, is not the norm.

Seen in this light, we can understand what happened next. When the auditors asked about the quarterly review, Andrew saw it as Kenichi's opening to offer his suggestions ("I thought you would say something"), but Kenichi, as a junior, felt uncomfortable speaking up without first being invited. Doing so would imply he was Andrew's equal, which would be insensitive and disrespectful. Andrew, knowing none of this, waits for Kenichi to speak. When he does not, Andrew assumes that Kenichi must be having second thoughts ("I wondered if you had changed your mind") and just changes the subject. Thus the suggestions never get aired.

In classic Japanese style, Kenichi apologizes for Andrew's faux pas (twice) and also states that he did not change his mind; the suggestions are still valid and should have been made. As to why he didn't say anything, Kenichi simply responds that he "did not find an opportunity." What he means, of course, is that Andrew never *gave* him an opportunity—but he would never be so rude as to say that directly to a superior. From Andrew's perspective ("But you were in the room"), Kenichi didn't have to "find" an opportunity; he just needed to take it.

Deference is not in the American DNA; it smells of inequality. America, after all, was founded by people escaping an inherently unequal hierarchy of social classes, an order sustained by deference to rank and status. Those who risked everything to escape were not about to recreate in the New World what they hated most about the Old World. "Americans dislike being made to feel inferior," Edward Hall writes, "and bristle at any system of arbitrary social ranking independent of achievement. The American belief in equality makes Americans dislike those who act superior or condescending or who attempt to 'pull rank'" (1990, 150).

While in Asia deference is mainly a way of showing respect, in America it inevitably carries a suggestion of inferiority. "There are many ways in which the Japanese publicly acknowledge a social hierarchy," Condon writes, "in the use of language, in seating arrangements at social gatherings, in bowing to one another.... All of this can be a source of irritation for many Americans [who] usually infer that if differences are stressed, then one [person] must be *better* than the other" (1984, 20).

We should not leave this explanation without briefly mentioning the Japanese love affair with the word "sorry." This is most often a slight mistranslation of the Japanese word *sumimasen*, which more accurately means "excuse me." If "excuse me" is not the first word a Japanese child learns, it's certainly the third (after "mother" and "father"). The Japanese will apologize at the drop of a hat or even if the hat doesn't actually drop but looks like it might. They excuse themselves when they behave inappropriately, when they neglect to behave appropriately, and even when *you* behave inappropriately. At the end of the day, it's always a good idea to excuse yourself *just in case*.

The Fix

This is hard for Americans, for whom a little bowing to authority goes a long way. But if you are working in a Japanese business environment, graciously accept the deference that comes your way. At the same time, be careful to defer to anyone senior to you, especially in public settings such as meetings. An American who behaves as the equal of her superiors in a meeting will embarrass herself, acutely embarrass any Japanese present, and lose a great deal of respect besides. Similarly, protesting too much when your subordinates defer to you will undermine your authority. Meanwhile, don't let all this deference go to your head; the Japanese resent any boss who does not treat them with respect.

Japanese working in American business settings should realize that Japanese-style deference towards one's superiors makes Americans very uncomfortable. You may think you're just being polite and respectful, but Americans will think you are either kowtowing or have low self-esteem. Meanwhile, Japanese managers should not be offended if American employees treat you more like equals; they do not mean any disrespect.

39. TRIAL RESULTS

CARLA: Hi, Yasuki. I got a call from my customer
           yesterday.

YASUKI: Yes, Carla.

CARLA: They wanted to know if the trial results could be aggregated by the end of next week.

YASUKI: I see.

CARLA: I told them I'd check with you.

YASUKI: Of course.

CARLA: So what do you think, Yasuki?

YASUKI: The end of next week?

CARLA: Right. They said that would be a big help to them.

YASUKI: I'm sure.

CARLA: So what do you think, Yasuki?

YASUKI: Excuse me?

This dialogue brings us face to face once again with the great cultural divide between direct and indirect communicators, quite possibly the greatest of all cultural divides, certainly if it is measured by the amount of frustration and confusion it causes in business interactions. The particular difference on display here is how people in indirect cultures communicate "no" in certain situations. (See also Dialogue 35, "Timing.") Indirect cultures tend to be collectivist and group-oriented, with group harmony as one of the highest values. Indeed, it is precisely this overarching need for harmony that predisposes the Japanese to indirectness in the first place. There is a general reluctance to tell others what they do not want to hear—to confront, argue, disagree, or object— which makes the word "no" inherently problematic. This is not to say that Japanese never give negative answers—disagreement is necessary and common in all cultures—but only that such answers do not involve the word "no." In "Trial Results," we witness one of the classic methods of communicating "no" in indirect cultures: never quite managing to say "yes."

Don't forget that Yasuki desperately wants to be helpful here; nothing would make him happier than to tell Carla what she wants to hear. And yet he never manages to say "yes" despite having four opportunities. When Carla informs him of the client's proposed deadline, Yasuki surely knows what would please her, and yet the best he can manage is a completely neutral "I see." She presses further ("I told them I would check with you"), giving him a second chance, and he lets this chance pass by also with a neutral remark ("Of course"). When Carla comes right out and asks ("So what do you think?"), he dodges his third chance to be agreeable ("The end of next week?"). And then he rounds out his miserable performance by completely ignoring the implication of her last statement ("They said that would be a big help to them") with his pitiful "I'm sure." Yasuki, the man who'd love to say yes, misses all four of his chances. Surely there is a message here.

In Japan, absolutely; indeed, the second Yasuki replied to the proposed deadline with his vague "I see," another Japanese would know that the timeline was impossible, and the conversation would be over. Imagine how excruciating it must be for Yasuki to have to turn Carla down three more times.

While it can be argued that Carla is being somewhat dense, that she should be picking up on Yasuki's evasiveness, the simple fact is that in a direct culture like the United States, where telling other people what they want to hear is not especially important, there's no reason to avoid the word "no." In other words, in cultures where there's no reason to avoid the word "no," there is accordingly no need to find more polite substitutes, such as never quite managing to say "yes."

This discussion begs a deeper question at the heart of the direct-indirect communication divide: How can what is *not* said—in this case, the word "yes"—be a message? By what logic, in

205

other words, in which parallel universe can something that is not expressed constitute communication? The short answer is that what is unsaid becomes a message when its omission is so obvious as to be literally remarkable. Which then leads us to ask an even deeper question: How can something that is not there be obvious?

To find the answer, we need look no further than Yasuki's collectivist culture. As noted in Dialogue 36, "The Production Schedule," people in collectivist cultures derive the lion's share of their personal identity by association with and membership in the group. Yasuki and his compatriots are all individuals, of course, but they tend to define themselves in terms of larger entities rather than personal attributes. Their sense of self, in other words, includes a large element of the other. In this paradigm, the survival and general well-being of individuals depends on the strength and well-being of the group, which in turn makes group harmony the lifeblood of a successful collective.

Consider the implications of this for everyday interactions between group members. Acceptable behavior is determined by— and restricted to—what is pleasing and will not offend, disturb, or otherwise upset the totality of the group members. In such a scheme, where many sensibilities must be taken into account and respected before action is taken, the range of acceptable behavior becomes severely circumscribed. There are common scripts for most interactions, in short, and people seldom depart from them.

Which brings us, finally, to how what is not said, what is omitted, what is absent, can become obvious. If people like Yasuki always say yes to certain inquiries, if saying yes in such circumstances is a completely predictable cultural imperative— if the script mandates yes—then the absence of yes is utterly conspicuous.

While Americans belong to many organizations, they are not group-oriented in the sense that they do not derive the lion's share of their identity from close association with a limited number of other people whom they know intimately. Harmony, the glue that holds a group together, is not an important value in the U.S., and accordingly the need to preserve harmony by choosing one's words carefully does not compute. Indeed, since maintaining harmony is not culturally mandated and since Americans do not know other Americans as intimately as people do in collectivist cultures like Japan, being direct, what Americans call speaking one's mind, is essential for successful communication. In Japan, there's no need to speak your mind; your fellow group members already know what you're thinking.

The Fix

In Japanese work settings, Americans must pay close attention to what is left unsaid, something you have almost no experience of doing. So be patient with yourself while you are acquiring this skill. Another suggestion is to study Japanese body language. As noted above, what the Japanese say in any particular situation may indeed be predetermined by a kind of script; the words are frequently not their own and they say what they must say. But their feelings *are* their own, scripts notwithstanding, and if you tune in closely to their nonverbal reactions, you'll get much nearer to the truth. You might also want to reassure your Japanese colleagues and direct reports that the word "no" is not considered rude. And as for using that word yourself: try to use one of the many polite alternatives that manages to get the point across.

For their part, Japanese in American work settings should understand that most Americans find your communication style vague and indirect and they often misinterpret you. You may think you are being clear, because you are *to other Japanese*, but not to Americans. If you can't quite manage to be as direct as

Americans, then try to be less indirect. If you are uncomfortable using the word "no," then try to use a few more obviously negative phrases, such as "I can try to get that done by next week, but it will be difficult," or "I'd like to be able to please the client, but I just don't think it's possible." Neither of these would be misinterpreted as "yes" by Americans—nor, just as important, would they ever be seen as impolite.

40. CHANGES

GAIL: Has your group had a chance to read the new procedures manual?

KYOKO: Yes, they have all read it.

GAIL: Are they happy with the changes?

KYOKO: Most of them, yes. All but two people.

GAIL: Two out of ten, that's great. I'm sure the others will be fine.

KYOKO: I can't say. We will be interested to get their comments.

GAIL: So we can start implementing the changes tomorrow, then?

KYOKO: That might be too early.

GAIL: Too early? Why?

Many readers may be surprised to hear that Japanese management style is highly decentralized in some respects, especially when it comes to decision-making. Both Dialogue 36 and Dialogue 39 have dramatized the exquisite sensitivity Japanese show toward their superiors. How, then, can a hierarchical society eschew top-down decision-making? The short answer is that another bedrock Japanese value—group-orientation—trumps many aspects of hierarchy in the workplace. An interesting study of three collectivist cultures—India, Iran, and Japan—looked at whether social collectivism carried over into the workplace in the form of strong work groups. While Indians and Iranians tended to become much more individualistic and competitive at work, the Japanese work culture was just as collective as the social culture. "Japan, although strongly hierarchical, is one of the most consensual societies in the world," Erin Meyer writes. "This seemingly paradoxical pattern grows from the fact that both hierarchical systems *and* consensual decision-making are deeply rooted in Japanese culture" (italics added, 154).

This means that decisions affecting the group in Japan are almost always made by the group, and until there is group consensus, no action is taken. "Decision-making in Japan is a collective process involving many people," Engholm writes. "The person pushing the plan spends a lot of energy to gain consensus before the formal decision. Getting consensus beforehand is a key to success" (62). Japanese managers readily acquiesce to this highly participatory decision-making, known as *ringi* in Japanese. They know that if everyone is not behind the decision, if everyone has not had the chance to weigh in and be heard, then group harmony—and ultimately productivity—can be seriously undermined. "People should talk and talk until some agreement emerges," Condon writes. "If the mood is such that no consensus is possible, then it may be best to defer making a decision. Japanese management gives much more authority and responsibility to those in lower ranking positions, so that sometimes the managers' function is merely to endorse what has come up the line" (1984, 10, 11, 21).

Americans are accustomed to what they regard as a more efficient, majority-rule style of decision-making, which is tailored to their work and business individualist culture. "One person, one vote" preserves the voter's individual rights, and if the vote goes against him, he happily acquiesces. If at least 51 percent of other individuals thought differently, they have the right to prevail. In a culture with no tradition of group identification, consensus is not a priority and its absence has fewer adverse consequences.

Which brings us to Gail and Kyoko. They are charged with implementing a new procedures manual, which is being circulated within Kyoko's team. When Gail learns that all but two of Kyoko's staff have approved the new manual, she's ready to move forward, assuming—as would be the case in American culture—that the other two will respect the will of the majority and go along with the plan ("I'm sure the others will be fine"). When Kyoko responds that she "can't say," this should give Gail pause—some other criteria for decision-making may be in play here. And when Kyoko adds that she'll "be interested to get their comments," it certainly sounds like this is not a done deal. Any doubt should be erased when Kyoko fears the next day is "too early" to implement the changes, but Gail obviously can't relate to her ("Too early? Why?") and is on track to be disappointed. "Japanese decision-making causes Americans great distress," Edward Hall writes, "because they don't understand the delays" (1983, 82).

Business gurus have argued about *ringi* for years. But most Japan-watchers agree that while getting consensus certainly takes longer, the initial delays are worth it because implementation is much faster when everyone is on board. Deutsch observes that

> there is a "slow, slow, fast, fast" dynamic operating in Japanese business. While they are initially slow in making decisions and getting the ball rolling, when it rolls, it rolls quickly. Their implementation of decisions is swift and usually surprises Americans who are used to the opposite: quick decisions, but considerable foot-dragging to get the decision into operation. (91)

Some years ago, a study was done in which 100 American and 100 Japanese students were each given a piece of paper. They were asked to write down on one side any decisions they wanted to make by themselves and on the back side any decisions they wanted to make with others. The Japanese had four times as many decisions on the back side as the Americans. (The only common one for the Americans was "When I die.")

The Fix

In the Japanese business environment, Americans would be wise to make their peace with *ringi* and let the locals do it their way. If in fact, as many studies have shown, the Japanese achieve liftoff just as fast as anyone else, does their initial runway speed really matter? In any culture where group cohesion is the key to workplace productivity, surely achieving consensus is well worth the wait.

Japanese working in a U.S. environment must accept that group cohesion is relatively unimportant in the American workplace. You should not expect it and you should not be offended if a decision is made that you disagree with; Americans mean no disrespect when they do that. Japanese who manage Americans should feel no pressing need to get consensus and should likewise be aware that once a majority of Americans agree on something, they expect it to be implemented without undue delay.

9

Mexico

We're going to be neighbors until this planet ceases to exist. Perhaps it's time to understand each other.

—Octavio Paz

Americans ought to have a tolerably good understanding of Mexican culture. People of full or partial Mexican ancestry comprise nearly 11 percent of the U.S. population, a total of 35 million, and make up 64 percent of all Hispanics or Latinos in the country. Moreover, Mexico is close—very close—one of only two countries that shares a border with the United States.

Americans (or more accurately for our purposes here, Anglo-Americans) ought to understand the Mexican culture that surrounds them, but many of them do not. For one thing, millions of Mexicans who live in the United States are second-, third-, fourth-, and even fifth-generation; they have never lived in Mexico, their parents have never lived in Mexico, and neither have their grandparents. While they are certainly Mexican in some respects, they are unquestionably American in many others. Anglo-Americans should not assume they understand the culture of present-day Mexico merely because they interact and work with Mexican-Americans in the United States. Indeed, many Mexican-Americans who travel to Mexico find they do not fit into their "home" culture.

While both Mexico and the United States were once controlled by European powers, any historical similarities end there. America was colonized for approximately 130 years, Mexico for over 300, followed by 100 years of military dictatorships. America's immigrants came from all over Europe to join the famous "melting pot"; Mexico's immigrants came mostly from Spain, and while they intermarried with indigenous Mexicans, cultural diversity was limited. The United States is a northern European culture, and Mexico is a Latin culture. One of the few things they have in common is their border.

In the end, Anglo-Americans must not let their familiarity with Mexican-Americans fool them into thinking they know Mexico; they do not. Carlos Fuentes puts it very well: "The culture of Mexico is far more intricate and challenging to the North American mind than anything in Europe; [it is] a country at times more foreign than anything in Asia" (De Mente, 7).

41. WRITING A REPORT

MR. MARTÍNEZ:	How is the data analysis going, Sharon?
SHARON:	The analysis? Oh, I finished that last week. I'm almost done with the report now.
MR. MARTÍNEZ:	You finished the analysis last week?
SHARON:	Right. That was the deadline we agreed to.
MR. MARTÍNEZ:	But I haven't seen your analysis yet.

214

SHARON:	No. I think it makes more sense if you get the analysis and the report together. Besides, I knew you were really busy last week with those visitors from the U.K.
MR. MARTÍNEZ:	I might have had some suggestions.
SHARON:	Excellent! I can't wait to hear what they are.
MR. MARTÍNEZ:	I'm sure.

Sharon, who works for Mr. Martinez, tries to be a good employee by requiring as little oversight as possible, freeing her boss to execute the important tasks managers at his level are responsible for. That more or less summarizes the American definition of a good direct report and a good boss. Except that Mr. Martínez is Mexican and has a rather different view of what constitutes the proper role of a manager.

Hierarchy and its cousin, the exercise of power, are front and center in Mexican business culture, and they are almost unmentionables in the United States. "Mexicans have never known a world without hierarchy," Ned Crouch observes.

More than most other Latin Americans, Mexicans hold to traditional hierarchical roles based on family, education, age, and position. Because of the value placed on self-respect and its mirror image—respect for others—a hierarchical system suits them well.

We find ourselves at nearly opposite ends of the spectrum in the United States. Of all the advanced nationalities in the world, we think of ourselves as among the most egalitarian. (133)

Power in particular is strongly deemphasized in American business culture. Rosabeth Moss Kanter, one of the leading management gurus in the United States, writes, that "power is one of the last dirty words. It is easier to talk about money—and much easier to talk about sex—than it is to talk about power. People who have it deny it; people who want it do not want to appear to hunger for it; and people who engage in its machinations do so secretly" (Kanter, 135). American managers are not averse to accumulating power, but they know better than to wield it with a heavy hand.

In Dialogue 8, "Phase II," we cited Geert Hofstede's study of "power distance." In high-power-distance cultures, people are more tolerant and accepting of the unequal distribution of power; in low-power-distance cultures, people have less tolerance and managers know better than to wear their power on their sleeve. Note that in Hofstede's study, Mexico had the second-highest score out of the eleven countries in this book. Indeed, of the fifty countries and two regions surveyed by Hofstede, only four other countries had a higher score, hence a higher tolerance for power gaps. Since Hofstede considers a difference of 10 points between two countries to be significant, the 41-point gap between Mexico (81) and the United States (40) suggests trouble is brewing for Sharon and Mr. Martínez.

The power question affects the degree to which managers delegate responsibility and how much supervision they exercise. Americans like Sharon are used to hands-off managers who lay out their expectations and then get out of the way. Bosses are careful to add that their "office door is always open" in case questions come up, but the onus is on the employee to initiate any requests for additional guidance or supervision.

This is the style Sharon is accustomed to, but it doesn't work with Mr. Martínez, who only gets more and more upset with every comment Sharon makes. To begin with, he expected her to check in with him when she finished her analysis so he could review it before she started working on the report ("But I haven't seen your analysis yet"). But Sharon used her own judgment and decided it was better if Mr. Martínez saw the analysis and the report together, a decision it was not her place to make. Nor was it her place to decide that Mr. Martínez was too "busy with those visitors from the U.K." to look at the analysis. A clearly frustrated Mr. Martínez ("I might have had some suggestions") must be wondering what other management prerogatives Sharon will seize next. For her part, Sharon assumed she should take ownership of these tasks and not bother her boss, who surely has bigger things to worry about.

But ownership is not so readily ceded in Mexico, and while Mr. Martínez may in fact have bigger things to worry about, that doesn't mean he appreciates being left out of the loop. "In Mexico there is no tradition of delegation of authority," Eva Kras observes.

217

> [The] concept itself is alien to most people. The boss is an extension of the autocratic, authoritarian father image. As a result delegation of responsibility normally takes the form of assignment of specific tasks, which are carried out in constant consultation with one's superior. Most subordinates prefer this approach since it saves them from making errors and from losing face [highlighting added].
>
> The smaller firms are nearly all completely autocratic . . . [and] even in the largest companies authority is still vested in a very few at the top. One finds considerable delegation of responsibility but rarely the authority to go with it. (45)

Geoffrey Gorer, a cultural anthropologist, explains:

> *Americans [are] rarely deferential to authority figures, whether political, professional, or parental. Just as the colonists had rebelled against paternalistic Britain, and the second-generation immigrants had escaped the patriarchal culture of Europe, so all American children were taught to reject and then to surpass their fathers. The result was a permissive, freewheeling, anti-authoritarian society, egalitarian in its human relationships. . . . Even those who held power retained the common touch (Pells, 170, 171).*

The Fix

218

Americans working in a Mexican business context should be ready to tolerate closer guidance and supervision from their Mexican bosses. You should get in the habit of checking in with bosses before making most decisions, even on matters actually delegated to you. Meanwhile, do not interpret any of this, as most Americans certainly would, as a vote of no confidence in your abilities or a symptom of paranoia.

If you are an American manager in Mexico, you should not be reluctant to be more intrusive, to offer additional guidance and direction to your subordinates. If this makes you uncomfortable, you should make it very clear to Mexican subordinates that you may be checking in with them less often than they are used to but that it's perfectly acceptable, indeed it's expected, that staff can ask you for help as often as they want.

I sometimes use an alternative version of this dialogue in my workshops in which Sharon is the manager and Mr. Martínez is the employee. He doesn't quite measure up to an American manager's ideal of a take-charge direct report:

SHARON:	How is the data analysis going, Carlos?
MR. MARTÍNEZ:	It's finished, ma'am. We can start on the report anytime now.
SHARON:	Good. How long do you think it will take?
MR. MARTÍNEZ:	Ma'am?
SHARON:	To write the report.
MR. MARTÍNEZ:	I couldn't say, ma'am.
SHARON:	You don't know how long it will take?
MR. MARTÍNEZ:	When would you like it, ma'am?
SHARON:	Well, I want to give you enough time to do a good job.
MR. MARTÍNEZ:	We'll do a good job, ma'am.

219

Mexican supervisors working in the U.S. business environment should be very careful not to micromanage. If you work under Americans, however, be willing to accept responsibility and use your own judgment in matters delegated to you. American managers will not appreciate it if you constantly check in with them before making most decisions. If you are afraid of making a mistake, know that managers are typically much more forgiving of mistakes in the U.S. than in Mexico—*as long as the decision you made was in fact delegated to you*. In that case, your only mistake is being afraid to accept responsibility.

42. MY COUSIN OCTAVIO

DAVID:	Hey, Raúl. I wanted to talk to you about the problems we're having in the sourcing department.

RAÚL:	Yes. The new person you put in charge, Mary, she's very nice.
DAVID:	I know, but she's not working out too well.
RAÚL:	Maybe she doesn't know many people down here. I know someone who would be very good.
DAVID:	Really, who?
RAÚL:	He's my second cousin, Octavio.
DAVID:	Great. Does he have a background in sourcing?
RAÚL:	I'm not sure. I can ask him.

220   Unless David is very tuned in to Mexican culture, this conversation leaves him scratching his head: How could Raúl say his cousin would be "very good" at heading up the sourcing division if Raúl doesn't even know whether Octavio has a background in sourcing?

As it happens, there are two clues in this conversation, if David could see them, as well as a clue to how David created this mess in the first place through an earlier mistake. Let's begin there. It appears that David picked Mary without much consultation with his Mexican colleagues, probably assuming his selection criteria for the position—skills, education, relevant work experience—would be as valid in Mexico as in the U.S. It's also possible, of course, that he did not think about his criteria one way or the other. Either way, David has now learned that business expertise accumulated in one's own culture (e.g., what constitutes being qualified for a position) doesn't always travel well.

But maybe David was more astute and *did* consult Raúl and others before selecting Mary. In that case, Raúl probably expressed his disapproval indirectly, the way he does in the dialogue ("Mary is very nice"), and David probably misinterpreted him. The significance of "very nice" after all, is that it is a completely neutral statement, conspicuously lacking in any praise, which makes it a polite form of criticism. Raúl reports to David, after all, so he would never flatly accuse his boss of exercising poor judgment (not now and not in the previous instance either).

Which brings us to the present conversation. Raúl twice tries to establish Octavio's qualifications by citing criteria that actually mean nothing to the North American. The first criterion is that Mary "doesn't know many people down here" and, by implication, that Octavio does. In the relationship-oriented and particularist Mexican culture, a major qualification for any senior position is contacts (also called the ingroup), a robust network of family, extended family, friends of family, college classmates—all those people who owe you favors. And because you helped them last time, these are people you can turn to when the system inevitably breaks down and has to be circumvented. The leverage and influence of contacts, the power of the ingroup—the essence of a particularist culture—is indispensable in Mexico precisely because the system cannot be relied upon to be impartial. When the bureaucracy is unresponsive, when regulations are applied inconsistently, when the need for permits impede even incremental progress, and when personal preferences—and personal animosities—count for more than following the rules, your only hope is the people you know. Over time, Mary might be able to build her own ingroup, but she didn't arrive with one, and that appears to have been a major handicap.

The other indispensable qualification Octavio possesses is his blood; he's part of Raúl's family. That doesn't make him an expert in sourcing, of course, but it is critical for another reason: His deep concern for the well-being and reputation of the family all but guarantees that he will do his utmost to acquit himself admirably—or risk incurring the wrath of Raúl and company. And because Raúl is well aware of this, he does not hesitate to

221

recommend his cousin. Moreover, Raúl will make it his business to closely monitor Octavio's performance to make sure he is working out. That much, at least, he owes to David. "In all Mexican businesses," Eva Kras writes,

> *from the largest to the smallest, hiring practices strongly favor relatives and friends of employees and avoid, as far as possible, unknown or unrecommended persons. . . . Few higher-level executive positions are filled without some personal knowledge of the candidate, even though a few executive placement agencies now operate. But it is to be remembered that trustworthiness, loyalty, and reliability are of paramount importance to employers, causing them to continue to rely on family . . . ties (50).*

That's all well and good—we can accept that contacts are invaluable—but *somebody* has to know about sourcing and actually do the job! True enough, but that doesn't have to be Octavio, at least not right away. Octavio is going to be the head of the division, not one of the worker bees, and while he will have to educate himself about sourcing in general, he can rely on staff for the particulars. For their part, moreover, staff will be extremely pleased to have someone of Octavio's caliber as their leader, someone from a well-connected family with the status and influence to make things happen—to open doors, get around bureaucratic obstacles, have his phone calls returned, get on people's calendars, and schedule important meetings. These are the "qualifications" that matter at Octavio's level.

David misses this because most Americans don't think in terms of contacts and connections, of leveraging one's ingroup; indeed, they don't even use the ingroup/outgroup terminology. The United States is a universalist culture, where everyone is treated the same, no matter who they are or who they know (those contacts, again). Indeed, because universalist systems are designed to be inherently fair and impartial, it *doesn't matter* who you are or who you know: the system works the same for everyone and should never need to be circumvented.

Mexico is also a collectivist culture, meaning Mexicans derive much of their identity and sense of well-being from the group, especially the family and extended family (the ingroup). But for collectives to work, the individual members must uphold the reputation of the group in all their actions. Raúl has such confidence in Octavio because he knows his cousin will discharge his duties to the best of his abilities, thereby protecting the family honor. In a more individualist culture like the U.S., the family does not exert nearly as much influence on the behavior of its members; hence, there is no special advantage in hiring a relative. Indeed, in many universalist cultures, there are strict regulations against hiring relatives, as giving preferential treatment to certain people undermines the core universalist principle of treating everyone the same.

223

The Fix

Americans making hiring decisions in a Mexican business context should be wary of hiring strangers and of selections based solely on North American criteria. Skills, experience, and education do not have to be thrown out the window, but you should weigh them along with considerations like family background, class, and what social networks the person can bring to the enterprise. If Mexican hiring decisions perplex you, if they hire people you think are "unqualified," remember that their concept of qualifications is probably broader than yours.

Mexicans working in an American environment should accept that good connections, family background, and social refinements carry little weight in the U.S. business environment, except perhaps at the highest levels. Americans are most interested in education (level and type), professional expertise, and work history.

43. WHY NOT?

CHARLES: So, Carmen. What do you think? Can your team take on that work?

CARMEN: Yes. Why not?

CHARLES: That's great. How long do you think it will take?

CARMEN: It might be a week.

CHARLES: A week? I was thinking three days at the most.

CARMEN: Of course. We haven't done anything exactly like that before. But Carlos' team has, so we can consult with them.

CHARLES: I don't know, Carmen. They're pretty busy on a rush job I asked them to do.

CARMEN: Of course.

CHARLES: So what do you say, Carmen?

This dialogue was inspired by an excellent piece of advice courtesy of Ned Crouch's *Mexicans and Americans: Cracking the Cultural Code*: "Never believe the first answer you get in Mexico" (3). This advice applies whether the first answer is "yes," as it is here, or whether it is "no" (although in Mexico, hearing "yes" is much more common). And while we are quoting Crouch, here is a very useful companion observation: "Of all the people in the world, only the Americans are so sure there is a clear distinction between *yes* and *no*" (xvii).

Carmen gave Charles several clues that her team was not right for this assignment, beginning with "Yes. Why not?" While "yes" could be interpreted as a positive response, the "Why not?" is troubling. At the very least, it introduces a note of ambivalence into Carmen's response, and in Mexico an ambivalent "yes" is very often as good as a "no." If Charles were a Mexican supervisor, in short, he would immediately start looking around for another team. The next hint is when Carmen says it could take her a week to do the job in question, and Charles ("I was thinking three days at the most") implies that this is not a week's worth of work. Carmen is well aware of this, which means that her deliberately unreasonable estimate is a way of telling Charles to look somewhere else.

If there is any doubt about Carmen's position, it disappears with her next remarks: "We haven't done anything exactly like that before. But Carlos' team has, so we can consult with them." If her team is so inexperienced that it needs help, her "yes" at the beginning of this exchange cannot have been anything but pure politeness. Charles, who is somehow still a believer, observes that Carlos is not in a position to help her. Carmen's "Of course" confirms the obvious: she can't do this without help; no help is available; Charles needs to ask someone else. When Charles responds with "So what do you say?" Carmen (and we hope the reader, too) must be completely puzzled.

While we have already encountered the "yes" phenomenon several times in these pages, it is such a common element in U.S.-Mexican relations, especially in manager-subordinate interactions, that it demands yet another airing in this chapter. Let's listen to more from Ned Crouch:

The confusion arises innocently enough out of a simple desire to please. Mexicans say yes or no because you say yes or no. "It will rain today, won't it?" Yes. "It won't rain today, will it?" No.

Infusing the world with sunshine, the Mexicans are exceedingly polite—polite as in agreeable, agreeable as in telling you what you want to hear. Whether you're dealing with a baker in Guadalajara, a roofing contractor in Michigan, a supplier in Monterrey, or a government official in Mexico City, ask a direct question and you'll rarely get no for an answer. Why? Because Mexicans are never overtly contentious. Because no would be uncooperative, even offensive. So to avoid no, most Mexicans will naturally answer yes. But don't take yes for an answer. (3)

226

Americans are not always comfortable saying no either, but they hardly ever say yes when they mean no. Instead of a direct no, they might give a conditional or qualified answer, such as "maybe," "perhaps," or "possibly." Disagreement and refusal are more acceptable in America than they are in Mexico, probably because the imperative to be polite is weaker in egalitarian cultures. Where people are acutely attuned to differences in rank and status, the need for sensitivity dictates a more nuanced (Americans would say confusing) communication style.

The Fix

Americans working in a Mexican context should listen for the absence of "yes" rather than the presence of "no." Since Mexican subordinates are usually reluctant to refuse requests outright, make your needs known without asking direct questions. Charles might have "asked" for Carmen's help by saying, "I was wondering, Carmen, if there is a team that is not too busy right now." Carmen would immediately understand Charles was asking for assistance and would offer to help on the spot if her team was free.

In dealing with Americans, Mexicans should not be so polite as to mislead, remembering that very often what sounds direct in your culture, especially from a subordinate to a manager, might not register at all with an American. Similarly, what you might think of as blunt or rude usually comes across to Americans as direct and nothing more. Rest assured that very few Americans ever accuse Mexicans of being rude, although the reverse is not always true.

44. UNHAPPY IN BOSTON

MIGUEL:	Hi, Al. I was just showing my team how to package the shipments more carefully.
AL:	Hey, Miguel. That's why I'm here, actually, to talk about that. I just got a call from Boston, and they're not very happy.
MIGUEL:	Sure. Just let me finish. Why don't you wait for me in my office?
AL:	Actually, it would probably help me to hear how you're doing this, if you don't mind.
MIGUEL:	It may take a little while.
AL:	No problem. I've got plenty of time.

Mexicans are a very proud people. "The first thing foreigners in Mexico . . . should know about Mexicans," Boyé De Mente writes, "is that their behavior, both private and official, is generally controlled by their code of *personalismo* [which] embodies the Mexican belief that personal dignity . . . takes precedence over all other considerations, including the ethical and the moral" (268).

Part of the fallout from *personalismo* is that in workplace and business contexts you must be very careful when delivering negative feedback. "Constructive criticism" is a complete oxymoron in any face-saving culture like Mexico, and *personalismo* leaves Mexicans especially vulnerable to embarrassment and humiliation. "Mexicans must exercise extraordinary care not to damage the dignity of others," De Mente continues, "something that can be done very easily by such things as failing to address them properly, by a remark that can be taken as a criticism, [or] by an action that can be taken as a slight" (268, 119).

Al embarrasses Miguel mightily—not to mention gratuitously—when he tells him in front of his team that people in Boston are unhappy. (Boston is presumably the headquarters of the company Miguel and Al work for here in Mexico.) That kind of criticism is never conveyed publicly in Mexico if there's any way to avoid it. What makes Al's remark gratuitous is that Miguel is in fact in the midst of correcting the problem: "I was just showing my team how to package the shipments *more carefully*." "More carefully" because he knows Boston isn't happy, and he's working on it. Indeed, as soon as Miguel sees Al approaching, he knows why, and, afraid that Al is about to blurt out something inappropriate, he tries to signal him that everything is under control ("I was just showing my team") before Al embarrasses everyone.

Al misses all this, but he should pick up on Miguel's next clue: the suggestion to move the conversation to his office. Al is having none of it, and moreover he seems determined to cause Miguel further embarrassment by insisting he observe as the team is taught how to do the job. The message here (from Miguel's perspective) can only be that Al doesn't trust Miguel to get it right and wants to correct any mistakes he might make.

Miguel's humiliation is more or less complete, but he makes one last attempt to limit the damage from Al by pointing out that the training "may take a little while." Al should come back later or at least make himself comfortable, maybe by sitting down and relaxing in Miguel's office. But Al is one very determined guy ("No problem. I've got plenty of time"). If we were to confront Al later about this exchange, he would probably say he was only "doing my job"—and so he was, even from Miguel's point of view. But it's *the way* Al does his job that is the problem.

People in all cultures have pride, of course, not just Mexicans—Americans can feel humiliated, too—but the degree of personal sensitivity varies greatly across cultures. Generally, people in family- and group-oriented cultures are more susceptible to taking offense, as they must worry about saving face and protecting the group. "Mexicans . . . are highly sensitive to criticism," Eva Kras writes,

> *because of a deep emotional response to everything that affects them personally (this includes criticism of their work, which is taken as personal). . . . Because of this sensitivity, non-Mexicans often consider Mexicans "thin-skinned" or victims of an inferiority complex. Such an interpretation, however, misses the importance of saving face in a close-knit society where one's standing with friends and colleagues is at stake. As one Mexican executive told [me], "You cannot criticize a Mexican in front of his friends. It is a disgrace, and he will hate you for the rest of his life." (31)*

This preoccupation with dignity also leads to *adulacion*, excessive flattery. It stands to reason that if people are wary of slights, it can't hurt to spread around the praise. It is "characteristic of Mexicans," De Mente observes, "to avoid criticizing and correcting others and to flatter and praise them no matter how incompetent and unproductive they might be, all in the interest of harmony" (34).

The imperative of saving face helps to explain Mexican sensitivity, but there is also a historical component. For centuries, the indigenous inhabitants were ruled and exploited by a political and religious elite that treated them, in the words of one Mexico-watcher,

> *with a combination of contempt, physical and mental abuse and outright cruelty. Both the government and the Church followed policies of denigrating the worth of the mixed-bloods and the Indians, literally brainwashing them into having low opinions of themselves. . . .*
>
> *In this environment it was impossible for the mixed-bloods and Indians to develop normal racial and cultural orgullo "pride." There was no way they could take pride for what they were because there was no foundation for any pride; no personal accomplishments; no great heroes who had succeeded in improving their lot; no grand dreams. The only pride they were capable of developing and expressing was personal. (De Mente, 256, 257)*

Once again we hasten to point out that Al doesn't have to have been aware of any of the above to have avoided his complete mishandling of the exchange with Miguel. He simply needed to listen more closely, to listen *differently*, to what Miguel was saying. As usual, the clues are all there.

The Fix

There is very little feedback, other than unmitigated praise, that should be given in public in Mexico. Feedback that American managers consider neutral—suggestions, subtle hints, even very mild praise (conspicuous for not being more substantial)—can easily be felt as slights by Mexican subordinates. If you have any fears of being misinterpreted, hold your observations for later.

Also remember that Mexicans will not give negative feedback in public, so no matter what they say or how they respond to something you say in the presence of others, always wait to see if they have anything to add later when they can talk to you one-on-one.

Mexicans in the U.S. must accept that Americans often give public feedback that, while humiliating and embarrassing in the Mexican workplace, is neither intended nor interpreted that way in American culture. Other Americans would not think worse of you if you were criticized in front of them. You should also feel free to give "constructive criticism" to Americans in public, provided the issue is not too serious.

45. REPLACING ENRIQUE

ROSITA: Now that Enrique has left the company, are you thinking about who will replace him as our team leader?

DIANE: I was thinking of Juan. He's a real self-starter.

ROSITA: The young guy who started last year?

DIANE: Yes. He's quite independent and thinks for himself.

ROSITA: He's very intelligent for his age. At our team meetings, he was always telling Enrique how he could do things differently, little improvements he could make in how we work.

DIANE: I know. He's not afraid to speak up.

ROSITA: Even with you. We all saw that at the meeting last week. He was your choice, we heard.

DIANE: Well, not exactly, but I did recommend him to Enrique.

ROSITA: That's what Enrique said. How did you know him?

DIANE: I first met him at the plant in Sonora before I was transferred here. High-potential new hires were paired with a senior manager. So I mentored him for a few weeks.

ROSITA: I see.

If dialogues can sink under the weight of cultural misunderstandings, this one is falling fast to the ocean floor. Where to begin? The first and most serious mistake Diane appears to have made was not consulting the team about this important decision. Rosita approaches Diane here—not the other way around, as it should have happened—to bring up the subject of Enrique's replacement and to let her know the team's suggestions. Much to Rosita's surprise, Diane already has a candidate and even makes the mistake of naming him, thereby strongly suggesting (to Rosita et al) that her mind is made up. Under the circumstances, the team would feel uncomfortable challenging Diane (as they would see it) by suggesting someone else. While selecting the team leader is certainly Diane's prerogative, especially in authoritarian Mexico, even top-down Mexican managers would never make such a decision without consultation. The fact that Diane neglects to do this is a considerable affront to the team.

But it gets much worse. Diane's candidate is a "self-starter," a dubious distinction in Mexico's team-oriented work culture. We learn that Juan is "young" and apparently started less than a year ago, two criteria that would make him a most unusual choice for team leader. Rosita has to be wondering what Diane sees in this guy that compensates for his youth and inexperience.

What she gets is that "he's quite independent and thinks for himself." These qualities might impress in the United States, but not in Mexican business culture. "Mexicans are strikingly group-oriented," Ned Crouch writes, "working easily together as a team. They don't break out of the pack . . . if it would upset the harmony of their household, their church, or their workplace" (92). Job number one in such a work environment is fitting in; independents and mavericks need not apply.

Rosita makes a sly reference to Juan's youth ("He's very intelligent for his age") and presents yet another reason Juan will never do: he has shown remarkable disrespect toward Enrique by criticizing him in front of his team. "He was always telling Enrique how he could do things differently, little improvements he could make in how we work." Next we learn that not only did he go up against Enrique, he also challenged Diane herself in front of the entire team. And finally, we learn perhaps the most damning thing of all: Enrique didn't want Juan on his team but was pressured into taking him by Diane ("He was your choice, we heard"). Diane would no doubt object—she only recommended Juan, she points out—but in the hierarchical Mexican management culture, if your boss makes a recommendation, you know what to do with it.

The dialogue concludes with a bombshell which explains everything that has gone on—and gone *wrong*—in this sorry episode. We learn that Juan was a protégé of Diane in her previous position where she mentored him for several weeks. We can't know for sure, but if Juan is young now, he was even younger when he started working in Sonora—meaning that in one of his first jobs he was coached by an American. No wonder he is so independent, freethinking, and outspoken—all qualities much admired in the American workplace. If Juan's colleagues in Sonora saw him as Diane's protégé, it's quite possible that none of them was willing to call him out on his inappropriate

233

behavior, and he thus managed against all odds to survive acting like an American in a Mexican workplace. Indeed, when Diane approached her former colleagues in Sonora about transferring Juan to her new location, they were probably very glad to get rid of him.

And now at last we understand why Enrique "has left the company," a most unusual move for a high-status Mexican team leader. By and large, Mexicans are loyal to their employers, and employers return the favor. The typical Mexican manager would think long and hard about leaving his company (although professional mobility is now becoming more common). Enrique would need a very good reason, and as it happens, he had one: Juan. Or, to be more precise, Diane's sponsorship of Juan. She went over Enrique's head to pick him in the first place, and then did nothing when Juan showed disrespect for Enrique. The message to Enrique was clear: my boss doesn't trust me to hire good personnel and thinks so little of me she lets this know-it-all embarrass me in front of my staff. It is a completely untenable position for Enrique, whose dignity and pride have been utterly undermined. For him to keep on working in such circumstances would be deeply humiliating. Enrique got the message—and has moved on.

Diane, an individualist, admires individualist qualities in others, and Juan, as it happens, has rather a lot of them: he's a self-starter and independent, thinks for himself, is not afraid to speak up, and challenges his superiors. Juan's only real problem is he's working in the wrong country. "Mexican factory and office workers assume that working together is the ideal," Ned Crouch writes. "[They] work better in solidarity with others, valuing loyalty to the group above individual effort. . . . A group-oriented workforce values group-harmony above all. In [this] environment, individual effort and self-starting are met with suspicion" (92, 94). And as for Juan's tendency to suggest improvements to his superiors—well, Juan should read Eva Kras: "Mexicans . . . are accustomed to giving only positive feedback to their superiors," she writes, "and to expressing only views which coincide with theirs. Mexican executives would consider it disrespectful of a subordinate to contradict them" (65). Let's give Ned Crouch the last word: "If you placed countries around the world on a scale of individual- versus group-oriented work styles, Mexicans and Americans would fall at the opposite ends of the continuum" (93). If it is surprising that Juan has survived this long in the Mexican workplace, it beggars belief that he might end up as team leader.

Since we're talking about teams in this dialogue, this might be a good place to address a seeming contradiction: If Americans are so individualistic, why is there so much emphasis in U.S. business culture on teamwork, a nonstop drumbeat of messaging about how critical it is to be a good team player? The short answer is that Americans have to talk incessantly about teams and conduct endless team-building workshops because they're just not any good at teamwork. Fons Trompenaars asked respondents in twelve countries which type of job they preferred:

A. Jobs in which no one is singled out for personal honor but in which everyone works together.

B. Jobs in which personal initiatives are encouraged and individual initiatives are achieved.

Fully 97 percent of Americans picked B. In Geert Hofstede's cultural study, Americans scored the highest on the individualism dimension of all fifty countries and two regions in the survey. Here are the rankings, from most to least individualist, for the cultures covered in this book. (Note that Mexico is second from the bottom.) The scores ranged from 91 to 11:

U.S.	91	India	48
England	89	Arab World	38
France	71	Brazil	38
Germany	67	Mexico	30
India	48	China	15
Japan	46		

Americans may be bad at teamwork, but they know it's important, so in recent years they have embarked on something of a cultural crash course. In other words, the emphasis on teams in the U.S. at the present time is largely aspirational. In this context, consider how the Japanese, who excel at teamwork, rarely talk about it. Why would they? It comes so naturally to them, instilled and internalized as early as their kindergarten years, that it's not something they would ever notice. People don't talk about things they're unaware of. Maybe one day Americans will be good team players, but for now it's a work in progress.

The Fix

Americans need to be sensitive to the importance of the team or work group in Mexico. You should always consult with the team before making important decisions, even though Mexican work groups readily defer to their managers. They defer out of politeness and respect for the hierarchy, but not because they think you have all the answers or because they don't expect to be consulted. And you need to understand that individuals who do not fit in, who are not willing to subsume personal goals for the greater good of the group, will disturb the harmony of the team in Mexico and could seriously undermine productivity.

Mexicans who want to succeed in the American workplace should try to emulate Juan. While good team players are appreciated, you will also be rewarded for being independent and the ability to work well on your own. You will find your American colleagues much better at competing than at cooperating. They will talk at great length about teamwork, of course, but don't expect to find it in their behavior.

10

Russia

> There are two ways you can tell when a man is lying. One
> is when he says he can drink champagne all night and
> not get drunk. The other is when he says he understands
> Russians.
>
> —Charles Bohlen

The consensus seems to be that Russians are impenetrable. Even
Winston Churchill famously gave up. "I cannot forecast to you
the action of Russia," he declared in an October 1939 radio broad-
cast to his nation. "It is a riddle wrapped in a mystery inside an
enigma." It doesn't help that nearly all those who write about
Russia almost always start with the subject of *dusha*, the Russian
soul, but souls, needless to say, are not easy to fathom. Even
Russians admit they do not really know themselves that well.
As the Grand Duke Aleksandr Mihailovich himself said, "I have
never met anyone who understood Russians."

Perhaps the failure to penetrate the Russian character can be
explained by the fact that Westerners look at Russia through a
Western lens, while Russia is not quite a Western nation. Only a

third of Russia, that part west of the Urals, is in Europe, and for much of its history Russia either faced east, to Constantinople, or simply gazed inward. It has only been since the reign of Peter the Great (1682–1721) that Russia has actively engaged with the West. To put that into perspective, the Mongols (called Tatars by the Russians) ruled much of the country for close to 250 years (1234–1480), roughly the same amount of time Russia has been facing west. "While the Mongol conquest did not make Asians of the Russians," Yale Richmond writes, "it did delay their becoming Europeans" (6).

Meanwhile, the central role of the Eastern Orthodox Church in the lives of ordinary Russians has left its mark on the collective psyche. Despite almost five decades of Communist suppression, many Russians have an abiding belief in the supernatural and an inclination toward mysticism, two characteristics most Westerners cannot relate to. In the end, if we in the West cannot understand Russians, if they regularly fail to behave rationally in our eyes, it's probably because they follow the dictates of a decidedly non-Western rationale.

Some Russians, anyway. But there are in fact two cultural strains to the Russian character—Slavophile and Western—and it would be wise to remember that when conducting business. "Russians with Western thought," Goehner and Richmond write,

> sought to borrow from the West in order to modernize. They were open to the Western enlightenment, rationalism, and political thought that came along with the technology. Russian Slavophiles also sought to borrow from the West but were determined, at the same time, to protect and preserve Russia's unique cultural values and traditions. The West has been seen as spiritually impoverished and decadent, Russia as morally rich and virtuous. (Goehner)

And finally there are the New Russians. Not much different from gung-ho businesspeople the world over, they are mostly concerned with making money and getting ahead—agents and exemplars of Russia's profound economic, social, and cultural change. But as former U.S. ambassador George Kennan reminds us, "Whatever happens and whatever restructuring of the Soviet society [occurs], Russia is and is going to remain a country very different from our own. We should not look for this difference to be overcome in any short space of time" (Goehner, Epilogue).

46. *DUSHA*: THE RUSSIAN SOUL

PHILIP: How do you think I did in the meeting?

ANDREI: You kept your cool. Is that the American expression? And you were very logical.

PHILIP: Thank you. I think the facts really do tell this story. I really didn't need to put myself into the presentation.

ANDREI: You had very strong data. Russians sometimes get emotional.

PHILIP: I know.

ANDREI: We like you to see a little piece of our soul.

"Russians prize the quality of soul above all others," Elisabeth Roberts observes. "They have a tendency to open their soul to complete strangers, telling everything about themselves" (10). Two other observers, Tomalin and Nicks, offer related advice: "If you're going to be dealing with Russia, you'd better first consider the great topic of the Russian soul. Note that we said consider and not understand, because even the Russians and some of their greatest writers continually debate the subject" (208). Part of the mystery about who the Russians are surely must stem from their deep romanticism, a strain of antirationalism in an otherwise down-to-earth and pragmatic people. Whatever the explanation, the logic of the heart often prevails over the logic of the head in interactions with Russians.

Russians like to "connect" with their business partners, and such a connection is impossible without at least a brief glimpse into the other's soul. The idea seems to be that once I have seen your soul, I know I can trust you. A "standard Russian complaint against Americans," Eliza Klose observes, "is that they lack *dusha* or soul" (Richmond, 164).

It's pretty clear that buttoned-up Philip revealed little of his soul during his presentation, which must have dismayed the Russian audience. Andrei tries to tell him this, politely, but Philip misses all the clues. The fact that Philip kept his cool—in a culture where trustworthy people "sometimes get a bit emotional"—suggests he should probably have let his hair down and displayed some feelings. "You can feel free to inject some emotion into your proposals," Tomalin and Nicks advise (212).

Andrei's observation that Philip was "very logical" makes a related point: Russians, especially the more traditional Slavophiles, are somewhat dubious of logic and regard feelings as more revealing and truthful. Furthermore, if Philip thinks "the facts really do tell the story," he's wrong again. Facts are cold, objective, devoid of passion; Russians are warm (in private), sentimental, and very passionate. "Logical categories are inapplicable to the soul," Tatyana Tolstaya observes. "In Russian culture emotion is assigned an entirely positive value, the more a person expresses his emotions, the better, more sincere, the more 'open' he is" (Richmond, 49).

And when Philip says there was no need to put himself into his presentation, he could not be more wrong; his Russian audience was waiting for exactly that, for a glimpse of the person behind all the data, someone they could connect with. "Russian business depends on good relationships," Tomalin and Nicks write. "Proceedings usually start formally but the business will only develop if good, informal relations are created" (210). Richmond writes "of the importance of the personal factor when doing business in Russia, where people are often more important than machines or technology. For an agreement to be truly successful, there should be a personal relationship between an American on one side and a Russian on the other" (164).

Russians are not irrational, but to them a purely rational appeal feels like it's missing something. They appreciate facts and data, but they also want to see the emotion. "Russians do have a rich spirituality," Yale Richmond writes,

> that does indeed contrast with Western rationalism, materialism, and pragmatism. . . . The rational and pragmatic approach does not always work for them. More often it is personal relations, feelings, and traditional values that determine a course of action. Westerners are more likely to depend on the cold facts and to do what works. (48, 49)

If you trust Russians with your feelings and give them a window into your private self, then they will trust you with their soul. And business will prosper.

The Americans have a much more clear-eyed, unsentimental, and "no-nonsense" approach to business. They feel no need to connect, be best friends, or even like each other to do deals—and they certainly don't have to be soul mates. Indeed, Americans believe that personal feelings might cloud their business judgment. They will take a "hard look" at the terms of a deal, giving them as unbiased and objective an evaluation as possible, and all other considerations are regarded as peripheral and secondary. Over time they may develop personal relationships with business partners or associates, but it is not usually a condition of doing business. If the terms are good, where do I sign? And as for the soul: Where's the proof?

The Fix

Americans might want to put a bit more of themselves into business presentations to Russians. And even if you think emotions have no place in business, you could at least let your hair down now and then in social situations. "Human feelings count for much in Russia," Richmond writes, "and those who do not share the depth of their feelings will be considered cold and distant. When Russians open their souls to someone, it is a sign of acceptance and sharing. Westerners will have to learn to drop their stiff upper lips and also open their souls" (47). If Russians put too much feeling into a pitch to Americans, do not consider them naïve or unprofessional; they're just reaching out and trying to connect.

244

For their part, Russians should not interpret American preoccupation with the terms to mean they don't want to know you or have anything other than a business relationship; it's just that Americans usually keep business and personal relationships separate. There will be time to get to know one another after the meetings. Meanwhile, make your proposals as detailed as possible; Americans will decide almost entirely on the basis of the terms of the deal, not personal feelings.

47. ANYTHING CAN HAPPEN

GEORGE: Hi, Vlad. How is everything going on those beta tests?

VLADIMIR:	We're working hard, George.
GEORGE:	Do you think we can announce the official release of the software for the third quarter, then?
VLADIMIR:	That's hard to say.
GEORGE:	Is there a problem?
VLADIMIR:	There can always be problems.
GEORGE:	I mean, anything you see now that would stop us?
VLADIMIR:	Maybe not right now, but that's still three months away. Anything can happen.
GEORGE:	So you think we should wait?
VLADIMIR:	I didn't say that.

If Americans are culturally ill equipped to deal with realists, as we saw in Dialogue 21, "Gloom," then what chance do they have working with pessimists? Indeed, if realists already come across to Americans as negative, then true pessimism must be utterly confounding.

From an American perspective, Vlad is a very negative guy. With the possible exception of his first comment ("We're working hard, George"), nothing Vlad says is the least bit reassuring: He's unwilling to commit to a deadline ("That's hard to say"); he insists on the likelihood of problems ("There can always be problems"); and he's more or less waiting for the other shoe to drop ("Anything can happen"). This is one troubled guy, not at all sure about the time line and clearly unwilling to commit. It *is* odd, though, that he apparently thinks there's no reason George should wait to announce the release ("I didn't say that"). If he didn't say that, what *did* he say?

But what if George were a Russian, a confirmed realist with an inclination toward pessimism? What would he hear in Vlad's comments? Let's take them one by one:

We're working hard, George.	From a Russian perspective, this is extremely encouraging. If a project were in trouble, no Russian would ever say something as neutral as "We're working hard."
That's hard to say.	Again, things are looking good. If Vlad thought it was a bad idea to announce the release, he would be much more unequivocal. "That's hard to say" is practically a green light.
There can always be problems.	Another very good sign. Vlad doesn't say there *are* problems, which he would have no hesitation whatsoever to announce. So he's merely being philosophical here.
Anything can happen.	Indeed, anything can always happen. This is just Vlad's Russian conservatism—and perhaps Vlad's way of covering himself just in case he's wrong.

Reading the exchange this way, Vlad actually feels quite good about the project and sees no reason not to announce the release. No wonder, then, that when George expresses anxiety ("So you think we should wait?"), Vlad is surprised ("I didn't say that").

Russians come by their pessimism as honestly as Americans come by their optimism. The place to start any discussion of the Russian psyche is with geography (just as it is, by the way, with the American psyche). "All civilizations are to some extent the product of geographical factors," George Vernadsky writes, "but history provides no clearer example of the profound influence of geography on a culture than in the [story] . . . of the Russian people" (Richmond, 5). And the aspect of geography that nearly all observers mention is the fact that most of Russia lies above the forty-fifth parallel, the same latitude as much of the U.S.-Canadian border. Russia's southernmost port, Novorossiysk on the Black Sea, is at the same latitude as Minneapolis, one of the two northernmost major cities in America. Moscow is at the same latitude as Hudson's Bay in Canada's far north. It's a cold, wind-swept, inhospitable environment two-thirds of the year, with a growing season of only five months. Life is not easy; Russians don't expect it to be easy; and if it should unaccountably *become* easy now and then, they know better than to get used to it. "The aim of civilization in the North is serious," the Marquis de Custine writes in *Empire of the Czar*. "There, society is the fruit not of human pleasures, not of interests and passions easily satisfied, but of a will ever persistent and *ever thwarted* which urges the people to incomprehensible effort" (italics added, Richmond, 8).

247

If that's not enough to incline sensible people toward pessimism, then consider the lot of the common man and woman throughout most of Russian history. If you were not actually owned by someone else, as millions of serfs were, your survival and well-being were almost entirely dependent on the all-powerful, land-owning noble class. When their interests coincided with yours, life might just be bearable; when they did not, you were the ones who made the sacrifices. Is it any wonder the long-suffering Russian peasant learned to be stoic and realistic? A famous Russian joke describes the difference between pessimists and optimists: A pessimist says, "Things can't be worse than they are now"; an optimist says, "Yes they can."

"Russian pessimism contrasts with American innocence and optimism," Yale Richmond writes. "Americans expect things to go well and become annoyed when they do not. Russians expect things to go poorly and have learned to live with misfortune" (42). The American national experience, hence the national outlook, contrasts vividly with that of Russia. During its admittedly short history, the United States has known few wars on its own soil, suffered only modestly from class struggles, and experienced no major plagues (though smallpox decimated several Native American tribes). On the other hand, the country is blessed with land that is both rich and abundant. Under the circumstances, to be optimistic is simply a matter of believing in your own national experience.

The so-called "immigrant mentality" is no doubt another factor underlying the positive American outlook. Immigrants are people who have decided not to accept life as they find it but to make their lives into something else. They are, accordingly, hopeful people who believe completely in themselves. It takes this kind of faith, after all, to leave behind all that is safe and familiar and cast off for alien shores. Scratch the surface of an immigrant, and you will find a person who has decided to create his own future.

The Fix

Americans must begin by acknowledging their optimism. You really do look at things as better than they are. There's nothing wrong with that, of course—it can be a great strength—but it does rub realists the wrong way. It makes Americans come off as naïve and unreliable; if you can't see things the way they are, then you may be caught unaware, not take necessary precautions, not have a plan for when things take longer than you expected, cost more than you estimated, or run into obstacles you minimized. With Russians, then, it's best to keep your optimism under wraps; you can still *be* positive on the inside, but you don't have to show it. Meanwhile, you can cheerfully acknowledge all the concerns, fears, and misgivings the Russians have, lending them credence and thus coming across as much more realistic.

Then by all means present your counterarguments. Russians *will* listen to you; they just need to know that you have both feet on the ground.

For their part, Russians should be careful not to come across as reflexively pessimistic because it's always safer to assume the worst. Assuming the worst is as annoying to Americans as their knee-jerk optimism is to you. Where you have legitimate concerns, by all means explain your position, but where things look good, admit as much. Just as you are more likely to listen to Americans if they have shown they can be realistic, Americans are more likely to listen if you have demonstrated you can be positive when that's justified. Remember also that Americans are more comfortable taking risks and even with failing than Russians are. Another reason for their optimism, then, is because they know they can handle whatever happens, including worst-case scenarios.

48. SIX MONTHS

DEBBIE:	Our shipping system has become quite inefficient.
NATASHA:	It has been in place for a long time.
DEBBIE:	I know. Headquarters is using a new system, just six months old. We could try it.
NATASHA:	Only six months?
DEBBIE:	Yes, it's brand new.
NATASHA:	So they're still learning about it?
DEBBIE:	I guess so.
NATASHA:	Has it been tried in the field?
DEBBIE:	I don't think so. We could be the first.
NATASHA:	Yes.

Americans and Russians have a very different relationship to what is new: Americans embrace it, while Russians are instinctively suspicious. If you're going to push something new on the Russians, you have to make the case for why they should adopt it, and the fact that something is new is not the case. Indeed, new is the case *against* it, which is precisely the sentiment behind each of Natasha's remarks in "Six Months."

When she observes that the shipping system "has been in place for a long time," Natasha is not implying, as Debbie thinks, that the system should be scrapped; she's saying, rather, that you don't abandon something tried and true, something that has endured for decades, just because of a handful of recent inefficiencies. When Debbie brings up the new system being used at headquarters, Natasha is immediately anxious; "new" means untested, hence risky and potentially unreliable. When Natasha hears the new system is only six months old, her worst fears are confirmed: "So they're still learning about it," meaning no one really knows if the new system works.

Against all her instincts, Natasha does try to be positive ("Has it been tried in the field?"). She's willing to consider this system if there's any evidence that it works anywhere else besides headquarters. When Debbie says no, Natasha probably assumes that now even Debbie might rethink this idea. But Debbie is undaunted: "We could be the first." No doubt, Natasha says to herself, the first in the field to fail.

America's love affair with the new was originally born of necessity. It was called the New World for a reason—because it was nothing like the Old World the immigrants came from. That was a world of cities and towns, roads and canals, institutions, universities, and culture—all the trappings of a developed, mature, centuries-old civilization. And America? America was a nearly pristine wilderness untouched by any trace of modernity. Among other things, nothing in the everyday experience of the early settlers would be of any use to them in their daily life in the New World. The skills they needed to survive were skills they did not have; the tasks they needed to complete were tasks they had never done before. To survive was to innovate.

The New World, Howard Jones writes, "was so incredibly filled with unpredictabilities, one wonders how the Europeans survived" (391). In the same vein, John McElroy observes that

> *[t]o understand American culture, one must always bear in mind that it developed from the situation of civilized men and women living in a Stone Age wilderness. Almost nothing in the cultural memory of the initial European settlers on the Atlantic coastal plain of North America prepared them for living in such a place. (17)*

251

Small wonder that experimenting, trying new things, and taking chances are all part of the American cultural DNA. Nor is it any wonder that tradition—the way we've always done things—was one of the first casualties of the American experience. Even today, Americans are always tinkering with successful, established products and practices to try to improve them. Americans don't fear the new; they fear being stuck in the past.

Now consider the lot of the Russian masses for most of that country's history, peasants and serfs eking out a subsistence living—when times were good—on the edge of the frozen north. Subsistence agriculture does not breed risk takers; if the risk does not pay off, people starve and die. And by definition, the new and the unknown are shot through with risk. "The harsh climate . . . explains the strength of Russians," Richmond writes,

> *their ability to endure extreme hardship, and their bleak outlook on life as well as their patience and submission. Climate has also made them cautious. In Russia's farmlands weather*

is often unpredictable and crop failure an ever-present possibility. In an agricultural society where survival depends on the weather, it is imprudent to take chances. And as in all traditional societies, the test of time is preferred to the risks of the new and untried.

The New World is indeed new, only some four hundred years old, compared with Russia's more than one thousand. Russians, moreover, have been living in their native environment from time immemorial and change has come slowly. The new has been welcomed in America, the old has been revered in Russia. (9, 14)

Another reason Russian commoners never trusted innovation is that more often than not it came from the top, and those at the top did not always have the interests of the peasants at heart. Indeed, in most cases the ruling class was neither aware of nor worried about the interests of the ruled. Moreover, the peasants knew from generations of experience that if the innovations failed, it would not be their rulers who bore the consequences.

The Fix

Americans who want Russians to try something new must make a strong case for it, which boils down to minimizing any risks. If you can find any data showing how this innovation succeeded elsewhere, that's a good start. Another good strategy is to give Russians more lead time to get used to the idea of change; if Americans would need two months' advance notice, give the Russians four.

Another tactic is to allow parallel systems, the old one alongside the new, until everyone is comfortable with the innovation. Many years ago, the American library in one of the former Soviet republics was digitizing its entire collection, doing away with the card catalogues and replacing them with computers. The staff had been trained in the new system over a two-month period, and the original plan was to make the switch over the weekend, removing the card catalogues and installing the computers in their place. The local staff approached the head librarian the week before the big changeover and asked if the card catalogues could be left in place for a few weeks and the computers set up nearby. This small accommodation led to a successful transition.

For their part, Russians should realize that risk taking, making mistakes, and even failure are not judged as harshly by Americans as they are by Russians. Accordingly, you should try to be more willing to experiment. Even if you fail, remember that Americans almost always manage to find something good in failure: a lesson that has been learned or some theory that has been disproven. While you should never be reckless—acting before you have done a careful analysis, gathered the available data, or consulted the experts—you should not be afraid to act merely because of the risk of failure. How will you know until you try?

49. MINSK MATES

NANCY: Has Yevgeny signed the agreement yet?

DMITRI: Not yet. He's still waiting.

NANCY: Maybe he didn't get the second set of projections I sent him.

DMITRI: No, he got them. They were very encouraging, like the first set, he said.

NANCY: I see.

DMITRI: By the way, did you ever find out where your ancestors came from?

NANCY: Excuse me?

DMITRI:	Yevgeny said you told him you thought they also came from Minsk.
NANCY:	Somewhere in that region is what we were always told, but I'm not sure where exactly.
DMITRI:	Maybe you could find out.

There is a mysticism in the Russian character that has no equivalent in the rest of Western Europe, perhaps because many Russians at their core are much more Eastern than Western. As one observer puts it, in Russia "the spiritual is predominant over the material" (Pavlovskaya, 67). One of the many ways this manifests is the Russian interest in the supernatural; while they *are* a very pragmatic people, that somehow does not hinder their tendency toward superstition. There was once a popular Russian television show that went around the country examining the unique superstitions of local towns and villages. "Over the last few decades," Pavlovskaya continues, "Russia has been overcome by a wave of mysticism and all sorts of fortune tellers, prophets and healers. The difficult conditions in which people live are fertile ground in which superstitions flourish" (66). In a way, it is unsurprising that people who accept that much of life is outside their control—because it always has been—would believe that unknowable and mysterious forces are at work in the affairs of men. There are some things we just cannot explain.

"Literature on astrology, palmistry, numerology, and the interpretation of dreams," Richmond writes,

can be found everywhere in bookstores and sidewalk kiosks, and interest in such subjects is not limited to common people. Gorbachev's horoscope was published in a Moscow newspaper. Brezhnev was treated by a Georgian faith healer in his final years. Boris Yeltsin had a team of Kremlin astrologers

254

whose sole job was to help him make decisions. . . . News-
papers advertise the service of clairvoyants, witches, and
sorcerers. (28)

This is the mind-set Nancy has come across in this dialogue. Her negotiations with a man named Yevgeny seemed to have stalled. Obviously, Yevgeny needs additional assurances that this is a good deal and he should sign, but the only forms of reassurance Nancy can imagine involve data and numbers. She assumes, in other words, that only objective, quantifiable, tangible evidence—say, a second set of market projections—will convince Yevgeny to act. But Yevgeny *has* this new evidence and he's still not happy.

Yevgeny is waiting for a sign, something more than data, to guide his decision. While such a sign may not be the deciding factor—he could very well initial the agreement anyway—it would add another layer of comfort. Dmitri hints at what that sign might be when he asks Nancy to find out where her Russian ancestors come from. If they do indeed come from Minsk, as she has apparently stated in casual conversation, that would be proof to Yevgeny, who also comes from Minsk, that this deal is not merely financially sound; it is also *meant to be*. Now *that* would be reassuring.

A related attraction here for Yevgeny is the possibility of establishing a connection to Nancy. We observed in Dialogue 46, *"Dusha*: The Russian Soul," how Russians like to form strong personal relationships with their business partners and have more than just a contractual arrangement. The fact that his and Nancy's forebears may have come from the same city—who knows, they might even be related—means this could be the beginning of a beautiful friendship. The terms of the deal, in short, are why the looming partnership makes sense, but the possible connection is why it will succeed.

There is very little fatalism or mysticism in the American national character. They are a practical, utilitarian, rational people; they believe in what they can see, touch, quantify, and measure. They don't have an especially deep spiritual or fatalistic side; everything has a logical explanation, and anything that does not is probably a hoax. There's nothing you can't explain if you try hard enough. As for superstition and the supernatural, it's all so much—take your choice—hocus-pocus or mumbo jumbo. Most Americans aren't even sure they believe in coincidence.

Why do Americans believe everything has an explanation? Surely it must be in part because Americans firmly believe they are in control of external circumstances, that things happen because you make them happen and for no other reason. There is nothing that is ultimately outside one's control; no mysterious, unknowable, external force behind the affairs of men, shaping their destiny. *You* shape it—and regularly *re*shape it as the mood strikes you. Is it any wonder that such devout believers in human agency are confirmed skeptics?

The Fix

If there's too much heart and not enough head in Russian decision-making, is that so bad? Does it cost you anything to indulge Yevgeny's superstition? If the man wants a sign, why not give him one? By all means use reason, logic, and data when persuading Russians, but appealing to their emotions, feelings, and sentiment will make your case even stronger. When Russians, for their part, become sentimental and try to appeal to your emotions, don't assume they lack confidence in their data. They're just adding icing to the cake. Meanwhile, never mistake Russian sentimentalism for naïveté; they may acknowledge the mysterious hand of fate, but they are anything but naïve.

Russians pitching to Americans should stick mostly to the facts. You can try to appeal to an American's spiritual side—if you can find it—but by and large they're more impressed by spreadsheets. If you don't give Americans enough information, they may become suspicious and think you're trying to hide something. Mention the supernatural and you will genuinely alarm them.

50. NOW OR NEVER

ROBERT: VitaMint looks like a very good acquisition.

TATYANA: They're a start-up, aren't they?

ROBERT: Yes, about eighteen months old now.

TATYANA: Have you had a chance to study their financials?

ROBERT: A little. They only announced their availability three weeks ago. What I've seen so far looks very good.

TATYANA: Three weeks? That's not long.

ROBERT: We may have to act fast. I heard there's a lot of interest.

Opportunities, or at least *real* opportunities, don't come along that often in Russia. And even when they do, a Russian's first instinct is to wonder where the catch is. Nor is there ever any need to act hastily in a culture where genuine improvement only occurs gradually, at the margins. Quick, decisive action (as Robert might call it) is scarcely ever necessary in the Russian business environment; on the contrary, a patient, methodical, and cautious approach is always best. Russia-watchers often comment on what Richmond calls "the Russian congenital inertia," citing the old proverb which holds that "the Russian won't budge until the rooster pecks him in the rear" (42).

In describing traditional peasant mentality, the anthropologist George Foster has called this belief system the "Image of the Limited Good." Foster writes that by

> *"Image of the Limited Good,"* I mean that broad areas of peasant behavior are patterned in such fashion as to suggest that peasants view their social, economic and natural universe—their total environment—as one in which all of the desired things in life, such as land, wealth, health, friendship, love, manliness and honor, respect and status, power and influence, security and safety—exist in finite quantity and are always in short supply, *as far as the peasant is concerned. Not only do these and other "good things" exist in finite and limited quantities, but in addition there is no way directly within peasant power to increase the available quantities. "Good," like land, is seen as inherent in nature—there to be divided and redivided if necessary, but not to be augmented* (highlighted added, Foster, 296).

In short, Russians come by their congenital inertia quite honestly. "Caution and conservatism are legacies of the peasant past," Richmond continues. "Barely eking out a living in small, isolated villages, peasants had to contend not only with the vagaries of nature but also with the strictures of communal life, authoritarian fathers, all-powerful officials, and reproachful religious leaders. . . . The experience of the twentieth century has given Russians no cause to discard their caution" (41). At a summit with George Bush, the Soviet president Mikhail Gorbachev "preferred not to act precipitously in resolving international differences. [He] advocated an approach that was 'more humane. That is to be very cautious, to consider a matter seven times, or even one hundred times before one makes a decision.' Americans will have their patience tested by Russian caution" (Richmond, 42, 43).

As Robert can surely attest. He wants Tatyana to seize an opportunity to acquire a start-up, but Tatyana, culturally more inclined to sniff opportunities than to seize them, is in no hurry. And the more she learns, the more concerned she becomes. To begin with, VitaMint is a start-up, only eighteen months old; it has very little history or track record, nothing on which to base a reliable prediction of how it might do in the future. When Robert admits he hasn't had time to look into VitaMint's financials in any detail, that gives the naturally cautious Tatyana even more pause. And when she hears VitaMint has only been on the market for three weeks, she must wonder what the rush is. Finally, the fact that "there's a lot of interest" doesn't resonate with Tatyana either; she's no doubt thinking that if there *is* a lot of interest, it isn't coming from Russian companies. If Americans want to act first and do their due diligence later—the "ready, fire, aim" strategy Americans are often accused of—that's not Tatyana's problem.

Americans are not deliberately reckless, although Russians would probably see them that way, but neither are they especially cautious. To an American an opportunity isn't something you dissect and analyze, looking for the hidden trap; it's something you seize before it's too late. Too much analysis and investigation lead to paralysis, or at least to a slow pace—which feels like paralysis to Americans. Americans are achievement oriented, in short—they are doers—and anything that gets in the way of doing is deeply frustrating. Analysis, discussion, planning, meetings, and data gathering all have their place, but they also have their limits and should never be confused with action. There is talking, in short, and there is execution; the sooner talk morphs into execution, the happier Americans are. Americans also tend to be spontaneous, inclined to act on the spur of the moment; they follow hunches and "listen to their gut" without worrying too much about the consequences.

But what if everything goes wrong? What if seizing the opportunity and acquiring VitaMint in unseemly haste leads to an expensive mistake? That's just the thing; Americans don't fear mistakes, at least not the way Russians (and many Europeans) do. They have great faith that they can handle mistakes, setbacks, and temporary failure—because failure is always temporary in the United States. Their national experience, quite unlike that of the Russians, has taught them that there's nothing they can't change or make better if they put their minds to it. In such a scheme, premature, precipitous action carries very little risk. Americans would much prefer to act and be wrong than to do nothing and miss a great opportunity. Hesitation is the only real mistake.

"The great wealth of America," Daniel Boorstin writes, "the abundance of our material resources, has encouraged a wholesome unconcern for material things. We have been able to afford to experiment" (54). If you believe in abundance and infinite possibilities, life takes on greater urgency. If *anything* can happen, then there's never any excuse to accept things the way they are. There is always the chance—a good chance, in fact—that timely action can make a difference. Under the circumstances, *not* to act always carries with it the possibility of some kind of loss.

The Fix

If you want Russians to act quickly, you must make a strong case; it goes against all their instincts—and uprooting instincts is a tall order. And the case, by the way, cannot be that you may miss an opportunity. True opportunities are much rarer in Russia than in the U.S. Try to show Russians that the risks are minimal, and even tell them what your contingency plan is in case everything goes wrong. Offer all the assurances you can. If the Russians are still hesitant and you insist on acting, then you will have to take full responsibility for any consequences.

For Russians working with enthusiastic, go-getter Americans, remember, first of all, that they have a high tolerance for risk and are more forgiving of failure. If they want you to act prematurely, make your reservations very clear. They *will* listen even if they ultimately disagree with you. If you want to stop them from seizing a dubious opportunity, explain the risks very carefully. If they are willing to shoulder the blame, you have nothing to lose.

11

Five Steps to Cultural Competence

This book has given you valuable knowledge about Americans and the citizens of the ten featured cultures. While these are eleven of the world's biggest economies, there are many other cultures out there. You may be wondering how this book is supposed to help you with them.

If you've read this far, you've already done most of the work. You've had the central realization that when you work with people from other cultures, there are certain ways you're not like them and they're not like you. You are different, in short, and as you've seen many times in these pages, differences have consequences.

If you'd like to avoid these consequences going forward, not just vis-à-vis the featured cultures but in *any* cross-cultural encounter, then we have one last piece of business together: Describing a simple, five-step process to identify what you need to know to succeed in doing business with any other culture. This process is the foundation upon which this books rests, so you've already seen this process at work in the preceding ten chapters; all we are doing here is making it more explicit.

Here are the five steps to cultural competence:

1. Understand what culture is and how it affects business and workplace interactions.
2. Identify the key assumptions and values of your own culture.
3. Identify the key assumptions and values of the target culture.
4. Identify the major differences between your culture and the target culture.
5. React as appropriate.

Step 1: Understand what culture is and how it affects business and workplace interactions.

We've never explicitly defined "culture" in these pages, as it's much easier to grasp what culture is by seeing it in action. Those actions, the things people say and do, together with the values and beliefs that prompt such actions, are what is generally meant by the term "culture." In these pages you have been introduced to the visible dimension of culture, behavior or the things people say in the dialogues, and then you have been taken behind the behavior to discover the invisible dimension, the values or beliefs that explain why the two speakers behave the way they do. In fifty different examples, you've seen this link between values and behavior, which is the essence of Step 1 in this process.

Step 2: Identify the key assumptions and values of your own culture.

Once you understand how values and beliefs influence behavior, the other steps in this process more or less suggest themselves.

If values and beliefs play such a key role, then people with *different* values and beliefs—people from other cultures—are bound to behave differently. If you want to work with others and succeed, you must understand those differences—which brings us to Step 2. The starting point for discovering differences is to become aware of the primary values and beliefs of your own culture, which will then enable you to compare your culture with any target cultures and identify the all-important differences.

But identifying your own values and beliefs is not easy because they are largely subconscious and internalized. While you may live by these values and beliefs, behaving in certain ways in certain situations and never in other ways—doing what is normal, in other words, and avoiding what is abnormal—you are usually not consciously aware of them. Indeed, if someone asked you to name the five most important values of your culture, you'd have to stop and think—and even then you would probably flounder.

So how do you identify your cultural preferences? Those who study culture have identified certain aspects of human experience that all people in all societies must come to terms with *but with respect to which different societies have evolved different attitudes and behaviors*. These include such things as sense of identity, attitude toward uncertainty, and concepts of time and fairness. Many of these topics have been described in these pages because they explain the differences illustrated by the dialogues.

To have a good grasp on your own culture, then, you must identify what it has taught you vis-à-vis these topics. Here is a list of the more common ones:

General Dimensions

- Sense of identity (individualism vs. collectivism)
- Locus of control/human agency (internal vs. external)

265

- Sense of fairness (universalism vs. particularism)
- View of human nature (benign vs. skeptical)
- Sense of limits (unlimited opportunity vs. limited opportunity)
- Sense of time (monochronic vs. polychronic)
- Communication style (direct vs. indirect)
- Concept of face (more important vs. less important)

Business/Workplace Dimensions

- Performance orientation (task vs. relationship)
- Management style (decentralized vs. centralized)

- Attitude toward power (high power distance vs. low power distance)
- Concept of rank and status (egalitarian vs. hierarchical)
- Attitude toward assertiveness (positive vs. critical)
- Decision-making style (top down vs. consensus)
- Attitude toward risk and uncertainty (risk tolerant vs. risk averse)
- Degree of guidance and supervision (high vs. low)
- Negotiating style (win/win vs. win/lose)
- Worker-employer relationships (opportunistic vs. mutual loyalty)
- Meeting style (problem solving vs. get-together)
- Short-term vs. long-term orientation

Numerous books in the field of intercultural communications discuss these factors in more detail, although authors may use different terms. The Reading List at the end of this chapter presents one or two highly recommended titles for each of the featured countries (and the United States). It also gives titles for a selection of other countries not featured in this book, as well as a list of general titles and websites. The Bibliography lists additional titles. You could also seek out classes or workshops in intercultural communication to further your efforts in completing Step 2. Or you can visit an online cultural resource such as the websites for GlobeSmart (www.globesmart.com) or Country Navigator (www.countrynavigator.com).

Step 3: Identify the key assumptions and values of your target culture.

Once you have a fix on your own culture, your next job is to compare it with your "target" culture, the country you wish to do business with. Using the same list presented above, identify how people in your target culture think and act vis-à-vis these key factors. Once again, we suggest consulting the Reading List for books and websites that will teach you more.

Step 4: Identify the major differences between your culture and the target culture.

After completing Steps 2 and 3, you will have all the information you need to complete Step 4. Contrast what you now know about your own culture with what you have learned about the target culture, and identify key differences. You can also identify similarities, of course. Although these should not present any serious business challenges, by noting similarities you will come to know the extent of difference between your own culture and your target culture.

Step 5: React as appropriate.

Seriously? I go to all this work and all I get at the end is "React as appropriate"? It does sound like a bit of a dodge, but think about it for a moment: What you should do when you encounter cultural differences in the course of doing business around the world depends entirely on the circumstances. In some cases, you should take a deep breath and try to act the way the locals do; in other cases, you should with good reason expect the locals to conform to your way of doing things; in still other cases, people from both cultures will have to shed some ethnocentrism and move toward a middle way that takes everyone outside their comfort zone. It depends on so many factors: Are you doing business in their country, or are they doing business in yours? Are you the buyer, or are you the seller? Do you work under someone from another country, or are you the boss? Are you managing folks in their own country, or managing a team of foreigners in your own country?

We have given a few suggestions for making accommodations in "The Fix" sections at the end of each explanation, but it is impossible to account for every situation. That said, we can offer a few general rules about how to decide who adjusts to whom:

- If the adjustment is between you and one other person, for whom is it easier to behave in a new way?
- If you are more familiar with the other person's culture than they are with yours, it may be easier if you do the adjusting.
- If you are in their environment, the expectation is that you will adjust.
- If they are in your environment, the expectation is that they will adjust.

- If everyone is in a third environment—such as a global team—the adjustment that requires the fewest number of people to travel the least distance outside their comfort zone is usually the best solution.

- If you are on a global team within a large multinational, chances are the national culture of the headquarters company is the one everyone will be at least minimally familiar with, hence, the closest thing to a common culture the team is going to have. It would at least be a good starting point for discussing team norms.

- If no one can agree on whose culture will prevail on any given team or in any given situation, the players should try to agree on the results they are looking for. They can usually then decide which culture's way is more likely to produce those results.

Being an American, I naturally want to end this book on a positive note. Let me say, then, that while this book has emphasized the challenges (Americans always say challenges, rather than problems) created by cultural differences, that's not the whole story. Cultural differences *do* cause misunderstandings, and misunderstandings *can* easily lead to all manner of unfortunate consequences. But there are also many benefits and advantages of encountering cultural differences: they make you think differently; they put your own culture into perspective; they offer alternative solutions to problems; they force you to be more flexible and tolerant; they make you curious; they prompt introspection.

We've emphasized the problems inherent in cultural differences because that's where you may need help. But you won't need any help reaping the benefits and enjoying the advantages.

Reading List

As you have just seen, Steps 2, 3, and 4 require you to process information about your own culture as well as the target culture and then make comparisons to discover key differences. The books in this list contain cultural information you can use to complete these three steps.

The Featured Countries

U.S.

- *American Beliefs: What Keeps a Big Country and a Diverse People United* by John Harmon McElroy
- *American Cultural Patterns: A Cross-Cultural Perspective* by Edward C. Stewart and Milton J. Bennett
- *Americans at Work: A Guide to the Can-Do People* by Craig Storti
- *Not Like Us: How Europeans Have Loved, Hated, and Transformed American Culture Since World War II* by Richard Pells
- *Out of Our Past: The Forces That Shaped Modern America* by Carl N. Degler

The Arab Middle East

- *The Arab Mind* by Raphael Patai
- *Understanding Arabs: A Guide for Westerners* by Margaret Nydell

Brazil

- *Behaving Brazilian: A Comparison of Brazilian and North American Social Behavior* by Phyllis Harrison
- *Brazil: A Guide for Businesspeople* by Jacqueline Oliveira

China

- *Encountering the Chinese: A Guide for Americans* by Wenzhong Hu and Cornelius Grove
- *Inside Chinese Business: A Guide for Managers Worldwide* by Ming-Jer Chen

England

- *Old World, New World: Bridging Cultural Differences: Britain, France, Germany, and the U.S.* by Craig Storti
- *Watching the English: The Hidden Rules of English Behaviour* by Kate Fox

France

- *Au Contraire! Figuring Out the French* by Gilles Asselin and Ruth Mastron
- *Cultural Misunderstandings: The French-American Experience* by Raymonde Carroll

- *French or Foe? Getting the Most out of Visiting, Living and Working in France* by Polly Platt
- *Old World, New World: Bridging Cultural Differences: Britain, France, Germany, and the U.S.* by Craig Storti

Germany

- *Germany and the Germans: An Anatomy of Society Today* by John Ardagh
- *Germany: Unraveling an Enigma* by Greg Nees
- *Old World, New World: Bridging Cultural Differences: Britain, France, Germany, and the U.S.* by Craig Storti

India

- *Being Indian: Inside the Real India* by Pavan K. Varma
- *Speaking of India: Bridging the Communication Gap When Working with Indians* by Craig Storti

Japan

- *Doing Business with the Japanese* by Mitchell Deutsch
- *Hidden Differences: Doing Business with the Japanese* by Edward T. Hall and Mildred Reed Hall
- *With Respect to the Japanese: A Guide for Americans* by John Condon

Mexico

- *Good Neighbors: Communicating with the Mexicans* by John Condon

- *Mexicans & Americans: Cracking the Cultural Code* by Ned Crouch
- *The Mexican Mind: Understanding and Appreciating Mexican Culture* by Boyé Lafayette De Mente

Russia

- *From Nyet to Da: Understanding the Russians* by Yale Richmond

Europe

- *The Europeans* by Luigi Barzini
- *We Europeans* by Richard Hill
- *Mind Your Manners: Managing Business Cultures in Europe* by John Mole
- *Understanding Europeans* by Stuart Miller

OTHER COUNTRIES

- *Into **Africa**: Intercultural Insights* by Yale Richmond and Phyllis Gestrin
- *A Fair Go for All: **Australian**/American Interactions* by George Renwick
- *From Da to Yes: Understanding the **East Europeans*** by Yale Richmond
- *Considering **Filipinos*** by Theodore Gochenour
- ***Finland**: Cultural Lone Wolf* by Richard Lewis
- *Exploring the **Greek** Mosaic: A Guide to Intercultural Communication in Greece* by Benjamin Broome

- *Among the **Iranians**: A Guide to Iran's Culture and Customs* by Sofia Koutlaki
- *Border Crossings: American Interactions with **Israelis*** by Luchy Shahar and David Kurz
- ***Korean** Etiquette & Ethics in Business* by Boyé Lafayette De Mente
- *Learning to Think **Korean**: A Guide to Living and Working in Korea* by Robert Kohls
- ***Latino** Culture: A Dynamic Force in the Changing American Workplace* by Nilda Chong and Francia Baez
- *Understanding Spanish-Speaking **South Americans**: Bridging Hemispheres* by Skye Stephenson
- ***Spain** Is Different* by Helen Wattley-Ames
- *Modern-Day Vikings: A Practical Guide to Interacting with the **Swedes*** by Christina Robinowitz and Lisa Carr
- ***Swiss** Watching: Inside Europe's Landlocked Island* by Diccon Bewes
- *A Common Core: **Thais** and Americans* by John Paul Fieg and Elizabeth Mortlock
- ***Vietnam** Today: A Guide to a Nation at a Crossroads* by Mark A. Ashwill

275

GENERAL & BUSINESS

- *Basic Concepts of Intercultural Communication* by Milton Bennett
- *Beyond Culture* by Edward T. Hall
- *Communicating Globally: Intercultural Communication and International Business* by Wallace Schmidt et al.

- *Communication Between Cultures* by Larry Samovar and Richard Porter
- *Cross-Cultural Dialogues: 74 Brief Encounters with Cultural Difference* by Craig Storti
- *The Cultural Imperative: Global Trends in the 21st Century* by Richard D. Lewis
- *Cultural Intelligence: A Guide to Working with People from Other Cultures* by Brooks Peterson
- *Culture, Leadership, and Organizations* by Robert J. House et al.
- *The Culture Map* by Erin Meyer
- *Culture Matters: How Values Shape Human Progress* by Lawrence Harrison

- *Culture Shock! A Survival Guide to Customs & Etiquette* (multivolume series)
- *Culture's Consequences: International Differences in Work-Related Values* by Geert Hofstede
- *Cultures and Organizations: Software of the Mind* by Geert Hofstede
- *The Dance of Life: The Other Dimension of Time* by Edward T. Hall
- *Doing Business in Asia: The Complete Guide* by Sanjyot P. Dunung
- *Figuring Foreigners Out: A Practical Guide* by Craig Storti
- *The Hidden Dimension* by Edward T. Hall
- *Intercultural Communication: A Global Reader* by Fred Jandt
- *Intercultural Communication: A Reader* by Larry Samovar and Richard Porter
- *Intercultural Communication: An Introduction* by Fred Jandt

- *International Dimensions of Organizational Behavior* by Nancy J. Adler
- *Managing Across Cultures: The Seven Keys to Doing Business with a Global Mindset* by Charlene Solomon and Michael Schell
- *Mind Your Manners: Managing Business Cultures in Europe* by John Mole
- *The Mindful International Manager: How to Work Effectively Across Cultures* by Jeremy Comfort and Peter Franklin
- *The Silent Language* by Edward T. Hall
- *When Cultures Collide: Leading Across Cultures* by Richard D. Lewis
- *The World's Business Cultures and How to Unlock Them* by Barry Tomalin and Mike Nicks
- *The Xenophobe's Guide* (multivolume series)

WEBSITES

There are many cross-cultural resources available online, but two of the best are:

Country Navigator by the TMA World Group (www.countrynavigator.com)

GlobeSmart by Aperian Global (www.globesmart.com)

Bibliography

General

Adler, Nancy (1986). *International Dimensions of Organizational Behavior*. Boston: Wadsworth.

Engholm, Christopher (1991). *When Business East Meets Business West*. New York: John Wiley and Sons.

Foster, George M. "Peasant Society and the Image of Limited Good." *American Anthropologist*, 67, no. 2, April 1965.

Hall, Edward T., and Mildred Reed Hall (1990). *Understanding Cultural Differences*. Yarmouth, ME: Intercultural Press.

Harris, Philip R., and Robert T. Moran (1987). *Managing Cultural Differences*. Houston: Gulf Publishing.

Hickson, David (Ed.) (1997). *Exploring Management Across the World*. London: Penguin Books.

Hickson, David, and Derek S. Pugh (1995). *Management Worldwide*. London: Penguin Books.

Hofstede, Geert (1988). *Culture's Consequences: International Differences in Work-Related Values* (abridged edition). Beverly Hills, CA: Sage.

House, Robert, et al. (Eds.) (2004). *Culture, Leadership, and Organizations: The Globe Study of 62 Societies*. Thousand Oaks, CA: Sage.

Joynt, Pat, and Malcolm Warner (Eds.) (1996). *Managing Across Cultures: Issues and Perspectives*. London: International Thomson Business Press.

Meyer, Erin (2014). *The Culture Map: Breaking through the Invisible Boundaries of Global Business*. New York: Public Affairs.

Tomalin, Barry, and Mike Nicks (2007). *The World's Business Cultures and How to Unlock Them*. London: Thorogood.

Yapp, Peter (Ed.) (1988). *The Traveller's Dictionary of Quotations: Who Said What, About Where?* London: Routledge.

Americans

Boorstin, Daniel J. (1976). *America and the Image of Europe: Reflections on American Thought*. Gloucester, MA: Peter Smith.

Boorstin, Daniel J. (1958). *The Americans: The Colonial Experience*. New York: Random House.

Bryson, Bill (1999). *I'm a Stranger Here Myself*. New York: Broadway Books.

Degler, Carl N. (1984). *Out of Our Past: The Forces That Shaped Modern America*. New York: Harper & Row.

Engel, Dean (1997). *Passport U.S.A.* San Rafael, CA: World Trade Press.

Faul, Stephanie (1999). *Xenophobe's Guide to the Americans*. London: Oval Books.

Foster, George M. "Peasant Society and the Image of Limited Good." *American Anthropologist*, 67, no. 2, April 1965, 296.

Hall, Edward T., and Mildred Reed Hall (1990). *Understanding Cultural Differences*. Yarmouth, ME: Intercultural Press.

Hendrickson, Paul. "Witness to the Unimaginable." *Washington Post*, F7, November 15, 1998.

Hutner, Gordon. (1999). *Immigrant Voices: Twenty-four Narratives on Becoming an American*. New York: Penguin Putnam.

James, Henry (1986). *The Ambassadors*. London: Penguin.

Jones, Howard M. (1968). *O Strange New World: American Culture: The Formative Years*. New York: Viking.

Kammen, Michael (1980). *People of Paradox*. Ithaca, NY: Cornell University Press.

Kanter, Rosabeth M. (1997). *On the Frontiers of Management*. Boston: Harvard Business School Press.

McElroy, John H. (1999). *American Beliefs: What Keeps a Big Country and a Diverse People United*. Chicago: Ivan R. Dee.

Pells, Richard (1997). *Not Like Us: How Europeans Have Loved, Hated, and Transformed American Culture Since World War II*. New York: Basic Books.

Schorr, Juliet (1993). *The Overworked American*. New York: Basic Books.

Stewart, Edward C., and Milton J. Bennett (1991). *American Cultural Patterns: A Cross-Cultural Perspective*. Yarmouth, ME: Intercultural Press.

Storti, Craig (2004). *Americans at Work: A Guide to the Can-Do People*. Yarmouth, ME: Intercultural Press.

Storti, Craig (2001). *Old World, New World: Bridging Cultural Differences*. Yarmouth, ME: Intercultural Press.

Tocqueville, Alexis de (1984). *Democracy in America*. New York: Penguin Books.

Wallach, Joel, and Gale Metcalf (1995). *Working with Americans: A Practical Guide for Asians on How to Succeed with U.S. Managers*. Singapore: McGraw-Hill.

Arab Middle East

Hamady, Sania (1960). *Temperament and Character of the Arabs*. New York: Twayne.

Kinglake, A. W. (1982). *Eothen*. London: Century Publishing.

Nydell, Margaret (2002). *Understanding Arabs: A Guide for Westerners*. Yarmouth, ME: Intercultural Press/Nicholas Brealey.

Patai, Raphael (1973). *The Arab Mind*. New York: Macmillan.

Brazil

Harrison, Phyllis (1983). *Behaving Brazilian: A Comparison of Brazilian and North American Social Behavior*. Cambridge, MA: Newbury House.

Herrington, Elizabeth (1998). *Passport Brazil*. San Rafael, CA: World Trade Press.

Oliveira, Jacqueline (2001). *Brazil: A Guide for Business People*. Yarmouth, ME: Intercultural Press/Nicholas Brealey.

Page, Joseph A. (1996). *The Brazilians*. Reading, MA: Addison-Wesley

Poelzl, Volker (2002). *Culture Shock! Brazil*. Singapore: Times Media.

China

Burns, Robert (1998). *Doing Business in Asia: A Cultural Perspective*. Melbourne: Addison Wesley Longman Australia.

Chen, Ming-Jer (2001). *Inside Chinese Business: A Guide for Managers Worldwide*. Boston: Harvard Business School Press.

Hu, Wenzhong, and Cornelius Grove (1999). *Encountering the Chinese: A Guide for Americans*. Yarmouth, ME: Intercultural Press.

Seligman, Scott (1989). *Dealing with the Chinese: A Practical Guide to Business Etiquette in the People's Republic Today*. New York: Warner Books.

Wang, Mary Margaret, et al. (2000). *Turning Bricks into Jade: Critical Incidents for Mutual Understanding among Chinese and Americans*. Yarmouth, ME: Intercultural Press/Nicholas Brealey.

England

Beadle, Muriel (1961). *These Ruins Are Inhabited*. London: Robert Hale.

Bryson, Bill (1995). *Notes from a Small Island*. New York: Avon Books.

Fox, Kate (2004). *Watching the English: The Hidden Rules of English Behaviour*. London: Hodder and Stoughton.

Miall, Anthony (1998). *The Xenophobe's Guide to the English*. Horsham, West Sussex, U.K.: Ravette Publishing.

North, Peter (1999). *Culture Shock: Success Secrets to Maximize Business in Britain*. Singapore: Times Editions.

O'Hanlon, Redmond (1988). *In Trouble Again: A Journey between the Orinoco and the Amazon*. New York: Vintage.

Europe

Barzini, Luigi (1983). *The Europeans*. London: Penguin Books.

Gannon, Martin J., et al. (1994). *Understanding Global Cultures: Metaphorical Journeys Through 17 Countries*. Thousand Oaks, CA: Sage.

Gibbs, Paul (1992). *Doing Business in the European Community*. London: Kogan/Page.

Hill, Richard (1994). *EuroManagers & Martians*. Brussels: Europublications.

Hill, Richard (1995). *We Europeans*. Brussels: Europublications.

Lawrence, Peter, and Vincent Edwards (2000). *Management in Western Europe*. London: Macmillan Press.

Miller, Stuart (1990). *Understanding Europeans*. Santa Fe, NM: John Muir.

Mole, John (1995). *Mind Your Manners: Managing Business Cultures in Europe*. London: Nicholas Brealey.

Moran, Robert T. (1992). *Doing Business in Europe*. Oxford: Butterworth-Heinemann.

Payer, Lynn (1989). *Medicine and Culture: Varieties of Treatment in the United States, England, West Germany, and France*. New York: Penguin Books.

Randlesome, Colin, et. al. (1995). *Business Cultures in Europe*. Oxford: Butterworth-Heinemann.

France

Asselin, Gilles, and Ruth Mastron (2001). *Au Contraire! Figuring Out the French*. Yarmouth, ME: Intercultural Press/Nicholas Brealey.

Barsoux, Jean-Louis, and Peter Lawrence. "The Managing of a French Manager." *Harvard Business Review*, July–August 1991, 60.

Carroll, Raymonde (1990). *Cultural Misunderstandings: The French-American Experience*. Chicago: University of Chicago Press.

Gramont, Sanche de (1969). *The French: Portrait of a People*. New York: G. P. Putnam's Sons.

Platt, Polly (1995). *French or Foe? Getting the Most Out of Visiting, Living and Working in France*. Skokie, IL: Culture Crossings.

Zeldin, Theodore (1996). *The French*. New York: Kodansha International.

Germany

Ardagh, John (1991). *Germany and the Germans*. London: Penguin.

Flamini, Roland (1997). *Passport Germany: Your Pocket Guide to German Business, Customs, & Etiquette*. San Rafael, CA: World Trade Press.

Lord, Richard (1996). *Culture Shock! Germany*. Portland, OR: Graphic Arts Center Publishing.

Lord, Richard (1998). *Culture Shock! Succeed in Business: Germany*. Portland, Oregon: Graphic Arts Center Publishing.

Nees, Greg (2000). *Germany: Unraveling an Enigma*. Yarmouth, ME: Intercultural Press.

India

Bagla, Gunjan (2008). *Doing Business in 21st-Century India*. New York: Hachette.

Bijlani, Hiru (1999). *Culture Shock! Succeed in Business: India*. Singapore: Times Editions.

Davies, Paul (2004). *What's This India Business? Offshoring, Outsourcing, and the Global Services Revolution*. London: Nicholas Brealey International.

Gudykunst, William B., and Stella Ting-Toomey (1988). *Culture and Interpersonal Communication*. Newbury Park, CA: Sage.

Kakar, Katharina, and Sudhir (2007). *The Indians: Portrait of a People*. New Delhi: Viking.

Kolanad, Gitanjali (2005). *Culture Shock! India*. Singapore: Marshall Cavendish.

Kumar, Rajesh, and Anand Kumar Seth (2005). *Doing Business in India*. New York: Palgrave Macmillan.

Makar, Eugene (2008). *An American's Guide to Doing Business in India*. Avon, MA: Adams Business.

Manian, Ranjini (2007). *Doing Business in India for Dummies*. Indianapolis, IN: Wiley.

Manian, Ranjini, and Joanna Huskey (2015). *Make It in India: Global CEOs, Indo-U.S. Insights*. Chennia, India: Westland.

Messner, Wolfgang (2010). *Working with India: The Softer Aspects of a Successful Collaboration with the Indian IT and BPO Industry*. Berlin and Heidelberg, Germany. Springer.

Sinha, Jai B. P. (1990). *Work Culture in the Indian Context*. New Delhi: Sage Publications.

Storti, Craig (2015). *Speaking of India: Bridging the Communication Gap When Working with Indians*. Boston: Nicholas Brealey International.

Tharoor, Shashi (1997). *India: From Midnight to the Millennium and Beyond*. New York: Arcade Publishing.

Varma, Pavan K. (2006). *Being Indian*. London, England. Penguin.

Wolpert, Stanley (2005). *India*. Berkeley, CA: University of California.

Japan

Barnlund, Dean (1975). *Public and Private Self in Japan and the United States*. Yarmouth, ME: Intercultural Press.

Clarke, Clifford, and Douglas G. Lipp (1998). *Danger and Opportunity: Resolving Conflict in U.S.-Based Japanese Subsidiaries*. Yarmouth, ME: Intercultural Press.

Collins, Robert (1992). *Japan-Think, Ameri-Think*. New York: Penguin.

Condon, John (1984). *With Respect to the Japanese*. Yarmouth, ME: Intercultural Press.

Deutsch, Mitchell (1983). *Doing Business with the Japanese*. New York: Mentor.

Fucini, Joseph J., and Suzy Fucini (1990). *Working for the Japanese: Inside Mazda's American Auto Plant*. New York: The Free Press.

Hall, Edward T., and Mildred Hall (1983). *Hidden Differences: Doing Business with the Japanese*. New York: Doubleday.

Lanier, Alison (1992). *The Rising Sun on Main Street: Working with the Japanese*. Morrisville, PA: International Information Associates.

Lu, David (1987). *Inside Corporate Japan*. Tokyo: Charles E. Tuttle.

Matsumoto, Michihiro (1988). *The Unspoken Way*. Tokyo: Kodansha.

Mexico

Condon, John (1997). *Good Neighbors: Communicating with the Mexicans*. Yarmouth, ME: Intercultural Press.

Crouch, Ned (2004). *Mexicans and Americans: Cracking the Cultural Code*. Yarmouth, ME: Intercultural Press/Nicholas Brealey.

De Mente, Boyé Lafayette (2011). *The Mexican Mind: Understanding and Appreciating Mexican Culture*. Phoenix Books.

Jessup, Jay, and Maggie Jessup. 1993. *Doing Business in Mexico*. Rocklin, CA: Prima Publishing.

Kras, Eva (1995). *Management in Two Cultures: Bridging the Gap between U.S. and Mexican Managers*. Yarmouth, ME: Intercultural Press.

Stephenson, Skye (2003). *Spanish-Speaking South Americans: Bridging Hemispheres*. Yarmouth, ME: Intercultural Press/ Nicholas Brealey.

Russia

Goehner. http://www.goehner.com/russinfo.htm

Mitchell, Charles (1998). *Passport Russia*. San Rafael, CA: World Trade Press.

Pavlovskaya, Anna (2007). *Culture Shock! Russia*. Tarrytown, NY: Marshall Cavendish Corp.

Richmond, Yale (2003). *From Nyet to Da: Understanding the Russians*. Yarmouth, ME: Intercultural Press/Nicholas Brealey.

Roberts, Elisabeth (1998). *Xenophobe's Guide to the Russians*. West Sussex, U.K.: Ravette Publishing.

Index